CONTESTED HOLINESS

JEWISH, MUSLIM, AND CHRISTIAN PERSPECTIVES ON THE TEMPLE MOUNT IN JERUSALEM

CONTESTED HOLINESS

JEWISH, MUSLIM, AND CHRISTIAN PERSPECTIVES ON THE TEMPLE MOUNT IN JERUSALEM

Rivka Gonen

KTAV Publishing House, Inc.
Jersey City, NJ

Library of Congress Cataloging-in-Publication Data

Gonen, Rivka.
  Contested holiness : Jewish, Muslim, and Christian perspective on the
Temple Mount in Jerusalem / Rivka Gonen.
      p. cm.
Includes index.
  ISBN 0-88125-798-2 (Hardcover) -- ISBN 0-88125-799-0 (Pbk.)
  1. Temple Mount (Jerusalem) 2. Jerusalem in Judaism. 3. Jerusalem in
Islam. 4. Jerusalem in Christianity. 5. Temple of Jerusalem
(Jerusalem) 6. Jerusalem--History. 7. Arab-Israeli conflict. I.
Title.
  DS109.28 .G66 2002
  956.94'42--dc21

                          2002014320

                        Published by
              KTAV Publishing House, Inc.
                   930 Newark Avenue
                  Jersey City, NJ 07306
                 Email: info@ktav.com
                     www.ktav.com
                    (201) 963-9524
                  Fax (201) 963-0102

In loving memory of my father Dr. Simcha Biger
Born in the Old City of Jerusalem
Passionate lover of the city

Table of Contents

"This world resembles the ball of the human eye. The white of the eye is the ocean, which encompasses the whole world, the black of the eye is the inhabited world, the pupil of the eye is Jerusalem, and the human face reflected in it is the Temple."

(Mahzor Vitry, p. 7)

Foreword

I began thinking about writing this book in the spring of 2001, several months after the beginning of the second Intifada (uprising), the so-called Al-Aqsa Intifada. This Palestinian uprising, which has disrupted the lives of both Israelis and Palestinians, allegedly began because of the much-publicized visit of Ariel Sharon, then head of the Israeli political opposition, to the Temple Mount in September 2000. It occurred to me that although everyone who reads newspapers, listen to the radio, and watches television must have heard about the Temple Mount, not many are aware of the numerous religious and political contests that had centered on it for the last 3,000 years, of the origin and development of its sanctity, nor exactly where it is located and what is its present-day configuration. The aim of the book is to give the reader a more in-depth view of this intriguing site, perhaps the oldest holy site in the world that is still revered and still fought over.

The Temple Mount has been part of my personal life since early childhood. As a young child in the pre-1948 years, my father would occasionally take me to the Western Wall, an imposing remnant of the Second Temple compound. We would wind our way through the narrow alleys of the Old City and eventually emerge in an equally narrow alley, bounded on its eastern side by the magnificent Wall with its huge stones. The sight of people praying by the Wall imprinted in my mind the notion of its holiness, but only when I grew up and took archaeology as my major at the Hebrew University of Jerusalem did I come to understand its full history and significance. The 1967 Six-Day War opened Jerusalem for intensive archaeological study, and I took part in both the Western Wall and the City of David excavation projects. Over the years I studied many aspects of past and present life in Jerusalem and headed several projects relating to the city. All my life I have lived and worked in Jerusalem, and its special atmosphere, its times of war and peace, its problems, joys, and pleasures are an inseparable part of me. The ongoing Jewish-Arab conflict has been a constant and integral part of my personal and professional life. I hope that I have managed to present a fair an account of the issue of the Temple Mount, in which the Jews and the Muslims are the major contestants, and the Christians, mainly evangelical sects, also play a part. Given the enormity of the problems that surround this site, and given the fact that I am a Jewish Israeli and thus, consciously and more so unconsciously, tend to stress one side of the contest, this was not an easy task.

I am greatly indebted to the numerous researchers, authors, reporters, artists, photographers, restorers and many others, who, over the ages, have been studying Jerusalem in general and the Temple Mount specifically from many and varied aspects. Jerusalem is probably one of the best explored cities in the world if not the best of them, and the assembled knowledge of all aspects of its life past and present is truly monumental. The eleven pages of bibliography in this book are but a fraction of what has been written about the history and other aspects of the Temple Mount. In adding one more book to this extensive and ever growing library, my aim was not to augment the research on the Temple Mount or further it, but to select from the extensive body of existing information what is relevant to its specific theme - namely the history and meaning of the contests over it - evaluate and organize it, and present it in a meaningful, lucid and visual manner.

I was fortunate to have access to several important libraries both in Jerusalem and abroad. The National and University Library at the Hebrew University, and the Yad Izhak Ben-Zvi Library, both in Jerusalem, have broadened my exposure to published and rare materials. The British Library in London, and the Robarts Library at the University of Toronto, had both graciously allowed me to use their facilities.

I would like to thank the various institutions that allowed me to use their illustrations: Israel Exploration Society; The Jerusalem Publishing House; The Holyland Hotel in Jerusalem, Haaretz Museum in Tel Aviv; and the Manuscript Library at the National and University Library in Jerusalem. The Photo Department of the State of Israel Government Press Office promptly and helpfully supplied the requested images, and photographer Bouki Boaz allowed the use of one of his photographs. My husband Amiram Gonen and myself also added images to the book.

Special thanks to Derek Diamond, Professor Emeritus at the London School of Economics for his valuable comments and sound advice.

My heartfelt thanks to Bernard Scharfstein, who agreed to take on the book almost at first sight. Throughout the process of writing, editing, selecting the images, and designing the book he was helpful, encouraging, and kind. His assistant Adam Bengal, with whom I was in almost day-to-day contact throughout the process, saw to it that the entire operation was smooth and swift. The designers of both the cover and the book did a superb job. Working with KTAV Publishing House was a fruitful and pleasant experience.

Rivka Gonen

Chapter 1
Laying the Foundation Stone for the Third Temple

On the Jewish festival of Succot (Tabernacles) in the fall of 1989, the Faithful of the Temple Mount, a group of national-religious Jews organized in 1982, added a new element to their yearly procession to the holy Mount. Every year at this time the group would come to the foot of the Temple Mount next to the Western Wall and try to go up the ramp that leads to the Mughrabi Gate, the one entrance through which non-Muslims could enter the Mount. Their clearly proclaimed intention was to conduct festive prayers on the Temple Mount, an act prohibited by both the Israeli and the Muslim authorities. In 1989 the participants brought with them a large stone; they hoped to carry it up to the Mount and there lay it as the cornerstone of the Third Temple. In preparation for the event, the group printed huge posters describing their aims. Posted on the walls in religious and national-religious neighborhoods where likely sympathizers of such an activity lived, the posters called upon the public to join the procession.

Similar posters have appeared every year since. The 2001 poster, for example, called the public to witness two stones weighing 4.5 tons each that would be taken up to the Temple Mount. It further promised what could not be

promised in 1989, when preparations to build the Temple were not yet far advanced: that the Temple's architect would present the plans as well as a large model of the Third Temple. The gilded incense altar and other Temple utensils would also be displayed during the procession. A priest (*kohen*) dressed in an exact hand-woven copy of the garment worn by the Temple priests, accompanied by members of the Tribe of Levi with musical instruments, would also be present. After placing the foundation stone on the Temple Mount, the procession, so the poster read, would proceed to the Siloam Spring at the foot of the City of David for the Pouring of the Water ceremony that is part of the Succot festivities. The poster ended with a message to "our enemies, our weak leaders, and the whole world that we will never give up our holy Temple Mount, Jerusalem, and one grain of the land of our fathers." [1] Although the 1989 procession did not achieve its aim and was not allowed on the Temple Mount to lay the cornerstones, the reaction of the Arab authorities and public was severe. Arabs who at the time of the procession were praying in the Muslim shrines on the Temple Mount began throwing stones at the Jews conducting their festive Succot

1

Procession of the Faithful of the Temple Mount marching
towards the Mughrabi Gate, 2002. Photographer: Amiram Gonen

Muslim women on the Temple Mount protesting and shouting at Israeli policemen.
Photographer: Tsvika Israeli, 1989. © 1997–1998, The State of Israel, Government Press
Office.

prayers at the Western Wall at the foot of the Temple Mount. The police on that occasion managed to quickly control the violence.

Because of the severe 1989 clashes instigated by the activities of the Faithful of the Temple Mount, the police prepared for Succot 1990 events. They announced in all Jewish and Arab media that the Faithful would not be allowed even to come close to the Temple Mount. The Faithful on their side proclaimed that they would not only attempt to bring a foundation stone but would erect a *succah* (temporary tabernacle commemorating the dwellings of the Israelites in the desert during the Exodus) next to the Mughrabi Gate. The Muslim authorities reacted in full force and called on their people to come up to the Mount and stop with their bodies the laying of the foundation stone. On October 7 masked people passed from house to house in one of the Arab neighborhoods of Jerusalem demanding that their residents participate in the organized rally.

The Palestinian media as well as the Hamas movement gave the issue much publicity. The next day, October 8, 1990, about 2,000 Arab demonstrators, including schoolchildren and their teachers, gathered on the Temple Mount, while some 25,000 Jews congregated at the Western Wall for the ceremony of the Priest's Blessing held during the Succot festival. Throughout the morning the Arab demonstrators attacked the Jewish border policemen stationed on the Mount. Several policemen escaped through the gates, which were immediately closed; others on the Mount locked themselves in the police station, which was set on fire. The demonstrators threw stones down at the Jews praying by the Western Wall. Police reinforcements forced their way through the blocked Mughrabi Gate

and controlled the multitude with rubber bullets, smoke grenades, and rifles. Seventeen Arabs were killed in the clashes and fifty-three wounded. Twenty-one policemen and nine of the worshippers at the Western Wall were also wounded.[2] These were the most severe clashes that ever took place over the issue of the Temple Mount. For fear the violence would spill over, the army put a curfew on towns and refugee camps in the West Bank. The entire Muslim world, many countries around the world, and the UN Security Council strongly denounced Israel for these events.[3]

Even after these deadly events, the Faithful of the Temple Mount did not stop their attempts to enter the Temple Mount on various festivals throughout the year and perform such ceremonies as lighting Hanukkah candles or sacrificing the Passover lamb. Their applications to the police to enter the Mount are always rejected, as are their repeated appeals to the High Court of Justice to force the police to allow them to do so.

Despite the huge posters in the streets of Jerusalem, the number of people who participate in this annual event is quite small and diminishing each year. However, every year the police must prevent the procession from entering the Temple Mount, and every year they push the demonstrators farther away from the gateway. Every year the Muslim authorities in charge of the Temple Mount use this rather extraordinary event to arouse widespread public anger against the manifest attempts of the Jews to build the Third Temple, an act that implies the destruction of the Muslim shrines on the Temple Mount. Many Jews, both secular and rabbinical as well as religious members of the Israeli parliament (Knesset), fervently denounce these activities of the Faithful of the Temple Mount on grounds that they only cause ongoing anger and sometimes, as in 1989, lead to violence. Some even remind the organizers of the processions that according to a time-honored Jewish belief the Third Temple will be not be built by human hand but by God himself.

The 1989–1990 incidents have all the elements of the contest over the Temple Mount. The two major contestants—the Jews and the Arabs—are well represented. To the Jews the Temple Mount is the holiest place on earth, the place where God manifested himself to King David and where two Jewish Temples—Solomon's Temple and the Second Temple—were located. It is also the place where, according to mystical beliefs, the world began and where it will come to an end. The sanctity of the Mount has been enhanced during millennia of Jewish exile through daily prayers, and special customs have evolved to keep the memory of Jerusalem and the Temple Mount alive. The unexpected victory of the Israeli army during the 1967 Six-Day War, culminating in the capture of Jerusalem and the Temple Mount, was viewed by some as a sign from God that the Days of the messiah were near. Now that Jerusalem and the Temple Mount were in Jewish hands, they believed, it was the duty of the people to begin making preparations for the building of the Temple, thereby accelerating the arrival of the messiah.

The Faithful of the Temple Mount have spearheaded many activities in Jerusalem and elsewhere since 1967 to prepare for the building of the Third Temple. Not everyone in the national-religious circles, however, agreed with the haste in which several sections of the movement began to operate. Indeed, there were conflicting views even among the sages of the past concerning the order of events relat-

ing to the coming of the messiah. According to a statement in the Jerusalem Talmud, the Temple may be built prior to the establishment of a Jewish kingdom that will be ruled by the descendants of King David (Ta'anit 5:1). The great rabbi and philosopher Moses Maimonides, on the other hand, proclaimed that the Kingdom of Israel and the Dynasty of David should come first, as indeed was the order of things in the past, and only then would the Temple be built.[4] There were also conflicting views on how the Temple will be built. As against those who preach "Temple now" and actively prepare for its construction, Jewish mystical thought placed the building of the Temple in the hands of God, believing that when the proper time comes the Temple will descend from heaven complete with all its finery and necessary utensils.

Similarly, there is no unified present-day Israeli-Jewish point of view regarding the future of the Temple Mount. National-religious circles such as the Faithful of the Temple Mount view our times as the beginning of the days of the messiah and believe it is necessary to take over the Temple Mount and build the Third Temple so that the messianic events will start rolling. They are working in various ways to get all the necessary aspects of Temple worship ready for that day. These circles see the Israeli-Arab conflict as a broad religious conflict between Judaism and Islam, centered on the control of the site of the Temple Mount, which they consider to be of exclusive Jewish holiness. They therefore are not prepared even to consider a compromise over it, let alone give it away to the Muslims.

On the other side stand the majority of the nonreligious and also many of the religious Jews in Israel and around the world who take a more sober view of the situation. They see the Israeli-Arab conflict as centering on political rather than religious issues. They realize that although no one doubts the sacredness of the Temple Mount to the Jews, the nation managed to live successfully without control over it for the 2,000 years since the Second Temple was destroyed. These circles believe that if Israel assumed total control over the Mount in preparation for the building of the Third Temple, the worldwide conflict that this act would create might lead to a third world war. These moderate circles are therefore ready to compromise over many territorial issues between Israel and a future Palestinian State, and some extreme left-wingers even consider giving up the Temple Mount to absolute Muslim control. Moderate views to the effect of putting aside, at least for the time being, the mystical aspirations and trying to contain any violence that may erupt have been voiced time and again by the Israeli government and Supreme Court, which have often been called upon called to express their view on the issue. This indeed was the reaction of the Israeli authorities in the 1989–1990 incidents. While pursuing this policy, the government of Israel and its parliament (Knesset) have been considering various options for a compromise over the Temple Mount and Jerusalem as a whole. These proposed options will be explored later in the book.

For the Muslims, who took over Jerusalem from the Christian Byzantines in 638, the Temple Mount in Jerusalem is regarded a holy Muslim site, third only to the mosques of Mecca and Medina in Arabia. It attained this position by being the assumed destination of the mythical Night Flight of the Prophet Muhammad. Influenced by Jewish legends, the Muslims also regard the Temple Mount the site where humanity will face the Last Judgment, an event that will mark the end of the days. Muslims have exerted full control over the Temple Mount for some 1,300 years, except for a short period between 1099 and 1187 when the Christian Crusaders established their kingdom in the Holy Land and turned the Temple Mount into a church site. When the British received a mandate over Palestine in 1920, and then when Israel assumed control over Jerusalem in 1967, the local Arabs came under non-Muslim rule. Rather than being overlords, they were now reduced to the position of subjects and turned to a policy of defending their holy sites against possible foreign incursion. The Arab reaction to Israeli control over the Temple Mount since 1967 has become extremely defensive, its authorities and population fiercely resisting any actual or suspected violation of the Temple Mount, the *Haram a-Sharif*.[5] Often backed by the rest of the Muslim world, the Arab reaction represents an ongoing apprehension that the Jewish national-religious circles will eventually have their way and the Jews indeed destroy their holy shrines on the Temple Mount. To prevent ceding any part of the vast 33.5-acre esplanade of the Temple Mount, the Muslims began referring to the entire area as the al-Aqsa Mosque, thus extending the sacredness over all of it, including the walls that surround it.

The apprehension about a Jewish takeover did not begin with Israel's 1967 victory. It had been the main issue of the Jewish-Arab conflict during the period of the British Mandate over Palestine (1920–1948) and was an important trigger in the development of an Arab national movement, as will be elaborated in chapter 5. Thus, as in the case of the Jews, Arab religious and national interests are intertwined, as is expressed by the demand that the future Palestinian State have Jerusalem as its capital, and the *Haram a-Sharif* be forever under Arab control. It is for this reason that photographs and posers of the Dome of the Rock, the dazzling Muslim structure on the Temple Mount, decorate every Arab house and office and are a favored background for official photos of the Arab leadership.

What is the role of Christianity in this complicated picture? The stake of Christianity in Jerusalem and the Temple Mount is twofold. Relations between Christianity and Judaism have always revolved around the notion that Christians replaced Jews as the people of the promise. Once the Jewish kingdom of Judah, with its capital Jerusalem and its Temple, fell to the Romans in 70 CE,[6] its people were exiled and became a dispersed and despised nation. These events occurred shortly after the life and death of Jesus and the formation of Christianity, a religion that was developed by the disciples of Jesus. After 300 years of persecution, the new religion became the state religion of the Roman Empire in the fourth century CE. It then began viewing itself as the victorious, true Israel, inheritor of all of God's promises.[7]

The establishment of the State of Israel in 1948 and the subsequent takeover of the Old City with all its holy Christian sites reversed the millennia-old order of things. The Vatican, speaking for the Christian world, could not agree to the new situation in which the Jews ruled over Christian sacred places. Not being particularly interested in the Temple Mount but rather in the Church of the Holy Sepulcher and other holy sites in Jerusalem, the Vatican attempted to pass a United Nations resolution to hand Jerusalem over to the rule of an international body that would include representatives of the Vatican.[8] This was one of the many pro-posals made to solve the Israeli-Arab conflict over Jerusalem and the Temple Mount, proposals that will be enumerated later in the book.

A completely different stake in the Temple Mount is taken by groups of fundamentalist-evangelical Christian denominations, based mainly in North America. These sects, which take the biblical prophecies literally, as do Jewish national-religious groups, view the return of the Jews to their homeland, followed by the establishment of the State of Israel in 1948 and crowned by its conquest of Jerusalem in 1967, as the fulfillment of such prophecies as Isaiah 52–55. The infallible words of God have come true. The time has thus come for the great drama of the End of Time to begin to unfold. These sects are also known as millennialists—those who foresee the millennium of the kingdom of God that will follow the advent of Christ.[9] But for the Second Coming of Christ to occur, the Temple in Jerusalem has to be built so that Jesus can enter it in glory.[10] During the last two centuries these evangelical movements have witnessed a remarkable upsurge in North America, where they now make up about a third of the practicing Christians and are said to be the fastest growing Christian-sects in the United States.[11] The Christian millennialists found natural allies in the Jewish groups who work to hasten the coming of the messiah. Although both groups want to build the Third Temple, each wants it for its own needs and reasons. And so it is not surprising that the activities of the Faithful of the Temple Mount are funded partially by fundamentalist groups in the United States, as are other activities geared to the same purpose.[12]

As against the Jews and Muslims who play the game of power, of domination over the Temple Mount, the interest of the Christians is

Christian participant (center, wearing a skull-cap) addressing the Faithful of the Temple Mount, 2002. Photographer: Rivka Gonen

not in the real estate. They do not want to control the Mount and are perfectly content to let the Jews fight the battle, win it, and eventually build the Third Temple to the benefit of the Christian world. The Christians refrain from taking an active part in the violent events that occasionally flare on the Mount. However, one of the most appalling events that occurred there, the burning down of part of the al-Aqsa Mosque, was the work of a deranged young Fundamentalist Christian, who believed he was sent by God to pave the way to the building of the Third Temple. His story will be related later in the book.

And thus Jews, Muslims, and Christians play their roles in the drama of the Temple Mount, each guarding their own interest and pursuing their own goals. The drama has often evolved into bloody conflict. No one knows yet how the conflict will be resolved, and the many suggestions made toward that end have not been accepted by either of the contesting sides. Since September 2000, when the al-Aqsa Intifada erupted, the Muslim authorities have completely closed the Temple Mount to all non-Muslims. The battles are now being fought elsewhere, in other parts of war-torn Israel/Palestine.

Let us now find out where the Temple Mount is located and learn about its long history, to understand how this complicated and dangerous contest over holiness came about.

Notes

[1] Translated by the author from a poster in her possession.

[2] Shragai 1995: 340–363.

[3] Berkovitz 2000: 95–97.

[4] Goren 1992: 2–3.

[5] Reiter 2000a: 156.

[6] Throughout the book the initials CE and BCE will be used. CE refers to "Common Era," a general term replacing AD (*Anno Domini*, "the Year of our Lord"). BCE refers to "Before the Common Era," replacing BC ("Before Christ").

[7] Conference on Jerusalem 1977: xi.

[8] Ferrari 1999: 143–165.

[9] Gorenberg 2000: 30–54.

[10] Lamy, Philip 2000: 257

[11] Whalen 2000: 329–332.

[12] Ariel 2000: 143–151.

Chapter 2
The Temple Mount: Location, History, and Contemporary Features

Where Is the Temple Mount?

For the past 3,000 years, the Temple Mount has been an integral part of the city of Jerusalem. Its situation within the city has, however, changed with the development of the city over time.

The hill known as the Temple Mount is the northern extension of a very narrow spur of hill that slopes sharply from north to south. On the east it is bordered by the deep Kidron Valley, also known as the Valley of Jehosaphat. In this valley, at the foot of its western slope, issues the Gihon Spring, the only perennial water source in the region that provides life-giving water to those in the vicinity. To the west of this narrow spur is the nameless "The Valley," known in the past also by the Greek name Tyropeon, translated as the Cheese-Makers Valley. This valley is now filled with refuse pilled into it over the centuries and is not clearly visible. The meeting point of the Kidron Valley with The Valley marks the southern end of the hill spur. Toward the north the hill spur widens but immediately narrows again by a valley that runs eastwards toward the Kidron Valley.

Aerial view of the Old City of Jerusalem surrounded by its walls. The Temple Mount in the lower right corner. Photographer: Moshe Milner, 1990. © 1998: The State of Israel, Government Press Office.

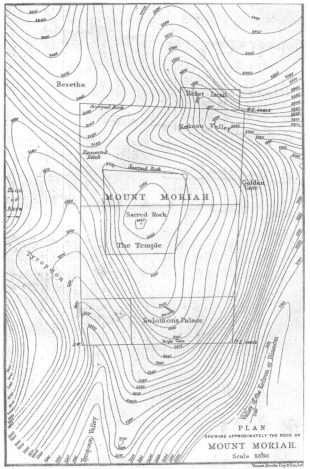

Topographic map of the Temple Mount and vicinity. Source: Wilson, R. E. and Warren R. E. The Recovery of Jerusalem, 1871.

As if in keeping with the forbidding topography of this hill, the climate of the area is also rather inhospitable. To the east of the north-south watershed, where the Judean Mountains begin their descent to the Dead Sea, the amount of rain that falls is usually minimal, hardly enough to sustain a permanent population. And yet, the southern part of this hill spur—small, narrow and bordered by very steep slopes, and dry most of the year— was the birthplace of Jerusalem. It began its long career as a walled city of the Canaanites at the beginning of the second millennium BCE, thousands of years after people began to frequent the site and buried their dead there, and perhaps also established a tiny village.

There can be no doubt that what made the hill fit for settlement despite its difficult topography and climate was the Gihon Spring, which issues at its foot. The spring provided water to people who had settled above it as early as the fourth millennium BCE, and continued to provide small amounts of precious water to the growing population of the city up to the first century BCE. At that time a system of channels, tunnels, and cisterns brought water to the expanding city from higher springs to the south of it.[1]

Only in the twentieth century were pipes and pumps installed, and now the city gets its water from the general water system of the country.

The City of David viewed from the south. The Kidron Valley is to the right, the Valley to the left. In the upper part of photo—the Temple Mount.
Photographer: Bouki Boaz.

Steps leading down to the Gihon Spring. Etching by W. Tipping, 1851.

The beginning of Canaanite Jerusalem around 1850 BCE preceded its conquest by King David of Israel by almost a thousand years. Having gained control over the city, David changed its name from Urusalim, as it was referred to in Egyptians texts, or from Salem, the city of Melchizedek (Genesis 14:18), and gave it his own name—the City of David. On the northern, somewhat wider extension of this hill, which was outside the walls of the City of David, King Solomon later built his Temple. Over the centuries this hill would become one of the holiest sites on earth, revered by Jews, Christians, and Muslims alike.

With time the city expanded beyond its original tiny location. Because of the difficult topography, it spread mainly to the north and west, while the southern areas leading toward the inhospitable Judean Desert and the Dead Sea, and the eastern area blocked by the high Mount of Olives were never settled. The first time the city spread out of its narrow borders was in the seventh century BCE, when a substantial influx of population necessitated annexing new grounds.

The city at that time expanded to the higher western hill, all the way to the Hinnom Valley in the west. This valley proved an insurmountable topographic barrier that prevented the city from further expanding westward until the middle of the nineteenth century. The city was now well protected from the east, west, and south by steep slopes and deep valleys.

The expansion to the north, where the ground slopes gently and provides wide, flat areas for easy construction, was more gradual, since this side does not have a natural defense and is therefore vulnerable. Only as late as the first century BCE did the city begin to expand in that direction. By then the Temple Mount had already achieved its present proportions and was situated, as it is now, in the extreme eastern side of the city, occupying only a very small area within it.

The topographic grandeur of a holy edifice towering over the residential section of the city, as it had done since it was built, was now lost. Now the higher grounds of the western hill that was within the city itself reduced the Temple Mount to a topographically lower position. Indeed it is reported that the kings who ruled Jerusalem in the first century CE were able to observe the rituals held on the Temple Mount from their palace on the western hill.

After its great expansion prior to the Roman destruction of 70 CE the city contracted, then expanded again under Christian Byzantine rule, and then contracted once again. Since the twelfth century it has had the form of a lop-sided square of about 25 acres, surrounded by walls about 1 kilometer by 1 kilometer each. Its eastern border has always been the Kidron Valley, its western border, the Hinnom Valley. The ancient City of David, as well as the southern section of the western hill known as Mount Zion, were left outside the city. This square, enclosed within its walls, has maintained its shape and size to this day and is known as the Old City of Jerusalem.

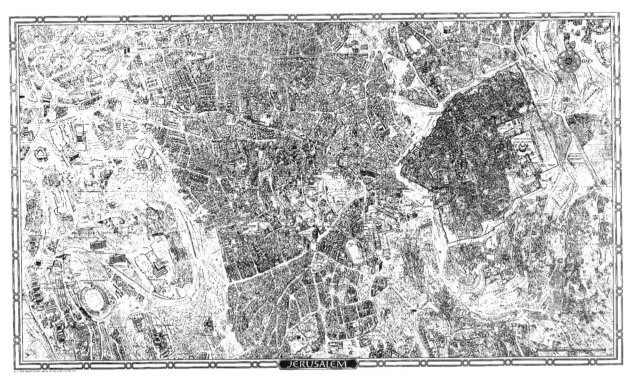

Aerial photograph of the center of Jerusalem. To the right—the Old City surrounded by walls with the Temple Mount in its lower right corner.

Since the middle of the nineteenth century, Jerusalem has expanded in an accelerated pace in all directions but the eastern side, and it now covers a huge area of almost 31,000 acres. The Temple Mount now occupies only a minute corner of the large and growing city. It has not, however, lost its significance as a locus of intense holiness and a source of contention between nations and religions.

A Short Historical Background

This section provides only a short sketch of the long history of the Temple Mount and the city of Jerusalem. Many of the events, edifices, and personalities mentioned here will be described in greater detail, and their significance to the story of the Temple Mount will be elaborated on in the later chapters of the book.

The Early Settlements (Fourth Millennium–1000 BCE)[2]

A scatter of pottery shards dating to the fourth millennium BCE unearthed in archaeological excavations on the eastern slopes of the City of David indicate that people had already found the site hospitable some 6,000 years ago. During the following millennia people continued to frequent the site and may even have built a permanent settlement that existed for hundreds of years. The Canaanites established the first walled town in about 1850 BCE as one of several fortified settlements. Although the town had its local king, it was under Egyptian domination, and its name, Urusalim, is mentioned in several Egyptian texts of the time.[3] The name Jerusalem is thus almost 4,000 years old, one of the oldest known place-names of a city that has been continuously occupied since.

The Monarchies of Israel and Judah (1000–586 BCE)

The Canaanite town survived until it fell to King David around 1000 BCE. Although David made it the capital of the expanding kingdom of Israel, the town did not grow beyond its Canaanite walls. This task fell to his son Solomon, who built a magnificent palace to the north of the town, and beyond it he erected a Temple to the God of Israel. This last project forever changed the nature of the hill to the north of the City of David, consecrating it as one of the most revered locations on earth. After Solomon's death, the kingdom split in two: the kingdom of Israel. with its capital Samaria in the northern part of the country, and the kingdom of Judah, with its capital Jerusalem to the south. David's dynasty continued to rule Judah from its capital city, and the Temple continued to function throughout this period, conveniently named the First Temple period. The consoling prophecies of Isaiah, Amos, Jeremiah, and other prophets ensured that King David and his dynasty, alongside Solomon's Temple, would be forever imbedded in the collective consciousness of the Jewish people, and also of the Christians and Muslims, as symbols of the most glorious period of Israelite history. An intense desire that those days will soon return is still pronounced three times every day in the Jewish prayers.

In 586 BCE the Babylonian army laid a long siege on Jerusalem and eventually captured and destroyed both city and Temple. That was the end of the kingdom of Judah. This destruction and that of the Second Temple many years later are mourned every year to this day on the ninth day of the Hebrew month of Av. The population of the kingdom was exiled to

Babylon, where they remained for some fifty years and wept when they remembered Zion and the Temple.

The Second Temple Period (538 BCE–70 CE)

The Second Temple period was a time of many changes, when the country frequently changed hands between foreign and Jewish rule. The weeping over Zion did not last long. Soon after the Babylonian kingdom fell to the newly established empire of Persia, Cyrus, king of Persia, declared a policy of religious freedom. In 538 BCE, only fifty years after their country was destroyed, Cyrus allowed the exiles of Judah to return to their homeland and rebuild their Temple. Only a trickle actually returned, however. The first years were difficult. The returnees had neither the power to withstand their envious neighbors, nor the resources to build the Temple, and they had to make do with only an altar. Although over the following years the Temple was built, it was poor compared with the former one. Only the leadership of Ezra the Scribe and the high official Nehemiah, who came to Judah about a hundred years after the first returnees, managed to curb the hostile neighbors and enforce adherence to the new religious codes developed during the period of exile. These codes became the foundations of the Jewish religion as it developed since then.

The uneventful period under Persian rule ended in 332 BCE, when Alexander the Great conquered the Orient and put an end to the Persian kingdom. After Alexander's untimely death, his kingdom was divided among Ptolemy, who became ruler of Egypt, Judah, and neighboring regions; Seleucus, who ruled over the vast area from Asia Minor to the borders of India; and Antigonus, who ruled over Greece. The times of peace Judah enjoyed under the Ptolemaic rulers came to an end when the kingdom fell to the Seleucids. The Seleucid ruler, King Antiochus IV, wished to Hellenize all his domains and consequently sacrificed a pig on the Temple altar. A mutiny broke out in Judah in 168 CE led by the rural priest Mattathias the Hasmonean and his five sons, one of whom was Judah Maccabee. Heroic victories on the battlefield ended with the creation of an independent Jewish state ruled by the Hasmonean dynasty. The consecration of the Temple is celebrated to this day in the festival of Hanukkah.

During a fierce competition between two Hasmonean princes in 63 CE over the throne, one of the contestants invited Rome to intervene. The Roman general Pompey sided with one prince and fought against the other, and consequently brought Judah under the yoke of Rome.

The last Hasmonean king was succeeded in 37 CE by Herod, who was placed on the throne by his powerful friends in Rome. He was the son of a convert and therefore never considered a true Jew worthy of replacing the royal Hasmoneans. Despite being rejected by the people and their religious authorities, Herod gave the country a period of security and prosperity. He built a series of palaces across the country and would retreat to them in the face of growing hostility against him; he also rebuilt the Temple Mount. With time Herod developed extreme suspicion against everybody around him, including his immediate family. His fears reached such a degree that he ordered the assassination of his wife, Miriam, a Hasmonean princess, and of his two sons by her.

With the death of King Herod in 4 BCE a period of unrest began in Judah, and the Romans appointed governors to rule the country with a firm hand. The unrest was not only political but also moral and ideological. Several charismatic leaders preached against the political and religious situation of the country and promised better days to come. The most famous of these was Jesus of the town of Nazareth in the Galilee, who traveled around the villages in the vicinity preaching a message of peace and love and performing miracles. When he went to Jerusalem in the company of several of his disciples to celebrate the festival of Passover, he was captured and brought to trial before the Roman governor as a prospective instigator of riots. He was found guilty and put to death on the cross. His disciples spread his message, and within a relatively short time a new religion—Christianity—was born.

During this stormy period, the people of Judah were divided between moderates, who believed in a peaceful existence under Roman rule despite its harsh measures, and zealots, who called for a war against the oppressor. A widespread anti-Roman revolt began in the Galilee in 66 CE and gradually spread to Jerusalem, which came under heavy siege. Jerusalem fell to the Roman army on the ninth day of the Hebrew month Av in 70 CE. The Second Temple period thus ended with a disaster to the Jewish people, who lost both their political and their religious center. With the end of their independence, the story of the Jewish people for the coming 2,000 years is the story of a people in exile.

The Roman Period (70–332 CE)

The 330 years of Roman rule in the country can be divided into two parts. For the first, from the conquest of Jerusalem to about 135 CE, the city was in ruins. The commanders of the conquering Roman legions stationed themselves in what was left of Herod's palace on the western hill, while the soldiers were stationed in a camp within the city, perhaps near the southwestern corner of the Temple Mount.

In 132 CE the Roman emperor Hadrian decided to build a new, pagan city on the site of Jerusalem. He changed its time-honored name to Aelia Capitolina—Aelius being his family name, and Capitolina in honor of Jupiter Capitolinus, the chief Roman god. The Jews who remained in the country after its destruction in 70 CE again rebelled against the Romans. Their leader was Simon Bar Kosiba, known as Bar Kokhba (son of a star), a name given to him by Rabbi Akiba, one of the important rabbis of the time, who hoped that the rebellion would succeed and the Jews would resume their independence. For three years Bar Kokhba led his army to victories and even captured Jerusalem. But these victories were short-lived, and when the Roman legions were mobilized the rebellion came to an end in 135 CE. The Bar Kokhba Revolt, known also as the Second War against the Romans, ended with the total demolition of Jewish existence in Judah. The Romans changed its name to Palestina, a name that survives to this day.

The Byzantine Period (332–638 CE)

The Roman period in Palestine came to an end through internal changes that occurred in the empire. Under pressure from invading barbarians from the north, the empire was divided in two, the Eastern and Western Empires. For the Eastern, or Byzantine, Empire, a new capital, Byzantium, was built on the Bosphorus. In 332 CE, the Byzantine emperor Constantine converted to Christianity, and under his orders the entire

Byzantine Empire became Christian. The pagan Aelia Capitolina again became Jerusalem, a holy Christian city filled with memories of the life and death of Jesus. Constantine sent his mother, Queen Helena, on a mission to Jerusalem to discover the exact location of the crucifixion. She discovered that place on a hill known as Golgotha (Calvary), the hill of the skull, which is now incorporated within the Church of the Holy Sepulcher. In a cave under Golgotha (Calvary), Helena also discovered the original cross of the crucifixion, which became the holiest Christian relic.

The Early Muslim Period (638–1099)

At the beginning of the seventh century a new religion, Islam, was born in the town of Mecca in Saudi Arabia. Muhammad, a merchant of that city, had a series of visions in which he was given the essence of the new religion. His pagan neighbors rejected his message, and Muhammad fled to the town of Medina. There he was free to preach, and within a short time he gathered around him many followers. Upon his death, his followers led a series of campaigns outside of Arabia, and within a very short period they forged an empire that stretched from Persia in the east to Spain in the west. Palestine came under their rule in 638. The Muslims adopted the tradition of the holiness of Jerusalem and the Temple Mount, transferring to it the story of the Night Flight of Muhammad from Mecca to a faraway place (al-Aqsa) from where he ascended to heaven to the presence of God. This story is the basis of Muslim reverence of the Temple Mount, a reverence that lies at the bottom of the Jewish-Arab contention over the site. The Muslims built two magnificent edifices on the Mount, the Dome of the Rock and the al-Aqsa

Mosque, both standing to this day. This early Muslim period lasted until 1099, when the Crusaders stormed Jerusalem and returned it to Christian rule.

The Crusader Period (1099–1187)

The Crusader period lasted less than a hundred years, and during that period Jerusalem was the capital of the Crusader Kingdom of Jerusalem. In fact, this was the only time between the destruction of Jerusalem of the Second Temple and the establishment of the State of Israel that Jerusalem was raised to the status of the capital of a country; during the Muslim period the capital was always elsewhere. The Crusaders converted the Dome of the Rock on the Temple Mount to a Christian church and handed over the al-Aqsa Mosque to the newly created Order of the Knights Templars to serve as their headquarters. Jerusalem returned to Crusader rule for another short period of ten years in the twelfth century following negotiations between the Christian and the Muslim rulers.

The Late Muslim Period (1187–1919)

The next 730 years were a long period of Muslim rule over the country and over Jerusalem. The period is divided according to the ruling dynasties into Ayyubid (1178–1250), Mamluk (1250–1516), and Ottoman periods (1516–1919). Throughout this time Jerusalem and the country as a whole suffered from gradual stagnation. Jerusalem was reduced to the position of a provincial town, but its religious status in the Muslim world rose, especially during the Mamluk period, when exiled officials settled there and built around the Temple Mount many buildings of religious nature, such as academies, libraries, and monasteries. For a short time in which the Ottoman ruler Suleiman the Magnificent showed interest in Jerusalem, restoring its walls, rebuilding some of its gates, and perhaps also repairing the Jewish place of prayer at the Western Wall,[4] but then the city sank into a long period of decline. Only the growing involvement of European powers in the affairs of the area after the Crimean War of 1853–1856 awakened Jerusalem from its long slumber and brought general improvement in many areas of public and private life.

The growing number of Jewish immigrants to the country, and especially to Jerusalem, created the need for new residential neighborhoods beyond the confines of the Old City walls. The first small extramural neighborhood, built in 1860, marked the beginning of the vast expansion of the new sections of Jerusalem, an expansion that continues to this day. The Temple Mount is now only a tiny square on the extreme southeastern corner of the large city of Jerusalem.

The Period of the British Mandate (1919–1948)

In the new world-order that followed World War I, Britain, one of the victorious countries, obtained a mandate over Palestine that lasted for some thirty years. The British did much to develop the country in general and Jerusalem in particular, but they did not manage to curb the growing hostility between the Jews and the Arabs, who were at the time developing their political awareness and national institutions. The Jewish-Arab conflicts centered at that time on the Jewish place of prayer at the Western Wall. This period ended with the 1948 war between the contending parties, which led to the creation of the State of Israel

The Israeli, Jordanian, and Again Israeli Periods

The new State of Israel encompassed only part of Palestine. The so-called West Bank, located west of the Jordan River and Dead Sea, came under the rule of the neighboring Kingdom of Jordan, while the small Gaza Strip, between Israel and Sinai, came under that of Egypt. Jerusalem was thereby divided. The New City was declared the capital of the State of Israel, while the Old City and other Arab neighborhoods became part of the Jordanian West Bank. The Six-Day War changed this situation when Israel took control of the West Bank and Gaza Strip, and united Jerusalem under its rule. Now the Temple Mount, for centuries under the exclusive sovereignty of Muslims, had a new Jewish sovereign. This gave rise to a severe contention that is with us to this day. The future of the Temple Mount, of Jerusalem, and of the region as a whole is shrouded in mist.

The Temple Mount Today[5]

The Temple Mount as it is today reflects the last 2,000 years of its long history, from the time of King Herod until the present. Remnants of the earlier periods, including those of Solomon's Temple, are buried under the Herodian fill. The Temple Mount is a large oblong of some 33.4 acres with a main north-south axis. A slight tilt in the northeastern corner mars its perfect shape. The shape and dimensions of the Temple Mount were established by the major construction work of King Herod, whose architects and builders diverted a stream in the north and the more substantial Tyropeon stream in the southwest, to create the planned shape. One can appreciate the enormity of this project by looking at the huge stones used for the construction of its walls. The huge Temple Mount esplanade is nowa-

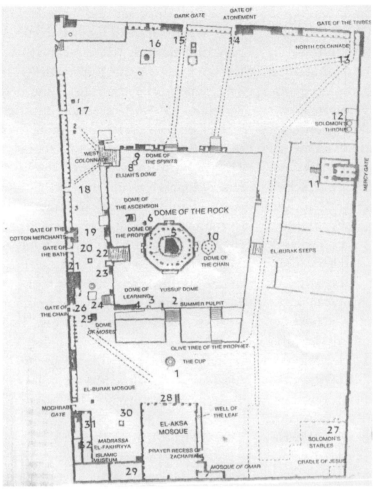

Plan of the Temple Mount / *Haram a-Sharif* prior to the conversion of Solomon's Stables into a mosque.

The Sites: 1. The Cup; 2. the Summer Pulpit; 3. Yussuf Dome; 4. Dome of Learning; 5. Dome of the Rock; 6. Dome of the Prophet; 7. Dome of the Ascension; 8. Elijah's Dome; 9. Dome of the Spirits; 10. Dome of the Chain; 11. Golden Gate; 12. Solomon's Throne; 13. Gate of the Tribes; 14. Gate of Atonement; 15. The Dark Gate; 16. Dome of Solomon; 17. Gate of the Inspector; 18. The Iron Gate; 19. Gate of the Cotton Merchants; 20. Gate of the Bath; 21. Madrassa el-Uthmanyya; 22. Fountain of Qayt Bey; 23. Fountain of Qasem Pasha; 24. Fig Tree Area; 25. Dome of Moses; 26. Gate of the Chain; 27. Solomon's Stables; 28. El-Aksa Mosque; 29. Women's Mosque; 30. Dome of Yussuf Agha; 31. Madrassa el-Fakhryya; 32. The Islamic Museum.

days divided into three levels. The upper platform is located more or less in the center of the Temple Mount. It is the highest section of the Mount and is crowned by the Dome of the Rock. The lower platform, on which the al-Aqsa Mosque is built, surrounds the upper platform and occupies most of the area of the Temple Mount. It is especially spacious on the north and south sides. Under the southern lower platform, where the Temple Mount was substantially enlarged, is an underground level.

The Upper Platform

The upper platform is not located in the center of the Temple Mount but is shifted to the west. It is trapezoid in shape, wider in the north and narrower in the south, and occupies some 6 acres. It is about 4 meters higher than the surrounding lower platform. Eight flights of steps mount the upper platform—two from the north, two from the south, one from the east, and three from the west. The west faces the Muslim Quarter of the Old City and is therefore the direction from which most peo-

Bird's-eye view of the Temple Mount from the south. Al-Aqsa Mosque is in the foreground, the Dome of the rock further up. Photographer: Moshe Milner, 1995. © 1998, The State of Israel, Government Press Office.

Aerial view of the upper platform of the Temple Mount with the Dome of the Rock in the center. Photographer: Moshe Milner, 1995. © 1998, The State of Israel, Government Press Office.

Decorative arches on the upper platform of the
Temple Mount. Photographer: A. van der Heyden,
1989. Courtesy of The Jerusalem Publishing House.

ple enter the Temple Mount. All the flights of
steps are surmounted by sets of decorative
arches, each different. Known as "The Scales,"
they reflect the Muslim belief that on the Day
of Judgment scales will be hung on the arches,
and the souls of the believers will be weighed
to determine who was righteous and will be
rewarded, and who did evil and will be punished.

The Rock

The focus of this elevated platform is the
sacred rock, the highest surviving exposed
bedrock on the entire Temple Mount. This
bare rock has attracted the imagination of generations of people who understood it to be the
local for monumental events in the past and

future of the universe. It is assumed, and gen-
erally accepted, that Solomon's Temple and
then the Second Temple were built on this
very rock, and on this same rock the Dome of
the Rock has been standing for some thirteen
centuries. Of the two Jewish Temples nothing
has remained, allowing several scholars to
doubt whether they indeed stood on this spot.

The gray bare rock that is seen today has
on its surface many natural depressions as
well as signs of artificial quarrying and cutting. Its western side is an artificially cut
straight line; perhaps it was one side of a foundation trench for a wall, or perhaps part of a
flight of steps cut to facilitate worshippers
going up to its summit. It is not known who
was responsible for this cut or when it was

The Rock inside the Dome of the Rock. Photographer: Eric Matson, 1915. © 1997–1998, The State of Israel, Government Press Office.

made. On the north and south sides of the rock are several additional artificial cuts, which again may have been foundation trenches of walls. These artificial cuts on the rocks are believed by some to strongly support the view that the Jewish Temples indeed stood over the rock. It has been suggested that the walls that stood in these trenches were the walls of the most sacred part of the Temples: the Holy of Holies.[6]

Other cuttings on the northern side of the rock and on the rock itself are attributed to the Crusaders, who built several altars over the rock and next to it. In the floor on this side is a tunnel covered with marble slabs. Perhaps this tunnel runs northwards and passes under a black slab embedded in the floor next to the northern door of the Dome of the Rock. The Muslims believe that this slab covers the entrance to Paradise.

On the south side is a natural depression in a section of the rock that is separate from the main rock and adjacent to it. It is believed by Muslims to have been caused by the heel of Muhammad when he ascended to heaven from this spot. A sort of cupboard, known as Jacob's Cupboard, surmounts this depression. Incense is put into the depression, and Muslim worshippers put their hands into it and touch the imprint of their prophet's heel. The Crusaders believed that this depression was the footprint of Jesus, who stood here when he chased the moneychangers from the Temple. In the center of the cupboard is a silver box containing, so tradition relates, three hairs from the beard of the prophet Muhammad.

The Cave Under the Rock

Under the south side of the rock is a cave, entered by a flight of steps. The original size of the cave was reduced when a wall was built on its southeastern side. Its shape was also modified over time. The round hole in its ceiling suggests that this cave may have been a typical burial cave cut around 2000 BCE. The possible existence of burial caves on the Temple Mount necessitated taking strict measures to allow the ritual defilement— caused, according to the Jewish religion, by a corpse— to seep out of the holy edifice. This cleansing was particularly mandatory during the Second Temple period, when preoccupation with ritual purity was very pronounced.[7] The cave today has an oblong shape, and various corners in it are believed to have been places of prayer of important personalities of the past—the patriarch Abraham, the prophet Elijah and other prophets, Kings David and Solomon, and Muhammad himself. The

Interior of the Dome of the Rock with Jacob's Cupboard.
Source: Charles W. Wilson, Picturesque Palestine, Sinai and Egypt, 1880.

The cave under the Rock. Source: Barclay, T. J., City of the Great King, 1858.

northwest corner of the cave is called the Seat of the Angel Gabriel, the angel whose task will be to proclaim the end of the days. In the floor of the cave is a round slab with a blackened star incised in it. Muslims believe that this is the entrance to Hell, and that the souls of the dead are buried under it. It is appropriately called the Well of the Spirits. Another belief suggests that all the waters of the world have their source under this slab.

It seems that during the First and Second Temple period the rock was covered by construction and thus was hidden from view and possibly may have been altogether unknown. Indeed, the steps that lead down to the cave are not cut in the rock but are constructed, perhaps by the builders of the Dome of the Rock.

The Dome of the Rock

This magnificent edifice was built in 691/92 by Caliph 'Abd al Malik of the Ummayad dynasty. Its English name is a translation of the Arabic *Kubbat a-Sakhra*. This oldest of all Muslim structures has been preserved intact to this day, although its external and internal ornamentation were at times replaced. Because of its perfect symmetry, harmonious proportions, and lively color scheme, it is considered one of the most beautiful structures ever built. Unlike the usual mosques, which are large spaces with rows of

The Dome of the Rock with the Mount of Olives in the background. Photographer: A. van der Heyden, 1989. Courtesy of The Jerusalem Publishing House.

The Dome of the Rock and the Dome of the Chain. Etching by E. Finden, 1835.

pillars, this concentric edifice befits a commemorative building for private prayer and meditation. Its plan is most unusual in Muslim architecture and is believed to have derived from earlier Christian prototypes.

Other Structures on the Upper Platform

To the east of the Dome of the Rock is the Dome of the Chain. It is a small structure, its roof resting on a circle of eleven pillars and its dome on an inner octagon formed by six pillars. Because its plan is somewhat similar to that of its larger neighbor, it has been suggested that it was an architect's model for the Dome of the Rock and thus contemporary with it.

To the northwest and southwest of the Dome of the Rock are several small domed structures, each differing from the others and

each built in a different period, most of them commemorating important personalities of the past. The closest to the northwest honors Fatima, the daughter of Muhammad, and next to it is the Dome of the Ascent, commemorating another place from where Muhammad ascended to heaven. It was built in the Crusader period. Further to the north is the Dome of the Spirits or the Tablets, the origin and significance of the name is not known. Its floor is natural bedrock, a fact that gave rise to an alternative theory concerning the location of the Jewish Temples. Next to it is the Dome of the Prophet Elijah. To the southwest of the Dome of the Rock is the oblong Dome of the Grammar, surmounted by two domes. It is said that here studies in grammar were conducted. It has a very ornate entrance flanked by two braided pillars, probably taken from

Dome of the Ascent. Photographer: Avi Ohayon. © 1997–1998, The State of Israel, Government Press Office.

some ruined Crusader structure. Today this structure houses the offices of the Muslim *waqf* (organization responsible for handling property donated to the upkeep of religious institutions) and the office of the officer who regulates the affairs of the Temple Mount. Next to it is the Dome of Joseph. Near the flight of steps that ascends to the upper platform is the marble Summer *Minbar* (preacher's pulpit) surmounted by a dome, which marks an open-air mosque for the used when there is an overflow of worshippers in the al-Aqsa Mosque. Next to it is a marble *mihrab*, a niche facing southward toward Mecca, the direction holy to the Muslims.

The Lower Platform

The al-Aqsa Mosque

Most of the area of the Temple Mount is occupied by the lower platform, extending on all sides of the upper platform. It is dominated by the al-Aqsa Mosque, situated against the southern wall of the Mount. This structure is specifically designed for communal prayer and is built in the typical style of such mosques, with eight parallel rows of columns

Façade of al-Aqsa Mosque. Source: Charles W. Wilson, Picturesque Palestine, Sinai and Egypt, 1880.

Muslim washing his hands at The Chalice. Photographer: A. van der Heyden, 1989. Courtesy of The Jerusalem Publishing House.

that hold the ceiling, creating seven aisles between the columns. The central aisle, which leads straight toward the *mihrab*, is the widest. This is the oldest mosque in this part of the world, and one of the largest and most important. The name of the mosque reflects the tradition that this is the Farthest Place (*al-aqsa*) mentioned in the Koran, to which Muhammad flew on his Night Flight. Built between 705 and 715 on the unstable artificial Herodian fill, it was destroyed many times by earthquakes. Its original vast space was reduced with time until it reached its present dimensions. The sections inside the mosque were built in various periods, and therefore the building lacks the harmony and unity of the Dome of the Rock.

The mosque has several additions both to the east and to the west of it. To the east, and leaning on the southern wall of the Temple Mount, is 'Omar's Mosque, added in the Ottoman period. Its name is a reminder of the first mosque built on the Temple Mount by Caliph 'Omar. In the east wall of the mosque are the Mosque of the Forty and the Chapel of Zechariah, both dating to the Crusader period. The three structures to the west also date to the Crusader period. The one closest to the main mosque was in the past a women's mosque and is now a Muslim religious school.

Water fountain of Kayyat Bey. Source: Charles W. Wilson, Picturesque Palestine, Sinai and Egypt, 1880.

Next to it is the Mughrabi Mosque, used in the past as a place of prayer for pilgrims from North Africa. The third, along the southern section of the west wall, has been converted into an Islamic Museum, which houses important relics from various periods of use of the Temple Mount.

In front of the main entrance to the al-Aqsa Mosque stands the Chalice (*el Kas*), a fountain that provides water for washing the hands and feet of the worshippers, who, according to Muslim custom, are obliged to enter the mosque clean. It was built in the Mamluk period and in the twentieth century was provided with taps and seats for comfort. Next to it grows an olive tree named after the Prophet Muhammad. The tree is said to be associated with the mythical Tree of Light mentioned in the Koran, which is rooted in Paradise and whose branches touch heaven. It is the Muslim form of the Tree of Life,[8] a very ancient and very widely spread symbol in the ancient Near East, transformed into the Jewish Temple candelabrum (menorah), as well as the Christian cross.

Other Structures on the Lower Platform

The lower platform to the east of the al-Aqsa Mosque, as well as the entire length of its eastern and northeastern sides, is empty of structures, except for the much-revered Solomon's Seat. This double-domed structure to the north of the Gate of Mercy is believed, according to a Muslim legend, to be where King Solomon sat and watched the demons build his Temple for him. King Solomon is one of the most highly esteemed personalities of the past, and many legends are told about him in both Jewish and Muslim folklore. King Solomon is again honored in the lovely Dome of Solomon in the northwestern corner of the Temple Mount. Built by the Crusaders, who named it the Seat of Jesus, this is an octagonal bedrock-based structure. It was originally an open structure, based on eight piers, but was later closed in. Other structures in this section of the Mount are the early nineteenth- century Dome of Suleiman, and a water fountain named after Sultan Suleiman.

The narrow western side of the lower plaza is rich with structures designed for the comfort of the worshippers who enter the Temple Mount from the west. There are several watering fountains, the most spectacular being the one built by Keyyat Bey during the Mamluk period. Three others fountains are named after their builders. The Dome of Moses commemorates the prophet revered by Muslims and Jews alike.

The Gates to the Temple Mount

Entry to the Temple Mount is only from the north and the west. Three gates give access from the north, seven from the west. Until September 2000, the beginning of the al-Aqsa Intifada, non-Muslims were allowed to enter only through the Mughrabi Gate, the south-ernmost of the western gates. Exit of non-Muslims was allowed through the Gate of the Cotton Merchants, a highly ornate gate built in the Mamluk period. Since then non-Muslims have been totally barred from the Temple Mount. The other gates serve only Muslims.

The blocked double Gate of Mercy, known to Christians as the Golden Gate, is in the east wall of the Temple Mount. This special entrance has a gatehouse, a structure divided by a row of columns into two halls, and a flight of steps that leads up to the lower platform of the Temple Mount. In its present shape the gate was probably built toward the end of the Byzantine period as a triumphal gate to celebrate the victory of the emperor Heraclius over the Persians. The gate was blocked at some point after the Crusader period. There are traces of an earlier gate of unknown date under it,[9] but no excavation has been carried out to ascertain their date.

The Underground Level

The Temple Mount is studded with underground halls, passages, and water cisterns, all hidden from the eye of the visitor.

Solomon's Stables[10]

The southern section of the Temple Mount is an addition to the original configuration of the Mount, the work of King Herod in the first century BCE. There are no contemporary or later records that describe how the huge subterranean spaces under the enormous esplanade were dealt with in the days of Herod. At present there is in the southeastern section an earth fill some 100 feet high, and on it are rows of piers and arches that hold the surface of the platform. All this massive construction is held in place by the south wall of the Temple Mount, which is about 150 feet

Interior of Solomon's Stables. Photographer: American Colony, 1910. © 1997–1998, The State of Israel, Government Press Office.

high. The space on the southeastern part of this monumental addition has been known since the Crusader period as Solomon's Stables. In the 1990s Solomon's Stables underwent major changes and were converted into a mosque. It is very possible that other, similar subterranean spaces exist on the southwestern part of the Temple Mount, but there is no access to that part.

The halls of Solomon's Stables now consist of twelve rows of piers of different lengths. Some of the stones of the pillars display cuttings typical of the Herodian period. The fact that they are in secondary use indicates that the construction dates to a later date, perhaps to the Early Muslim period when the entire Temple Mount was reshaped. Other stones

are typical of the Crusader period, proving that repairs and alterations were carried out in the structure in later periods.

We do not know what these vast spaces were used for in the time of their construction. Before recent research and careful examination of the structure, it was assumed that in the time of Herod there was a system of piers and arches perhaps on two or three levels under the esplanade level. It has been suggested that the spaces between the piers were left empty to allow the ritual defilement caused by assumed ancient burial caves to seep out. Already in the early Byzantine period, if not earlier, these subterranean spaces were attributed to King Solomon. The Bordeaux pilgrim who visited Jerusalem in

Remnant of the flat arch surrounding the blocked Double Gate
under the al-Aqsa Mosque. Photographer: Rivka Gonen, 2002.

333 CE attributed these spaces to Solomon's palace and noted especially one chamber roofed with one stone, where, he believed, Solomon wrote his wisdom literature. Theodosius, a fifth-century CE pilgrim, alludes to a convent of virgins in these subterranean spaces, who received their food from the walls above them and drew water from cisterns. It was recently suggested that a spacious building of the Byzantine period located to the south of the Temple Mount wall may actually have been the convent.[11]

The Crusading Knights Templars, who had their headquarters in the al-Aqsa Mosque, which they believed was Solomon's palace, used these spaces for their horses. Holes in the pillars for tying the horses and traces of mangers testify to this use. It was they who gave the spaces the name Solomon's Stables, a name that survives to this day.

The Crusaders opened a gate in the south wall of the Temple Mount to facilitate exit and entrance to the Stables from the outside. This gate, known as the Single Gate, was blocked as part of a restoration carried out after the expulsion of the Crusaders, and in the last centuries the entrance to the Stables has been through a narrow flight of steps in the southwestern corner of the Temple Mount esplanade. Halfway down these steps is a small room where, according to tradition, Mary placed Jesus in his cradle after she pre-

Passage of the Double Gate under the al-Aqsa Mosque. Source: Le Strange G. Palestine under the Moslems, 1890.

sented him at the Temple. A small dome resting on four slender pillars surmounts the traditional place of the cradle.

Underground Passages[12]

The entrances to the Herodian Temple Mount from the south were through long tunnels that passed under the artificial construction that held the platform. There were two sets of such entrances—the Triple Gate and the Double Gate, known together at the Hulda Gate, Hulda being a prophetess who resided in the late First Temple period in a house nearby. Both gates are blocked from the outside.

The arches that surmount the blocked Triple Gate date to a period later than their original construction. The underground passageway of this gate, located very close to Solomon's Stables, is a double passage divided by a row of piers.

A massive structure built sometime in the Middle Ages blocked most of the outer opening of the Double Gate. The shallow decorated arch that surmounts it dates perhaps to the Early Muslim period, a time of large-scale repair and construction on the Temple Mount. The underground passageway of the Double Gate, which passes under the al-Aqsa Mosque and comes out next to its facade, is well documented, as it was carefully surveyed in the nineteenth century. This is a well-constructed passage between two walls. A row of stout pillars that hold decorated domes divide the passage in two.

Decorated dome of the Double Gate.

Blocked Triple Gate. Photographer: Rivka Gonen, 2002.

These passages are well preserved despite the earthquakes that often damaged the mosque above it. Its southern part with the decorated domes is the only preserved section of Herod's Temple Mount. Its middle part was repaired in the Early Muslim period, and the northern part, which comes out in front of the al-Aqsa Mosque, was added after the earthquake of 1033, when the mosque was extended northward. Known for generations as al-Aqsa al-Kadima—the ancient al-Aqsa—it too, like its neighbor, Solomon's Stables, has lately been converted into a mosque.

A massive lintel that can be seen on the southwestern section of the west wall of the Temple Mount, just to the south of the Western Wall, suggests that here was another of the gates that gave access to the Herodian Temple Mount. Only part of the lintel is visible, the rest being buried under the ramp that leads up to the Mughrabi Gate. Its original name was most likely the Kiponos Gate, but it is now known as Barclay's Gate, honoring its discoverer, James Barclay. The gate's threshold is many meters below the present surface of the Western Wall plaza. Like the southern gates, it had an underground passageway, but only the first part of it, just behind the gate, is known, the rest having been blocked by later repairs.

Water Cisterns[13]

The Temple Mount is studded by thirty-seven water cisterns of different shapes, depths, sizes, and dates. They are fed by rainwater falling on the Temple Mount, and by water from distant springs to the south of Jerusalem conveyed by gravitation in a system of conduits and open cisterns. Some of the underground cisterns are very large, the largest with a capacity of 2 million gallons of water. The oldest cisterns may have been cut as early as the Hasmonean period, prior to Herod's major modification of the Temple Mount, and were designed to provide water for ritual use in the Temple and for the multitudes of pilgrims who congregated on the Mount. Other cisterns were added in the Herodian, Early Muslim, Ayyubid, and Mamluk periods, and modifications and repairs were carried out at all times. In later periods, and up to the beginning of the twentieth century, when pumps and pipes were installed to bring water to Jerusalem from other parts of the country, these cisterns provided precious water to the city. They were particularly essential in the frequent years of drought when the small private cisterns and the Gihon Spring dried out. It has been calculated that in times of need the Temple Mount cisterns could supply the entire population of the Old City of the 1860s with a whole year's supply of water. The unusual shape of some of the cisterns indicates that they were originally intended for other uses, such storage or as secret passages, but in time they were converted to their new use of holding water.

Notes

1 Rubin 2000: 2–9
2 Maeir 2000: 33–65.
3 Malamat 2000: 15–16.
4 Ben–Dov 1983: 34.
5 Schiller 1989: 45–145
6 Ritmayer 1996; 46–55.
7 Gonen 1985: 44–55.
8 Milstein 1999: 35–39.
9 Fleming 1983: 24–37; Ritmayer 1992: 24–43.
10 Gibson 1996: 268–279.
11 Mazar E. 1998: 15–48.
12 Gibson 1996: 253–268.
13 Ibid 191–223; 225–233.

Chapter 3
Locating Holiness

How Does a Place Become Holy?[1]

The Temple Mount, on which so many temples have stood for the last 3,000 years, must have been a place of special significance since very ancient times. It is one of the outstanding examples of a "place of power," a place that caught the imagination of people in the past for a variety of reasons and was interpreted as sacred.[2] A place may be regarded as holy because it possesses something special, an awe-inspiring element, such as a very high mountain, or a particularly crooked rock or tree, or a life-giving river or a spring. In other cases the gods may be said to reveal themselves through signs, such as an animal, a majestic eagle, or even a sow coming to a rest in a particular place, or a bush burns but is not consumed.[3] There are places that become consecrated because an event of special significance occurred there, such as the location of the cosmic event of the first emergence of the primordial hill out of the abysmal waters, shown in the ancient Egyptian Temple in Hermopolis.[4] There are also sacred places of less cosmic occurrences, such as where a person was believed to have been brought back from the dead or where water was turned into wine. The location of the tomb of some legendary hero, a particularly esteemed person,

or a religious or political martyr may be turned into a holy site, as indeed are the tombs of Jesus and of his mother Mary in Jerusalem as well as the tombs of lesser saints around the world. In many cases, even a relic of a highly esteemed personality is enough to sanctify a place. There are sometimes less exalted reasons that make a place holy. For example, a Temple may be built to enhance the prestige of a ruler or to serve a community, and it later may become sanctified by its very existence.

Divine revelation seems to be the most prevalent reason for the development of a sacred site.[5] For the aboriginal people of Australia, sacred sites are those places where the divine spirits transformed themselves into all the visible natural phenomena—the hills, the rocks, the waterholes, the animals, the trees, the people.[6] Places where Jesus revealed himself became holy to the Christians. This is how Mount Tabor, the site of the Transfiguration, obtained its sacredness, and this is why the Mount of Olives, the location of the Ascent of Jesus to Heaven, is so revered. Many places in Europe and Latin America where Mary is said to have revealed herself have become sites of Marian churches, and some developed into major pilgrimage centers.[7]

The belief in the power of a holy place does not diminish when the Temple built on it is destroyed or when the people who first noted its special qualities are replaced. Its holiness can extend over generations, and a succession of Temples of different religions can be built on the same spot, usually proclaiming the victory of the new arrivals over the local population. Examples of such occurrences abound around the world. The conquering Spaniards built their cathedral of Mexico City over an Aztec Temple and built numerous churches over Temples of the Inca in South America. The story of the cathedral of Cordoba is illuminating. Following the reconquest of Muslim Spain by the Christians, a cathedral was built not over but inside the great Muslim mosque, which was built over the ruins of an earlier Visigoth church, itself built over the destroyed Temple of the Roman goddess Venus.

A more recent and still relevant contention over ownership of a holy site centers on the disputed shrines in Ayodhya in India. The place has been holy to the Hindu population for over 1,000 years as the city of their god Rama. When the Muslim Moghul Dynasty took control over northern India in the sixteenth century, a Muslim mosque that was built over the site sacred to Rama. The gradual deterioration of the power of the Moghuls and the growing interest of the British in India to the point of turning it into a British colony in the nineteenth century brought about an awakening of Hindu sentiments and a wish to reclaim their holy site. The Ayodhya mosque became a bone of contention between Hindus and Muslims, causing much unrest and violence that eventually led to the destruction of the mosque by Hindus in 1992. Further violence between Hindus and Muslims over the ownership of the holy site erupted in Ayodhya in 2002, causing much damage and a loss of many lives on both sides.[8]

Choosing the Temple's Location

With the creation of the United Monarchy of Israel and the choice of Jerusalem as its capital, King David set out to build a Temple in Jerusalem, around which to forge the twelve tribes of Israel into a unified nation under one God. His first mission was to choose a proper location for his scheme. The Bible gives us a description of how the choice was made in II Samuel 24, at the very end of the book and out of context with anything that came before.

The story is rather sinister. God was angry with his people for an unspecified reason and incited David against them by giving him orders to conduct a census. David, who had forgotten the procedure for conducting a census of the Israelites as laid out in Exodus 30:11, obeyed, but Joab refused at first to carry out the census because "Should it be a cause of trespass to Israel?" (I Chronicles 21:3). He was overruled, but when he counted the people he left out the tribes of Levi and Benjamin, "for the king's word was abominable to Joab" (I Chronicles 21:6). The census was conducted, but "David's heart smote him after that he had numbered the people" (II Samuel 24:10), and he asked to be personally punished. God, however, was interested in punishing the people of Israel and, through the prophet Gad, gave David three options as to how many of the people would perish: seven years of famine, three months of war, or three days of pestilence. David chose the third. A devastating plague struck Israel and 70,000 of the people died. When the plague reached Jerusalem, an angel of God stood by Aravna's threshing floor with his arm stretched ready to strike the city. At that point God repented the evil, had mercy on Jerusalem, and ordered the angel not to strike.

David was then ordered to build an altar on the threshing floor, and for that purpose he purchased the place from its owner for 50 silver shekels. I Chronicles 21 elaborated the story and introduced a startling change: not God but Satan incited David. It also relates that after David built the altar he put on it whole offerings and called upon God. God answered with fire coming down from heaven and consuming the offerings. Then David said, "This is to be the house of the Lord God, and this is to be an altar of whole-offerings for Israel." Indeed, Solomon later built the Temple on Aravna's threshing floor. And so Chronicles tells us the fire from heaven signaled that God chose the threshing floor as the location of his Temple.[9]

This was not the first time God revealed himself to his people. He did so in several places, as in the many unnamed places where God spoke to Abraham, in the Burning Bush in the desert where Moses first encountered God, and on Mount Sinai—the site of the most spectacular revelation of God to his entire people. It is interesting that the holiness of these places was not perpetuated. They are not mentioned again in the Bible, and they did not become places of Israelite worship. Even their exact location was forgotten, and scholars to this day speculate on the location of Mount Sinai. Bethel, where Jacob dreamed of a ladder that spanned heaven and earth, is an exception, since it was a place of worship in the times of the Judges (I Samuel 10:3) and eventually became one of the two sacred sites of the kingdom of Israel. Even burial places of the illustrious have not become places of reverence and pilgrimage, and regarding the bur-

ial place of Moses the Bible specifically says, "He was buried in a valley in Moab opposite Beth-peor, but to this day no one knows his burial-place" (Deuteronomy 34:6). Jewish pilgrimage to tombs of the righteous, including those of the patriarchs and matriarchs in Hebron, began thousands of years after they passed away, perhaps only around the middle of the first millennium CE.

What, then, were the places of worship of Israel prior to the building of Solomon's Temple? We have reference to three such places: Shechem, Shiloh, and Gibeon. No revelation that marked any of them is mentioned in the Bible, and we have no way of contemplating the source of their sacredness. Shechem was the site of the gathering of all the elders of Israel convened after the conquest of the land of Canaan was completed, and the place where Joshua retold the story of the Israelite nation from the time of Abraham until his own days (Joshua 24:1). Shiloh became a place of worship because it was for a while home to the Ark of the Covenant (I Samuel 4:3–4). When the Philistines took the Ark hostage, Shiloh lost its status as a holy place. There is no mention of how Gibeon came to be a place of worship. According to I Chronicles 21:29–30 it was home to the holy Ark of the Covenant in the time of David, although the earlier (and more reliable) version in II Samuel insists that the Ark was in the City of David (6:17). The conflicting versions are further complicated by the story that "King Solomon went to Gibeon to offer a sacrifice, for that was the chief hill-shrine" (I Kings 3:4). And thus the true significance of Gibeon is left unclear. Bethel and Dan, the two places chosen by Jeroboam as sites of religious reverence, were border posts of the newly formed kingdom of Israel—Dan in the north,

Bethel in the south. In order to dissuade his citizens from going to Jerusalem to worship, he installed in these two towns golden calves as representations of the God of Israel (I Kings 12:26–33). It is not clear whether the worship there was indeed to the Israelite God or to foreign, pagan gods and goddesses.

With the disregard to choosing places of divine revelation as holy sites, and the choice of other places that had no apparent virtue, the case of Jerusalem is outstanding. A close consideration of the biblical verses reveals that the fire that came down on David's altar as a sign that God chose the place appears only in Chronicles, books that were compiled after the return of the exiles from Babylon. The original story in Samuel does not mention this fire. It may thus be suggested that the revelation by fire had been added to the original version in later days, after Jerusalem had already become holy by the very presence of the Temple in it. The addition may have been made to conform to a new understanding of the nature and origin of a holy place, adopted in the land of exile.

Why, then, did David choose the place of the threshing floor as the proper site on which his son Solomon would later build the Temple? There may have been several reasons, some bringing to the fore ancient, pre-Israelite sacredness, others perhaps political. The most obvious and practical reason would be that the northern, topographically higher extension of the hill on which the City of David was built was not settled at the time and therefore a natural place for a large-scale project. This makes sense especially when one takes into account the very small size of the City of David and the fact that it may have been quite densely built at the time. Yet Zaphon, which means "north" in Canaanite

and Hebrew, had a special meaning in the cult of the Canaanites, predecessors of the Israelites in the land. Mount Zaphon was the abode of the gods of Ugarit, a major Canaanite city in northern Syria.[10]

The cultic associations of Zaphon are imbedded in Psalms 48:2: "Beautiful for situation, the joy of the whole earth, is Mount Zion, on the sides of the north."

Thus even what seems a practical reason for the choice of location is connected with early cultic associations. There are various other such associations. Canaanite gods, especially the god Baal, were connected with topographically high places and mountaintops, so much so that a high place was equivalent to a holy place.[11] Temples in Babylon were called "House of the Mountain of All Lands" or "Mountain of the House" (like the Hebrew *Har haBayt*, designating what in English is called the Temple Mount) and also "link between Heaven and Earth." The chosen hill, the future place of the house of God, was indeed higher than the residential City of David, and the cultic associations of a high mountain seem to have been most relevant.

These pagan associations infiltrated Israelite religious norms, a fact clearly expressed in the prophecy of Isaiah (2:2–4). "And it will come to pass in the last days, that the mountain of the Lord's house shall be established in the top of the mountains, and shall be exalted above the hills, and all nations shall flow unto it. And the people shall go and say, Come ye, and let us go up to the mountain of the Lord." That indeed there was a place of worship in Canaanite Jerusalem can be gathered from the story of Abraham and Melchizedek , king of Salem (short form of Jerusalem), who was priest of El-Elyon, or God most High, El being the name of the supreme god of the Canaanite pantheon. The sanctity of Jerusalem thus preceded the Israelite conquest. It should not come as a surprise that the Israelites adopted the holiness of Canaanite Jerusalem. They also adopted the alphabet, literary style, and other, less evident elements of Canaanite culture. In the same vein Christians and then Muslims later adopted the Jewish holiness of Jerusalem alongside many of the myths and legends relating to it.

Further connotations of holiness may have been centered on the threshing floor of Aravna (or Ornan), king of Jerusalem, at the time it was conquered by David. A threshing floor is in many cultures, especially agricultural ones, a place where the bounty of the fields is gathered and where the gods of fertility were revered.[12]

The Israelites were again not beyond adopting the Canaanite reverence of such a place. Another aspect of the sacredness of threshing floors is their association with burial. When the body of Jacob was brought up from Egypt it was at one point placed in the "threshing floor of the thorn, which is beyond Jordan, and there they mourned with a great and very sore lamentation" (Genesis 50:10).

The connection between threshing floors and burials lends support to the possibility that the hill was in the first half of the second millennium BCE a Canaanite burial ground. Because the site has changed beyond recognition by many centuries of building and destruction, it is difficult to prove the hill was indeed a cemetery. However, the only cave on the Temple Mount that had preserved some of its original features, the cave under the rock inside the Dome of the Rock, is connected to the surface of the rock by a round, rock cut shaft. This shaft is equivalent both in shape

and in size to numerous shafts of burial caves in the many cemeteries scattered in the hill country of Judah and Samaria. There may have been similar adjacent burial caves which, over the generations, were transformed into the many water cisterns that dot the hill. Burial grounds are always connected one way or another with holiness, and this may have been the case with the hill above the City of David.

It is interesting that in the days when the Second Temple stood on that hill, there was apprehension lest the place be defiled by the presence of death, which is the ultimate source of ritual defilement. One rabbinical tradition claims that when the exiles returned from Babylon and built their Temple, they found the skull of Aravna, the original owner of the site, under the Temple altar (Sotah 20a, Nedarim 39b). Another passage in the Talmud relates that the skull was found even earlier, when Solomon's Temple was redecorated or by the returnees from Babylon (Palestinian Talmud, Sotah 20a, Nedarim 39b). Perhaps more suggestive is the saying that "He who is buried in the Land of Israel is as if he were buried under the altar [of the Temple]. . . . And he who is buried under the altar is as if he were buried under the throne of the Divine Majesty" (Sayings of the Fathers 26:8, Tosephta Abodah Zara 4:3). Measures were taken when the place was built, so the Mishnah tells us (Mishnah Parah 3:3), to avert this danger. All this points to the probability that the sages knew that there were ancient graves on the site.

The accumulation of pre-Israelite holiness on the hill north of the City of David is perhaps the main reason for its choice as a place fit to house Jewish sanctity. However, there may also have been a political angle to the transformation of Aravna's threshing floor to an Israelite place of worship.[13]

The Bible tells us that David purchased the plot from its owner for a large sum of money—50 shekels in Samuel, 600 shekels in Chronicles. This is interesting, because David, as the conqueror of Jerusalem, could have simply confiscated the plot. The elaborate haggling that took place between Aravna, who offered it free, and David, who insisted of paying, is reminiscent of the argument between Abraham and Ephron in Hebron over the purchase of the Cave of Machpelah as a burial place for his wife Sarah (Genesis 23:3–18).[14] By buying the threshing floor, where an angel of God stood and on which he was about to built an altar, David perhaps felt the need to establish his legitimate ownership over the sacred site, as his great ancestor Abraham did in Hebron. It is also possible that by relinquishing this piece of real estate outside of the city, the deposed king of Jerusalem was stripped of the last vestige of his royal status, which was now transferred legally to the new king. Perhaps this transaction was another way for David to establish himself as the legitimate ruler of the city.[15]

Thus one of these reasons, a combination of several, or all of them together may have led to the choice of the hill above his city as the site on which the Temple to God would later be built. The choice was made by a human being, King David. The attribution of the choice to God came only later, when the Temple was already standing and functioning. All the biblical literature that succeeds the early story in the book of Samuel, especially the prophets and Psalms, is devoted to the glorification of the Temple as the place where God chose to put his name.

On the site of the threshing floor Solomon later built the Temple (II Chronicles 3:1) that lent it everlasting holiness. From the Jewish Temples the holiness passed on to the Christians and the Muslims. Domination over this most holy spot has become the source of a centuries-long contention between Judaism, Christianity, and Islam, one that is with us to this day.

What Was the Exact Site of the Temple?

The Bible does not deliberate on the exact site on which the Temple stood. The only reference to a location is in II Chronicles 3:1: "Then Solomon began to build the house of the Lord at Jerusalem on Mount Moriah, where the Lord appeared unto David his father, in the place that David had prepared in the threshing floor of Ornan the Jebusite." This verse is the one and only place Mount Moriah is mentioned in the Bible. The early reference in Genesis 22:2 is to the *Land* of Moriah, where on one of the mountains Abraham was commanded to sacrifice his son Isaac.

The substitution of the Land of Moriah, a vague geographical location, with the universally known mountain on which Solomon built his Temple could not have occurred during the First Temple period, because Mount Moriah is not referred to in any other book save Chronicles. It has already been mentioned that Chronicles is a late book, the work of the editor sometime after the return of the exiles from Babylon. It would seem that the substitution of Mount Moriah for the Land of Moriah was meant to endow Solomon's Temple, and more so the newly constructed Second Temple, with the aura of the place where the monumental event of the Binding of Isaac occurred. Thus the verse in II

Chronicles began the tradition of identifying Mount Moriah with the Temple Mount. After the destruction of the Second Temple, the name Mount Moriah was so strongly identified with the Temple Mount that it was even considered the origin of other mountains of Jewish significance. Thus the Jerusalem Talmud relates that Mount Sinai is only a piece torn out of Mount Moriah, as a piece of dough is torn to make a hallah bread.

The exact location of the threshing floor of Ornan (Aravna) on the hill is not given in the sources. Threshing floors must be located in open places, preferably high on a hill, where the prevailing winds would aid the threshing and winnowing of the grain. Tradition, following the verse in Chronicles, pointed to the hill above the City of David as both Mount Moriah and the place of the threshing floor. The question is: where on that hill was the threshing ground located, and subsequently where exactly was the Temple built? Being the highest point on the hill, the bare rock that is now under the Dome of the Rock, and which may have had a different configuration before various constructions were built on it, is considered most suitable for a threshing floor.

Thus the prevailing view on the location of the Temple, endorsed by the majority of scholars, archaeologists, and rabbinical authorities, locates the Temple in relation to that rock. Most agree that the Holy of Holies was situated over the rock, while others think that it was the basis for the big altar of sacrifices in the courtyard of the Temple. A whole body of Jewish legends that developed mainly after the destruction of the Second Temple surrounds this rock. It includes, for example, the location of the Binding of Isaac, and the belief that it is the center of the world, the very place where God began the creation of the universe. This

very long and varied tradition of holiness makes the rock a likely candidate for having been the basis of the First and Second Jewish Temples. Moreover, despite the destruction of both Temples and the changes that occurred in the area, the Muslims adopted the sanctity of this very rock and built their magnificent Dome of the Rock over it.

Since this evidence is only of a circumstantial nature—no trace of either the First or the Second Temple has been found, and it is doubted that anything will ever be found—several other locations for the Temples have been suggested. Sir Charles Warren, the great nineteenth-century archaeologist who devoted much time to measuring and surveying the Temple Mount and its surroundings, and who also delved into the subterranean water cisterns to survey the natural bedrock, opted for a location other than the traditionally held one. Warren located the Holy of Holies of Solomon's Temple some 50 meters southwest of the Dome of the Rock, in a direct line to the summit of the Mount of Olives. The great bronze altar in the courtyard of the Temple he placed at the western edge of the great water reservoir (cistern 5) located under the southeastern corner of the upper platform of the present-day esplanade. This cistern, he argued, may have served in whatever original form it originally had as a collector for the blood of the sacrifices. Warren also made the assumption that the northern part of the present-day Temple Mount was not part of the Mount in the days of Solomon's Temple or of the pre-Herodian Second Temple.[16]

The area of the Temple Mount according to this suggestion would be a square of 250 by 250 meters (500 by 500 cubits) designated by the Mishnah as the holy section of the Mount in which strict restrictions were imposed.[17]

However, with this arrangement the rock, which is today some 6 feet higher than the surface of the upper plaza, would loom high behind the Temple. Later scholars who dealt with the subject of the location of the Temple did not embrace Warren's proposition, which was all but forgotten.

The Northern Option

Some twenty years ago a new suggestion was presented, locating the Holy of Holies of the Temple on a flat section of bedrock under the small Dome of the Spirits, located on the upper platform of the Temple Mount to the north of the Dome of the Rock.[18] This suggestion is based on the fact that a direct axis connects this dome with the Gate of Mercy, supposed to have been built exactly over Susa Gate of the time of the Second Temple. This straight axis then continues further on to the summit of the Mount of Olives, where several rituals were performed.

To lend plausibility to this theory, several cuttings in the bedrock in the vicinity of the Dome of the Spirits were noted and interpreted as the foundations of the west and north walls of the courtyard surrounding the First Temple. A thick wall built of large stones discovered in a pit dug into the ground to the northwest of the Dome of the Spirits was identified as the west wall of the Second Temple. When the lines of these cuttings and the wall were put on paper, it became apparent that they do not follow the same axis, and thus it was concluded that for some unknown reason the First and the Second Temples did not overlap, as is commonly assumed.

When published, this "northern option" aroused some interest, which at first did not spread beyond a small group of interested people. It was immediately refuted by most archaeologists as well as by rabbinical and other circles, but it was picked up by several Christian evangelical ministers and preachers. These evangelical Christians are eagerly looking forward to the building of the Third Temple as a necessary step toward the Second Coming of Christ and the events that will lead to the millennium of the Heavenly Kingdom. But they are well aware of the insurmountable difficulty of executing this project while the Dome of the Rock stands on the traditional place of the Temple. Although some preached the destruction of the Dome of the Rock to make way for the Third Temple, and one adherent actually put fire to the al-Aqsa Mosque to hasten the building of the Temple, others gladly adopted the alternative to the site on which the Temple may have stood.

If the Temple was not built where the Dome now dominates the Temple Mount, the way is paved for building the Third Temple. When the dimensions of the Jewish Temples were calculated, distances measured, and the outer courtyards of the Temples omitted, then the small building that both Temples were would barely fit into the corner of the upper platform of the Temple Mount. The idea of the "northern alternative" was very popular among evangelical Christians in the 1980s and 1990s, and its originator was a welcome guest in churches across the United States, where multitudes came to hear him present his proposal. But since the beginning of the al-Aqsa Intifada (Palestinian violent disturbances against Israel), it became clear that defining the exact location of the Temple was not the only problem facing those who wish to build the Third Temple. They have not lost hope, however, as the bloody events of the Intifada can be viewed as part of the Tribulations, natural and man-made catastrophes that according to Revelations 16–17 will be the first stage in the drama of the End of the Days. [19]

The Southern Option

A second alternative to the location of the Temple on the Temple Mount places it farther south than Warren proposed, between the Dome of the Rock and the al-Aqsa Mosque.[20] This proposition is revolutionary on many levels. First, it attributes the formation of the Temple Mount as we know it today not to King Herod of the first century BCE but to the Roman emperor Hadrian of the second century CE. This huge project, so it is reasoned, was connected to the emperor's scheme to dedicate a holy site to the Roman god Jupiter Capitolinus in the new city of Aelia Capitolina, which he built over the ruins of Jewish Jerusalem. However, the meager sources that mention Hadrian's holy site do not refer to a built Temple. It is therefore assumed that if indeed Hadrian initiated such a project it was only an open-air holy site, which would not necessitate such massive construction as the large Temple Mount that altered the topography of the hill and changed the course of two streams.

The reasoning behind the changing of dates is based on the history of architecture in the Roman Empire. It is argued that if the Temple compound was indeed built by Herod, it would have been of a scale unknown in the first century BCE in the entire Roman Empire. In the days of Hadrian, on the other hand, a time of "Roman Peace" and of great prosperity in the Roman Empire, a compound of comparable magnitude dedicated to the combined god Baal-Zeus was built on the site known today as Baalbek in neighboring Lebanon. If this historical reconstruction is correct, then the walls surrounding the Temple Mount and the ancient gates, including the subterranean passages of the Double and Triple Gates, are to be dated to the time of the Emperor Hadrian in the second century CE.

The archaeological excavations carried out at the foot of the south and part of the west walls of the Temple Mount refute this historical reconstruction. One of the amazing finds uncovered in these excavations was a huge stone that fell from the southwestern pinnacle of the Temple Mount and landed on the paved street that ran below it. The stone carried an unfortunately broken inscription in Hebrew "to the house of the blowing of the trumpet to announce," probably to announce the advent of the Sabbath.[21] This stone could have come only from a Jewish Temple compound where the custom of announcing the Sabbath was observed every week. Moreover, only a handful of objects dating to the period of the emperor Hadrian were found in these large-scale archaeological excavations. On the other hand huge quantities of pottery vessels, coins and other finds were securely dated to the period between the first century BCE, the building of the compound in the days of King Herod, and 70 CE, when it was destroyed by the Romans. There can be little doubt, therefore, that the Temple Mount as it has been preserved to this day was built by in the time of King Herod.

This "southern option" leaves the northern part of the Temple Mount, including the rock under the Dome of the Rock, outside the much smaller Second Temple–period Temple Mount compound, which is confined to the southern section of the Mount, much as Warren proposed many years ago. The protruding rock, it is suggested, formed the basis for the Antonia Fortress, built by King Herod on the northern outskirts of the Temple Mount to protect it on that vulnerable direction. But the new "southern option" goes much beyond Warren, suggesting most surprisingly that the level of the Temple Mount both in the time of the First and the Second Temples was some 50 feet lower than the level of the present-day lower platform. The Temples must have stood on a level some 30 feet lower than the level of the present-day Western Wall platform.

This astonishing hypothesis was probably designed to discard the disturbing walls and gates of the present Temple Mount, which has been proven, as was stated above, to date to the first century BCE, the time of King Herod. The Holy of Holies, according to this theory, was under the Chalice—the fountain in front of the al-Aqsa Mosque. All these revolutionary suggestions are allegedly supported by sophisticated radar tests, conducted on and around the Mount, that located a system of subterranean spaces in the area between the upper platform and the al-Aqsa Mosque. These spaces may, of course, be the under-structures that hold the Temple Mount esplanade, or they may be unknown subterranean water cisterns. In addition, infrared photographs taken from a helicopter are said to have detected a thick wall running north-south some 100 feet to the west of the present western wall of the Temple Mount. This would be, then, according to this proposal, the true Western Wall.

The "southern option," refuted by archaeological excavations as well as by the many myths and legends that center around the rock under the Dome of the Rock, was surprisingly picked up, not by evangelical Christians, but by political circles. They found expression in President Clinton's suggestion to solve the problem of sovereignty over the Temple Mount. Clinton, whose advisers must have heard of the "southern option," proposed to divide the sovereignty over the holy site horizontally, with the entire upper esplanade with its Dome of the Rock, the al-Aqsa Mosque, and other minor shrines allocated to the Muslims. The subterranean spaces would be allocated to the sovereignty of the Jews. This amazing and unrealistic suggestion and the actions taken in its wake will be discussed again in chapter 7.

Notes

[1] Brereton 1987: 526–535.
[2] Friedland and Hecht 1991: 27.
[3] Eliade 1961: 27–28
[4] Clifford 1972: 26.
[5] Eliade 1961: 10–13.
[6] Hubert 1994: 9–19.
[7] Turner and Turner 1978: 149–171.
[8] Zilberman 2000: 241–249.
[9] Zakovitch 1999: 23–26.
[10] Clifford 1972: 32.
[11] Ibid 57–79.
[12] Mazar B. 1969: 28.
[13] Friedland and Hecht 1991: 27–28.
[14] Zakovitch 1999:27–28.
[15] Cogan 2000: 71.
[16] Wilson and Warren 1871: xxx, Warren 1976:59, 78–79, illustration facing p. 62.
[17] Ritmayer 1992: 24–43, especially 30–33.
[18] Kaufman 1983: 40–59.
[19] Gorenberg 2000: 55–67.
[20] Sagiv 2001: 1–27.
[21] Mazar B. 1986: 58–60.

Chapter 4
Contesting Shrines

The First Temple

King David Chooses Jerusalem as a Political and Religious Capital

The conquest of Jerusalem, which in the time of David was called Jebus, the town of the Jebusites, opened the way to the unification of the territories of the tribes of Israel. The enclave of Jerusalem, situated on the border between the territories of the tribes of Benjamin and Judah, was until the days of David a Jebusite-dominated buffer zone between the southern and the northern tribes of Israel. In the early days of the conquest of Canaan there was a successful attempt to take Jerusalem, as the Bible reports: "now the children of Judah had fought against Jerusalem, and had taken it, and smitten it with the edge of the sword, and set the city on fire" (Judges 1:8). Yet the people of Judah could not have held the city for long, since in the early days of David it was still a foreign non-Israelite city.

The story of David's conquest of Jerusalem is somewhat obscure, and it is reported that the Jebusites resorted to magical incantations in order to hold the attacking Israelites back.[1] "Nevertheless David took the stronghold of Zion . . . and called it the city of David" (II Samuel 5:6–9). The version of the capture of Jerusalem in I Chronicles 11:4–7 adds the detail that David had to offer a prize to whoever would smite the Jebusites first. All this points to Jerusalem's having been well fortified, as indeed has been validated by archaeological excavations. By naming the conquered city after himself, David left an everlasting stamp on its history, for since then Jerusalem has been intimately connected with David and his dynasty.

The choice of Jerusalem as the capital of David's expanding kingdom of Israel was probably motivated by several considerations. Being the conqueror of this last foreign enclave within the densely settled Israelite territory, David must have viewed Jerusalem as his own personal prize. A further consideration for this choice was no doubt of a political nature. Despite the early conquest of Jerusalem by the tribe of Judah, the tribe failed to hold it permanently and the city fell back to the Jebusites. It thus maintained an extra-territorial status outside the tribal territories. It was thus a neutral place, and no tribe could claim supremacy because the capital of the kingdom was within its territory. By wisely choosing this unclaimed city, David achieved his goal of consolidating the constantly competing and even warring tribes into a unified nation around a new capital city.[2]

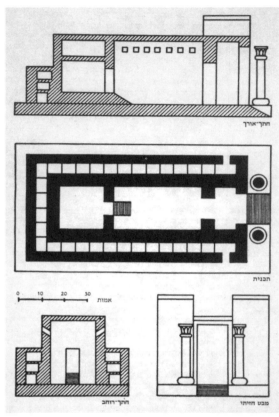

Plan of Solomon's Temple. Source: Watzinger, C.,
Denkmaler Palastinas I, 1933.

Suggested reconstruction of Temple with Dvir as a wooden cube.

David took a further crucial act in his attempt to solidify the twelve tribes of Israel into a unified nation. He brought to his new capital the Ark of the Covenant, which contained the Tablets of the Law received by Moses on Mount Sinai; it had not had a permanent home since it was captured by the Philistines many years before. David thus combined his own personal sense of achievement with political and religious motives that have been the hallmarks of Jerusalem ever since. After bringing the Ark and temporarily housing it in a tent, David made up his mind to build a Temple that would be the permanent abode of this holy object.

King David, so the Bible informs us, was not the only one who wished to build a permanent home for the holiest object of the Israelite religion. God himself, voicing his desire through the prophet Nathan, commanded: "Go tell my servant David, Thus saith the Lord, Shalt thou build me a house for me to dwell in? Whereas I have not dwelt in any house since the time that I brought up the children of Israel out of Egypt, even to this day, but have walked in a tent and in a tabernacle" (II Samuel 7:5–6). God did not want a house for the Ark of the Tabernacles that contained his words, but a house for himself. This notion seems to conflict with the later understanding of the Jewish God as a spiritual god without earthly needs, and yet Solomon's Temple was indeed conceived throughout the First Temple period as the house where God actually dwelt. The idea that God wanted a house to dwell in was adopted from the pagan world that surrounded Israel at the time, in which each god had his earthly abode. David, a son of his period, did not question God's request and began to make preparations to build him the house.

The actual task of building it, however, fell to his son King Solomon, as indeed was prophesied by Nathan: "He [your son] shall build a house for my name" (II Samuel 7:13). This first Israelite Temple in Jerusalem was inaugurated about 954 BCE and replaced the sacred edifice in Gibeon, north of Jerusalem. The Temple gave its name to the First Temple period, which began around 1000 BCE with the ascension of David, the first king of unified Israel, prior to the actual building of the Temple, and ended with the destruction of the Temple by the Babylonians in 586 BCE.

Solomon's Temple

The only available sources describing Solomon's Temple are in I Kings 6–7 and II Chronicles 3–4, but the two do not always coincide. The I Kings source is probably the earlier and therefore is considered the more reliable. Both descriptions are rather vague and do not give a very accurate picture of the building. Because no physical evidence of the Temple has survived, even its exact location is only assumed. If the Temple was indeed built over the old threshing floor of Aravna, it was most likely located on the summit of the hill, in relation to the exposed rock seen to this day inside the Dome of the Rock. Indeed, this is the most widely accepted view, although a few scholars place the Temple to the north or to the south of the Dome.

According to the biblical descriptions, the Temple was a small, elongated building, built on an east-west axis, and entered from the east, the direction of the rising sun.[3]

Its walls were thick, built of large, finely cut stones with intertwined wood beams that lent the walls flexibility and prepared them to better withstand the frequent earthquakes that occur in the area. Its internal dimensions were about 35 meters long,[4] about 10 meters wide, and about 15 meters high. These small measurements befit a private dwelling rather than a place for public activities. Along the northern, western, and southern outer walls was a three-story annex with many rooms for storage, entered from the outside. It is possible that this annex was added later.

The Bible refers to three sections within the building: *ulam*, *hechal*, and *devir*. The ulam (an Acadian word meaning the front side) was an entrance hall that divided the sacred from the profane. In it, or in front of it, stood two spectacular pillars, which bore private names, Jachin and Boaz.[5] These enormous pillars, 11 meters high and 2 meters thick, were cast hollow from copper and were surmounted with decorative copper capitals. The pillars probably had a decorative or symbolic rather than a constructive function.[6]

Beyond this entrance hall was the main hall (*hechal* = Temple). The walls of this 20-meter-long space were lined with cedar wood planks, carved with palm branches, flowers, and winged mythical winged beings (*cherubim*), all gilt. All these decorative motifs were widespread in contemporary ancient Near Eastern art. Several ritual objects stood in the *hechal*: a golden altar for burning incense, one (or ten as in Chronicles) golden tables for the loaves of showbread, and ten golden candelabra with their various cleansing implements.

Beyond the *hechal*, at the western end of the building was the *devir* (Holy of Holies), the most sacred part of the Temple. The *devir* was a perfect cube of 10 by 10 by 10n meters. Its dimensions presented generations of scholars with a problem, because its roof was 5 meters lower than that of the Temple. Some scholars suggested that the floor of the *devir* was high-

er than that of main hall and was ascended by a flight of steps. Despite the fact that such steps are not mentioned in the Bible, this suggestion gained favor since it placed the *devir* over the rock inside the Dome of the Rock. Others suggested there was a gallery above the *devir*, and yet others that the roof over the Temple was stepped, higher above the main hall, lower above the *devir*. A new solution to the problem of the *devir* was set forth some thirty years ago, based on I Kings 6:16, 19: "And he built twenty cubits on the sides of the house, both the floor and the walls with boards of cedar: he even built them within . . . [and] prepared in the house within." These verses suggest that the *devir* was a separate wooden cube assembled inside the Temple and placed in the far end of the *hechal*,[7] perhaps evoking the memory of the portable shrine carried by the Israelites in the Sinai desert during the Exodus.

The *devir* contained the most sacred item in the Temple, the Ark of the Covenant, which stood under the spread wings of two huge sculptured and gilt wooden mythical beings (*cherubim*). The outer wings of these immense *cherubim* touched the walls of the *devir*, their inner wings touched each other. In front of the Ark was a gilt cedar wood altar. The Ark of the Covenant with its protecting *cherubim* was viewed as being God's throne, as indeed witnessed by the prophet Isaiah: "I saw the Lord sitting upon a throne, high and lifted up, and his train filled the Temple" (6:1). The Ark of the Covenant as the seat of God fits well into the general picture of the Temple as the house of God, his earthly abode. Moreover, the various implements in the Temple were designed to satisfy several other earthly needs that God may have, as light (candelabra), food (showbread), and a pleasant aroma (incense). The

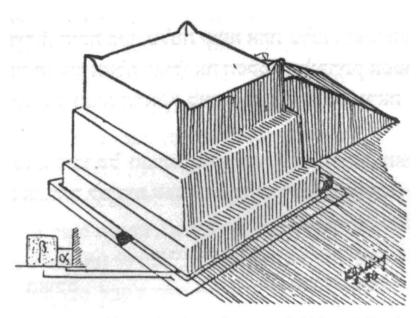

Reconstruction of the sacrifice alter in the courtyard of Solomon's Temple.
Source: Galling, K., Biblisches Reallexicon, 1934.

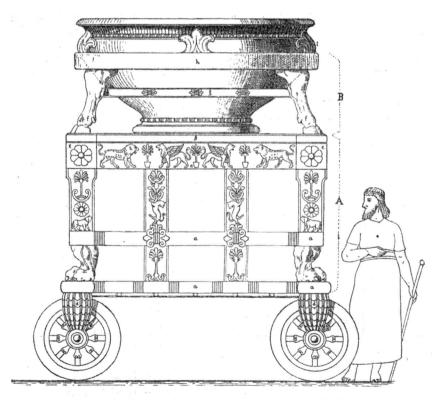

Reconstruction of wash basin in the courtyard of Solomon's Temple. Source:
Stade, Bernhard, Geschichte des Volkes Israel, 1887.

devir was always dark, for it had no windows, and no means of lighting it are described. The High Priest, who entered this mysterious and dark holy place once a year on the Day of Atonement, could do nothing in the dark but meditate on the power of God and pray for the expiation of the sins of the people.

When the Ark of Covenant was finally placed in its proper place in the Temple, God descended into it, as it is related: "when the priests came out of the holy place, the cloud filled the house of the Lord. The priests could not stand to minister because of the cloud, for the glory of the Lord had filled the house of the Lord" (I Kings 8:10–11).

In the courtyard outside the Temple was a huge stepped and horned copper altar, on which a constant stream of animal was sacrificed. Next to the altar was an enormous cast copper basin that stood on twelve cast copper bulls arranged in groups of three, each group facing a point of the compass. This spectacular vessel was most appropriately known as the "sea," a word evoking the mythological sea, home of the primordial Babylonian goddess Tiamat. Only after she was killed by her son Marduk could the world come into being.[8]

This vessel contained about 10,000 gallons of water, used by the priests to wash themselves after finishing the daily sacrifices. Ten smaller wheeled basins were used to wash the sacrificial meat.

Archaeological research in Israel and neighboring countries placed Solomon's Temple within the general style of contemporary Temples, especially those of northern Syria, where similar structures are known from as early as the third millennium BCE.[9]

The decorative motifs of Solomon's Temple were also within the well-established artistic vocabulary of its time and place. The sumptuous and highly sophisticated copper work, however, especially the huge cast items, which the Bible attributes to a coppersmith from the town of Tyre, were unique; nothing of this magnitude is known either in contemporary literary sources or in material unearthed in archaeological excavations.

Solomon's Palace

Another great structure built by King Solomon in his capital city of Jerusalem was his palace. The palace occupied the Ophel, the area between the residential City of David and the holy edifice of the Temple. The fact that it took thirteen years to built as against the seven years it took to build the Temple indicates both its size and its splendor. The palace was actually a compound that included several buildings. The one described in greatest detail in the Bible is the House of the Forest of Lebanon. This large 50- meter-long building had rows of cedar pillars that probably gave it its name. Another large pillared building of an unknown function was 25 meters long. The main building had an area designated for the public functions of the king. It had a large and imposing entrance with two pillars,[10] behind which was the hall of judgment, where King Solomon sat to judge his people. Here stood his amazing ivory throne inlaid with the best gold. It had "six steps, and the top of the throne was round behind, and there were stays on either side of the place of the seat, and two lions stood beside the stays. And twelve lions stood there on the one side and on the other upon the six steps, and there was not the like made in any kingdom" (I Kings 10:18–20). The private quarters of the king were build around an inner court. Everything was built of the finest materials—well-dressed stones,

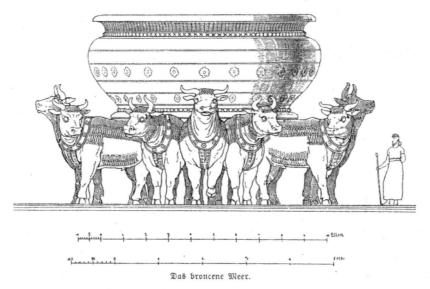

Das broncene Meer.

Reconstruction of the Sea in the courtyard of Solomon's Temple. Source: Stade, Bernhard, Geshichte des Volkes Israel. 1887.

A king sitting on an elaborate throne. Incision on an ivory object found in excavations at Megiddo.

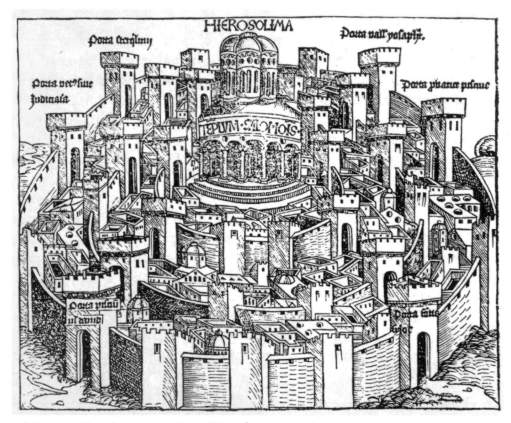

Solomon's Temple as viewed by a fifteenth century painter.

cedar wood, and gold inlay. A large court-yard surrounded the entire compound.

Much of the area to the south of the Temple Mount as it stands today has been exposed in archaeological excavations but nothing related to the magnificent compound of Solomon's palace was revealed. It is there-fore possible that the palace was located under the southern extension added to the Temple Mount by King Herod and thus forev-er buried. Since the days of King Solomon, the area between the City of David and the Temple that now forms the southern part of the Temple Mount was devoted to secular, royal use and was not part of the Israelite holy edifice. This observation has recently become most relevant in connection with discussions in rabbinical circles regarding which part of

the Temple Mount Jews could visit without trespassing on holy ground. This issue will be elaborated in chapter 7.

Solomon's Temple in Legend and in Early Artistic Depictions

The description of Solomon Temple and palace, with their vast quantities of precious materials, the superior wood and metal tech-nology, and the fine workmanship in gold and copper, has placed them on a legendary plateau. Solomon himself became an almost supernatural figure, and over time various magical qualities were attributed to him. The Bible itself states that "Solomon's wisdom excelled the wisdom of all the children of the east country, and all the wisdom of Egypt. . . . And he spoke three thousand proverbs, and his songs were a thousand and five. And he spoke of trees . . . beasts, and of fowl, and of creeping things, and of fishes" (I Kings 4:30–33). Legend relates that Solomon did not speak of the trees and animals but that he could converse with them, and that he also had power over the demons and spirits.[11] These beings of the night in fact built the Temple, which explains its excessive splendor.[12] In this vein it has been suggested that the Temple with its profusion of floral design and with the *cherubim* that shielded over the Ark of the Covenant, was intended to evoked the memory of the mythical Garden of Eden with the *cherubim* that guarded its entrance.[13] Was the Temple indeed as sumptuous as the Bible tells us, or was its description an exaggeration, composed by later generations to glorify the dynasty of King David by presenting an idealized picture of wealth and creativity? Indeed, not only the Temple and palace, but the warrior and poet David, and Solomon with his immense wealth and lavish spending, his wisdom, his numerous wives and exotic relations with foreign emissaries, all left a lasting mark on the imagination of generations to come.

The idealization of Solomon's Temple and its everlasting significance finds symbolic expressions in scenes worked into floors of synagogues of the fourth to seventh centuries CE unearthed in several locations in Israel.[14]

These floors are divided into three horizontal sections. The first, closest to the synagogue entrance, depicts the Binding of Isaac. It has been suggested that this scene commemorates sacrifices that were carried out in the courtyard of the Temple. It also evokes the identification, already widespread by the time the synagogues were built, of the hill in the Land of Moriah where the Binding took place with the Temple Mount in Jerusalem. Theme

on the central, largest section of the mosaic floors is the zodiac. This section is equated to the *hechal*, the largest space of the Temple, where many of the priestly rituals took place. The zodiac has been interpreted as reflecting the glory of God and his dominance over the heavens and the seasons of the year, and thus the power that controls the rain and the sun and the success of the agricultural year. Finally, the upper band is centered on a depiction of the Ark of the Covenant flanked by angels or by birds, reminiscent of the *cherubim* that shielded over the Ark of the Covenant in Solomon's Temple.

The depiction of Solomon's Temple on the floors of several synagogues built hundreds of years after it was destroyed reflects strong messianic aspirations for the return of the glorious times of King Solomon, aspirations that never died. They found expressions not only in artistic depictions but also in the Jewish daily prayers that were structured to coincide with the time of the priestly services in the Temple.

Changes and Repairs in Solomon's Temple

During the 350 years or so of the existence of Solomon's Temple it needed occasional repairs and underwent many changes. Several major restoration projects are mentioned in the Bible, one in the days of King Joash, another in the days of King Josiah. Other kings replaced elements of the Temple or added new ones. At some point new chambers were added for the use of officers, scribes, and guards. King Jotham built the higher gate of the Temple, and King Ahaz removed the large copper altar and replaced it with a new one built to the design of an altar he saw in Damascus. The Temple treasure was often used to pay foreign rulers in order to avert the danger of invasion and ward off enemies. This was done in the

Synagogue mosaic from Beit Alpha

days of King Ahaz, who cut up some of the large copper items and sent them to Tiglath-Pileser, king of Assyria, to avert an invasion (II Kings 16:8). Similarly King Hezekiah, "cut the gold from the doors of the Temple of the Lord and from the pillars . . . and gave it to the king of Assyria" (II Kings 18:16). When Nebuchadnezzar, king of Babylon, besieged Jerusalem, King Jehoiachin "carried out thence all the treasures of the house of the Lord, and the treasures of the king's house, and cut in pieces all the vessels of gold which Solomon, king of Israel, had made in the Temple of the Lord" (II Kings 24:13).

Twice foreign gods and pagan worship were introduced into the Temple. The first to do such an act was King Amaziah, who, after having conquered the Edomites, "brought the gods of the children of Seir, and set them up to be his gods, and bowed down himself before them, and burned incense unto them" (II Chronicles 25:14). Perhaps King Manasseh, who built altars in both courtyards of the Temple and installed a statue of the Canaanite goddess Ashera inside the Temple proper (II Kings 21:7), committed the greatest sacrilege. He may also have removed the Ark of the Covenant.[15, 16]

Opening page from a prayer book from Spain, 13th century,
depicting Temple vessels. Courtesy of the Manuscript Library,
The National and University Library.

During renovations of the Temple ordered by King Josiah, a book of the law was found in the Temple. The priests read the book to the king, who thus became aware of the true nature of the Israelite religion. Josiah then initiated a major religious reform that involved purifying and repairing the Temple. In the course of these activities the images of foreign gods that had been placed in the Temple by his predecessor, and all the vestiges of pagan cult throughout all the kingdom of Judah, were smashed and their priests killed. Thus foreign cultic activities were abolished, and the feast of Passover was observed properly for the first time since the days of the Judges (II Kings 22:3–23:25).

The Destruction of the Temple and the Whereabouts of Its Ritual Objects

In 586 BCE the First Temple was destroyed by the Babylonians. The Israelite population was exiled to Babylon, and the precious gold objects that remained in the Temple and in the king's palace were taken as booty (II Kings 24:13). The bronze items were cut up (ibid 25:13–15) and carried to Babylon as scrap metal. The Ark of the Covenant was not mentioned in the lists of booty, nor among the precious Temple items that were brought back to Jerusalem when the Second Temple was built.

Despite the early disappearance of the Ark of the Covenant, and the explicit biblical reference to the removal of the remaining objects to Babylon, popular mind could not agree about its disappearance. The rabbinical sages suggested that the prophetess Hulda told King Josiah, the instigator of the religious reform in his kingdom, that despite his good deeds the Temple would be eventually destroyed. Josiah was worried that the enemy would desecrate the holy items, and he apparently hid the Ark of the Covenant and related objects in a cave under the Temple. Indeed, the Palestinian Talmud (Shekalim 29:2) picked up this idea and noted that discarded holy objects were placed in a cave under the Temple. Sir Charles Warren, the great explorer of Jerusalem, believed that objects of the greatest interest were hidden under the Temple Mount. The possibility that holy objects are buried under the Temple Mount aroused hopes of locating them when a tunnel issuing eastward from the Western Wall Tunnel was found. News of the tunnel spread rapidly. When the Muslims became concerned that the tunnel would lead under the Temple Mount and undermine it, the Israeli government ordered the tunnel blocked.

Some sages with a poetic mind suggested that it was the prophet Jeremiah who was entrusted with protecting the ritual objects of the Temple[17],[18] but that an angel removed the most important items: the Ark of the Covenant with the two Tablets of the Law, the gold incense altar, and the vestments of the High Priest, including his breastplate with precious stones. The angel hid them on Mount Nebo, the mountain from which Moses observed the Promised Land before he died. Jeremiah col-

lected all the other objects, including a vessel that contained a sample of the manna consumed by the Israelites during their exodus from Egypt as a witness to the miracles God showed to his people, and hid them in a large cave. No one but Jeremiah knew the whereabouts of the cave, which will be revealed by God himself when the messiah comes. The musical instruments on which the Levites played during the rituals, the gold candelabrum, the seventy-seven gold tables, and the gold that covered the walls of the Temple were also hidden, while the golden gates sunk into the earth. In the Days of the Messiah a stream will burst under the location of the Holy of Holies and flow to join the Euphrates River. On its way this flow of water will uncover the hiding places of the treasures and reveal them (Mishnah Tractate Kelim 88–91).

In expectation of the arrival of the messiah, the Jews of Spain in the thirteenth and fourteenth centuries added to their Bible books an illuminated opening page with illustrations of the Temple vessels. Numerous items are depicted: the Tablets of the Law, the candelabrum and its tweezers, the golden table of showbread and incense altar, the altar of burnt offerings, and basins, shovels, scrapers, and firepans needed for performing the sacrificing. Other items were the silver trumpets, *cherubim*, snuffers, the manna jug, and Aaron's blooming rod. These pages, arranged in a variety of combinations, like the mosaic synagogue floors, express the yearning for the rebuilding of the Solomon's Temple with its Tablets of the Law. This yearning is explicit in the invocation on one of the pages: "All [the implements existed] while the Temple was upon its site and the holy sanctuary was upon its foundation. Blessed is he who beheld the splendor of the beauty of its greatness and all the acts of its power and its might. And happy is he who hopes and lives to see it. May it be your will that it [the Temple] be speedily rebuilt in our days so that our eyes may behold it and our hearts rejoice."[19]

To some the loss of the Ark of the Covenant, in particular, is inconsolable, and many speculations as to the place where it was hidden have developed over the ages. One hiding place is believed to be Ethiopia, to where, so this story relates, the Queen of Sheba took the Ark upon her return from her visit with Solomon. Another way the Ark is said to have arrived in Ethiopia is connected to the Order of the Knights Templars, whose headquarters during the Crusader period was on the Temple Mount. These knights used the subterranean spaces under the Temple Mount as Stables for their horses, and thus they found the Ark. It is rumored that the Ark has been in hiding for many centuries in a church in Ethiopia, where the monks closely guard it. Many have tried to penetrate the church and view the Ark, but no one except the guardian priest has access to it.

The Ark is also believed to be buried in various places in Ireland, having been brought there in 585 BCE by the prophet Jeremiah. In 1899 a group of British Israelites who believed that they were descended from the Ten Lost Tribes of Israel excavated in the Hill of Tara, the ancient seat of the great Celtic kings of Ireland, with the hope of discovering the Ark of the Covenant. The Mormons believe that the Prophet Lehi brought the Ark to America and that it is buried on the "outskirts of Utah."

The First Temple and Early Israelite Religion

What was the meaning and function of Solomon's Temple in the context of the ancient religion of Israel? The God of Israel is described as unique, transcendental, shapeless, and so vast that he filled the entire universe, in marked contrast to the many gods worshipped in the pagan world that surrounded ancient Israel. And yet it was felt in the early days of the development of the Israelite religion that God needed a home to dwell in, much in accord with the need of the neighboring pagan gods, and had expressed a desire for a house. Indeed, at the inaugural ceremony of the Temple, King Solomon proclaimed, "I have surely built thee a house to dwell in, a settled place for thee to abide in forever" (I Kings 8:13). Solomon's Temple was thus conceived as the private domain of God,[20] and, unlike modern places of worship, such as a synagogue, church, or mosque, not a place for the people to worship in. The people did not enter God's dwelling and did not participate in the ritual, which was conducted by a closed circle of priests who officiated in the Temple and carried out the prescribed daily and the festive ceremonial activities. The daily rituals executed by the Temple priests centered on symbolically attending to the physical needs of the divine God in his home. They sacrificed animals, baked special showbread, and burned incense to provide God with a pleasing aroma (e.g., Leviticus 1:17, 2:9, 3:5, 16).[21] They lit candelabras to provide light in the semidark space.

Another aspect of the Temple was its political function, reflected in its close connection to the royal house. The Temple, situated near the king's palace, was meant to symbolize the unity of the kingdom and the position of Jerusalem as its capital, as well as the special position of the royal dynasty of King David. Throughout its existence the Temple was a royal chapel, located in the farthest section of the royal acropolis, far away from the residential sections of the city, in keeping with the locations of Temples in royal courts of neighboring countries. It was not a place where the people could visit and perform the ceremonies, sacrifices, and offerings prescribed in Leviticus. No wonder the people, and even many of the kings, often resorted to idol worship. The many clay figurines of idols unearthed in private Israelite homes in Jerusalem and throughout the kingdom of Judah testify to idol worship, as are the harsh words the prophets continuously heaped on the idolaters.

Throughout the existence of the First Temple there were several attempts to reform the Israelite religion and abolish pagan practices, but they did not hold for long. Perhaps the worst idol worshipper was King Manasseh (seventh century BCE), who revived many Canaanite pagan practices, and even, as already mentioned, placed a statue of the pagan goddess Ashera inside the Temple (II Kings 21:6). Even the final attempt at a religious reform led by King Josiah following the Manasseh regression did not succeed, and the people continued their pagan practices up to the destruction of the Temple.[22]

The disillusionment of several prophets regarding the activities in the Temple is reflected by the visionary Temple described by the prophet Ezekiel (chaps. 40–43). His Temple is not related to the actual Temple that was still standing in Ezekiel's early days, before its destruction by the Babylonians, but reflects the ideal Temple that will be built one day, in which there will be no trace of idolatry or mishandling of the services and rituals.

The unity that David aimed to achieve by linking palace and Temple broke soon after King Solomon died, when the kingdom split in two. The ten northern tribes turned their back on the dynasty of King David, chose another capital, built other temples, and often turned to idol worship. The southern tribes of Judah and Benjamin, despite frequent religious transgressions, remained loyal to David, and through them the holiness of the Temple was sustained to become the sacred legacy of the entire Jewish nation. Solomon's Temple, despite its mixture of Israelite and pagan elements, as well as the Second Temple, which replaced it, became symbols not only of religious but also of national independence. Their construction symbolized national rejuvenation; their destruction, national catastrophe

The Second Temple

The Returned Babylonian Exiles Rebuild the Temple

The Babylonian exile was very short, lasting only forty-seven years. In 539 BCE Cyrus, king of Persia, conquered Babylon and, as part of his general policy of restoring the temples of local gods throughout his kingdom, allowed the exiles to return to their home country, Judah, and rebuild their Temple. While most of the exiles preferred to remain in their new home, a trickle returned to Judah. They brought with them several Temple items taken as spoils of war by the Babylonian army when the First Temple was destroyed and released to them by Cyrus.

The returnees began to make preparations to build a new Temple, but at first they were able to build only an altar.[23] On the festival of Succot (Tabernacles), just after the altar was completed, people from various parts of Judah made a pilgrimage to Jerusalem and sacrificed on the new altar, thus resuming the obligation to sacrifice, even though the Temple was not yet built. Shortly afterwards the foundations for the Temple itself were laid, but severe economic difficulties and strained relations with hostile neighbors brought the work to a halt.

However, fifteen years later, when another wave of returnees came to Jerusalem, work was resumed and brought to completion. This second wave was headed by two personalities with impressive genealogies: Zerubbabel, son of Shealtiel and grandson of Jehoiachin, the last king of Judah and thus a descendant of King David, and Jehoshua, son of Jehozadak, grandson of the last High Priest in Solomon's Temple. The Second Temple was inaugurated in 517 BCE. At first it was small and simple, reflecting the small number of returnees and their meager economic situation. Those who had survived the destruction of Jerusalem and the exile and lived to see the new Temple wept on the day of its inauguration, remembering the glory and riches of the First Temple.[24]

Although the Temple was standing, the people were quite reluctant to bring the obligatory tithes required for the performance of the rituals and for the upkeep of the Temple staff. The condition of the Temple was so poor that the priests and Levites left their office and retired to the countryside to find other occupations. It took the determination of Ezra the Scribe and Nehemiah, a high official in the Persian administration, who came to Jerusalem about a hundred years after the first wave of returnees and instituted social and religious reforms, and established the orderly routine of Temple activities. In times of need, Ezra congregated the people in a street outside the Temple precinct, where he read to them excerpts from the book of the Law of Moses. He also prayed there. Perhaps from then on prayers, which were held at the exact

hour of day when the priests performed the daily cult, could substitute for participation in the events of the Temple. In the course of the Second Temple period, synagogues were built around the country, including Jerusalem, and people would meet and pray in them.

Despite its modest beginnings, the Second Temple rose to great importance and left an everlasting mark on the development of the religious and national life of the Jewish people. The apex of the First Temple was right after it was built by King Solomon, after which it gradually declined because of idolatrous worship and the stripping of many of its treasures. The Second Temple, on the other hand, had a humble beginning, but its situation only improved over the centuries until it reached its apex in Herod's Temple.

There were other differences between the two Temples. Whereas the First Temple had occasional competing places of worship around the country, such as the temple that was discovered in the southern town of Arad, the Second Temple was the undisputed and exclusive holy place for all Jewish people, the center of their religious, national, and economic life. There was also a theological difference between the two Temples. The Second Temple was no longer conceived as God's dwelling place, as was expressed by the Second Isaiah, who claimed in the name of God that "The heaven is my throne, and the earth is my footstool: where is the house that ye build unto me? And where is the place of my rest? (66:1).

Several Psalms (e.g., 27:4, 84:2, 116:17–19) relate that the people longed to visit and even did visit the Temple courtyards, if not the Temple itself, a situation not known in the First Temple. The function of the Temple thus drastically changed during the Second

Temple period from a dwelling of God to a sanctuary open to the people. The Temple cult in Solomon's Temple centered on sacrifices. The importance of sacrifices continued in the Second Temple, but new ceremonies were added, such as the pouring of water on the seventh day of the festival of Succot. There was also a gradual acceptance of prayers as a substitute for Temple offerings,[25] and this was a step toward the purely abstract Jewish religion that had been gradually developing since the return from the Babylonian exile.

The sages of the Talmud conceived the First Temple as holier than the Second, since it had housed the Ark of the Covenant and other sacred items that were now missing. And yet the words of the prophet Haggai, "The glory of this latter house shall be greater than of the former" (2:9), proclaimed when the Second Temple was still very humble, were realized in full. The Temple cast its influence not only on Judah, but also on the expanding diaspora, from Persia in the east to Spain in the west, and on the development of Jewish religion, thought, and aspirations.

The term "Second Temple" is somewhat misleading, because in the first century BCE. King Herod transformed the shape of the Temple Mount and destroyed the old Temple to build a new, larger, and more impressive one. Because there was hardly any time gap between the two Temples, however, they were from the start considered as one.

The Plan and Dimensions of the Early Second Temple

Because the Temple Mount was left in ruins only for a very short time, the builders of the Second Temple must have seen stumps of the walls of the old Temple. They attempted to build on them or in relation to them so as to continue the First Temple as much as possible and absorb its sanctity. The inner dimensions of the main hall and the Holy of Holies together were identical to those of the First Temple: 35 by 10 meters.

No descriptions of the style of this building and its decorations have survived. What we do know is that the returnees added a closed outer courtyard to the inner courtyard. Both Israelite men and women were allowed into this new courtyard, but only men could enter the inner one. The outer courtyard was therefore named the Women's Court, and here all ceremonies not connected with sacrifice were performed. The inner court was called the Court of the Israelites, and those who brought sacrifices proceeded to it. Both courts had chambers in their corners used for storage, and a wall enclosed both the Temple and courts. It seems that the separation of the men from the women reflects the extra care taken by the Babylonian returnees in matters of ritual purity, under the guidance of their spiritual leader, Ezra the Scribe. Preoccupation with ritual purity characterized the Second Temple period, as witnessed by the numerous ritual baths discovered in residential neighborhoods of the period in Jerusalem.

The Persian and Hellenistic kings recognized the Temple as a Jewish holy place, and decreed that non-Jews were barred from entering it. The authorities also exempted from taxes the priests who served in the Temple.

We have no information regarding the Temple's ritual objects, but it seems likely that with time and the gradual improvement of the economic situation of Judah, an incense altar, candelabra, and tables for the showbread were introduced to the main hall. The Holy of Holies was totally empty, as it seems to have already been toward the end of the First Temple peri-od. Aristeas, a Jew from Egypt who visited Jerusalem in the third century BCE, wrote an enthusiastic letter to his brother in which he expressed his deep impressions of the Temple, of its walls and its gates, and of the thousands of animals sacrificed there on festive days. Aristeas also praised the priests for doing their work in a silent, dignified manner.[26]

To grant the Temple protection against the many enemies that threatened the province of Judah, a fort (*bira*) was built to the north of the Temple. Like everything that existed on the Temple Mount prior to the major renovations of King Herod, no traces of either the early Second Temple or the fort remained.

The Kings of the Hasmonean Dynasty Enlarge the Second Temple

The next phase in the story of the Second Temple was in the Hasmonean period, named after the dynasty that ruled independent Judah in the second and first centuries BCE. This period began with a religious-national Jewish revolt headed by the priest Mattathias and his five sons against the Hellenistic rulers of the Seleucid Dynasty, successors of Alexander the Great, who conquered the coun-try in 332 BCE. King Antiochus IV attempted to enforce the Hellenistic culture on all his sub-jects, and introduced foreign rituals to the Temple. A pig was sacrificed on the Temple altar, and the king's own statue was installed in its courtyard. He also looted the Temple treasures. Because of these acts of desecration, coupled with the breaking of the compound walls, the Jews deserted the Temple for three years during which battles raged between them and the Seleucid army.

The rebels succeeded beyond expectation. The foreign army was defeated in several bat-

tles, and Judah Maccabee, the most celebrated of the five sons of Mattathias, entered Jerusalem in triumph. Judas destroyed the desecrated altar and had the stones stored in one of the chambers of the Temple's court-yards, cleaned the Temple, mended its bro-ken walls, and built a new altar. The inaugu-ration of the consecrated Temple took place in December 165 BCE, an event commemorated to this day by the festival of Hanukkah.

The newly formed Kingdom of Judah soon came under the cultural influence of the Hellenistic world, and it has been suggested, although without proof, that the Temple was modified to look more like a Greek temple. Although we have no information on the activities of the Hasmonean kings in connec-tion with the Temple, it would seem likely that with the growth of their kingdom they devoted resources to its beautification.

In those days a major attempt to enlarge the Temple Mount was undertaken. The small natural hill summit was enlarged to a platform of 250 by 250 meters (500 by 500 cubits in the words of the Mishnah, almost 16 acres). To create this platform, strong terrace walls were built around the designed space, and the area behind them was filled and lev-eled. The exact location of these terrace walls can only be assumed, although a still-stand-ing section of the eastern wall of the Temple Mount probably dates to this period, since it is built of the small and roughly cut stones typical of that time. This section of wall may have been the southeastern corner of the Hasmonean Temple Mount.

The main entrances to the Temple Mount at that time were from the south, as they would be in the much-enlarged Temple Mount of the time of King Herod. Two ritual baths that may have flanked one of these entrances were recently identified. These baths again indicate the strict observance of ritual cleanliness throughout the Second Temple period. Except for these ritual baths, and perhaps the above-mentioned section of the eastern enclosure wall, nothing remains of the Hasmonean Temple Mount compound or of the Temple itself. They are all buried under the fill of the Herodian construction.

King Herod Rebuilds Temple Mount

King Herod introduced the major change in the configuration of the Temple Mount, determining its present-day shape. We know much about Herod's project from various sources. The two most important literary sources are the books of the Jewish historian Josephus Flavius and the Mishnah, a collection of sayings and deliberation of Second Temple and post–Second Temple period sages compiled in the second century CE. Josephus knew the Temple Mount intimately, having been a priest who served in the Temple. The sages of the Mishnah wrote down their knowledge of the Temple Mount for the future generations that might one day rebuild the Temple. Another important source is the discoveries made by the extensive archaeological excavations carried out along the southern and western walls of the compound in the 1970s; these added much important information on the walls, gates, and passageways of the compound.

Why Did King Herod Rebuild the Temple Mount?

About halfway through his reign, Herod decided to double the size of the Mount and rebuild the Temple. He must have had several reasons when he committed himself to such a grand project. His main aim seems to have been his desire to provide proper conditions for pilgrimage to the Temple. During the Second Temple period more and more people fulfilled the obligation to make an obligatory pilgrimage to the Temple on the three major yearly festivals of Passover, Shavuot (Pentecost), and Succot (Tabernacles). As economic conditions in Judah improved, more and more people were able to make the pilgrimage and bring offerings to the Temple. Not only local Jews fulfilled this obligation; numerous diaspora Jews joined their brothers in undertaking the pilgrimage. The Temple Mount became the meeting ground for Jews the world over, thus helping to strengthen the ties between the scattered segments of the nation and between them and their national and religious center in Jerusalem.

With the increase in their numbers, the Hasmonean compound became much too small to contain them all. Herod, who was considered a foreign, unaccepted ruler, perhaps wanted to appease his hostile subjects by presenting them with a magnificent new holy compound that would satisfy the needs of the multitudes of pilgrims. Herod, as quoted by Josephus Flavius, presented his project to the people as an act of thanksgiving: "Since, by the will of God, I am now the ruler, and there continues to be a long period of peace and abundance of wealth and great revenues, and what is more important, the Romans who are, so to speak, the masters of the world, are [my] loyal friends, I will try to remedy the oversight caused by the necessity and subjection of that earlier time [the old Temple was believed to have been 30 meters lower than Solomon's Temple], and by this act of piety make full return to God for the gift of his kingdom" (*Jewish Antiquities* 15:387).

The very well preserved south-east corner of Herod's Temple Mount compound. Courtesy of Israel Exploration Society.

But Herod must have had a further motive. Being a titular ruler of Judah by the favor of Rome and owing his throne to his Roman benefactors, he felt the need to impress the Romans with his wealth and ability. An enlarged and beautified Temple Mount, surpassing the largest and most beautiful Temples in the contemporary world, was probably just the right project to increase his prestige. Indeed, Josephus comments that Herod was also sure that "this project of his will be praised more than anything he did—and so it was" (*Jewish Antiquities* 15:380).

Herod's grand project took forty-six years to complete and came to an end only in the year 64 CE, many years after Herod's death and only seven years before Jerusalem fell to the Romans and the Temple Mount was destroyed. The people of Judah had no reason to oppose Herod's grand project, and both Josephus and the sages of the Mishnah report that the compound was divinely blessed, since it was rained on only at night, whereas during the day it was dry. Despite the inconvenience that the ongoing construction work no doubt caused to everyday life in Jerusalem, it was beneficial to the social and economic situation, providing long years of work to its citizens and those of the neighboring regions. Indeed, the completion of the work during the reign of King Agrippa, grandson of King Herod, caused a severe problem of unemployment in Jerusalem.

The Temple Mount Compound[27]

To double the size of the Hasmonean compound to the 36-acre Temple Mount that has been preserved intact to this day, Herod had to overcome major topographic obstacles. His engineers had to divert two streams on the west and northeast sides, to lower the rising slope on the northwest and to level the steep down-slope on the south side. To fulfill this grand plan, they surrounded the planned compound with high walls founded on bedrock. The height of the walls was in some places 60 meters. The upper 30 meters were exposed above the surrounding streets, while the lower section went all the way down to bedrock and was hidden under fill. The thickness of the walls is unknown, but it is estimated that to be constructively sound and hold the enormous weight of the fill behind them, they were at least 5 meters thick. The walls were built of huge, well-dressed stones, the largest being 12 meters long, 3 meters wide, and 4 meters deep. Its weight was calculated at some 400 tons. The larger stones were installed close to the base of the walls, reinforcing them and lending them stability that has proved itself to this day. For the upper courses, smaller stones, weighing on average 50 tons, were used. No mortar was put between the stones; they hold together by their sheer weight.

Wherever the space between the newly built walls and the natural configuration of the hill was shallow, it was filled with stones and earth. On the south side, however, where the natural ground slopes steeply, simple filling would have created too much pressure on the wall, so an arched structure was built to support the platform. The southern wall of the Temple Mount thus functions as a retaining wall. No wonder it suffered damage over the centuries, especially from earthquakes, and was often repaired. The strength of the walls won the acclaim of the famous Roman historian Tacitus, who wrote that the Temple was built as a citadel surrounded by extremely strong walls, and that more labor was invested in building them than for any other known fortification.

The Entrance Gates

The Temple Mount was thus a partially artificial platform raised above its natural surrounding, and special arrangements for entering it were required. Nine gates provided entrance to the Temple Mount from the streets surrounding it. The gates were of three types: directly from street level, through tunnels, and up flights of steps. The main entrances were through four gates in the west wall and two in the south wall. The other three served for ritual purposes. The function of the northern Tadi Gate is unclear. The eastern Susa Gate was aligned with the Temple entrance and with the summit of the Mount of Olives on which various rituals were held. It was from the eastern gate close to the southeastern corner of the Temple Mount that the scapegoat was sent to the desert on the Day of Atonement, carrying the sins of the people. The double and triple Hulda Gates in the south wall, the main entrances into the Temple Mount, were much lower than the Temple Mount platform and communicated with it through long underground sloping tunnels.[28] The tunnel of the western gate has survived to this day, and has two finely cut stone walls and stout square columns that hold large domes delicately carved with fine floral and geometric motifs. Pilgrims would enter the Temple Mount through the eastern, triple Hulda Gate and exit from the western, double gate. Mourners would go in the opposite direction so that people could console them. One gate in the west wall, the so-called Barclay Gate, also had a tunnel that led to the surface of the platform.

Three gates, two in the west wall and one in the east wall, were located high up at the level of the platform, and were reached by flights of steps. Nothing remains of the gates themselves, but their position has been calculated by the stump of an arch (Robinson's Arch) protruding from the southern section of the west wall, and by another stump of an arch in the east wall. The large-scale archaeo-logical excavations carried out at the foot of the Temple Mount mainly in the 1970s revealed traces of arches on which a flight of steps that led to the Temple Mount esplanade was built. Based on calculation of the full height of Robinson's arch, it was established that the original level of Herod's Temple platform was about 4 meters higher than the level of the lower platform of today's compound. Unlike today's two-level platform, Herod's Temple Mount was on one level.

The Royal Basilica[29]

The huge platform was surrounded by porticos in Greek-Roman style with two rows of pillars and a flat roof. On the south side of the platform stood the Royal Basilica, praised by Josephus Flavius for its size and beauty. The roof of this very large building was supported by 160 pillars arranged in four rows of 40 pillars each. Two additional pillars probably demarcated the apse at its eastern end.

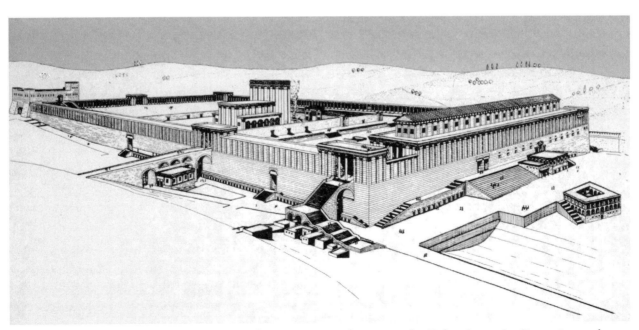

Reconstruction of Herod's Temple Mount, with Robinson's Arch carrying the flight of steps leading to its southwestern entrance. Courtesy of Israel Exploration Society.

Huge stones in Temple Mount compound wall. Photographer: Rivka Gonen.

Sections of pillars that fell from the Royal Basilica to the foot of the southern wall of the Temple Mount are 1 meter thick, contradicting Josephus, who wrote that the pillars were so thick that it needed three men holding hands to embrace them. The capitals were fashioned in the Corinthian style.

The Royal Basilica, a secular rather than a religious building, was used for a variety of official, public, national, and economic functions. Structures of the same architectural and functional nature are known from other religious compounds around the contemporary Hellenistic-Roman world.

Antonia Fortress

To complete the Temple Mount project, King Herod built a mighty fortress just outside the northwestern corner of the Temple Mount, which he named Antonia in honor of his Roman friend and benefactor Mark Antony. It was necessary to protect this vulnerable point,

because here the ground rises gradually and does not offer a natural barrier as exists on the other sides. The valley in the northeast corner of the Temple Mount was converted into a series of open water cisterns that offered good protection to the holy site on that side, while to the east the deep Kidron Valley and to the west The valley protected it from attack. On the south, the very high southern wall of the compound was in itself a mighty barrier. The Antonia Fortress must have been built on the 5-meter-high rock on which a school is built nowadays, although Josephus relates that the rock was 25 meters high.

King Herod's Temple

With all the splendor of the Temple Mount compound, the jewel in the crown was the newly built Temple itself. The demolition of the old Temple and the building of a new one were delicate matters, enough to enrage the people and their leaders. To avert the expect-

Carved stones of the time of Herod found among the debris along the south wall of the Temple Mount. Perhaps they once adorned the Royal Basilica. Courtesy of Israel Exploration Society.

ed anger, Herod first assembled all the necessary building materials, animals of burden, 1,000 wagons to transport the stones, and 10,000 workers. Among the workers were 1,000 priests trained in stone and woodwork, who were entrusted with the building of the Temple itself. Once the old Temple was demolished, work on the new Temple was done with the utmost reverence and the greatest care. The Mishnah relates that lightweight temporary walls were placed around the Temple area so that no one could get a glimpse at what was happening in the holy space. The stones for the altar were quarried in the Galilee without the aid of iron, because, as the Mishnah remarks, iron was created to shorten the days of man, and the altar's function was to lengthen them. The building of the Temple took a year and a half.

What we know about the reconstruction of the Temple is based on Flavius Josephus and the Mishnah, both sources dealing mainly with the final shape of the Temple, a short time before the Romans destroyed it in 70 CE. They are sometimes vague and are not always in agreement. Unlike the outer walls and gates of the Temple Mount, sections of which had been preserved, nothing of the Temple proper

Robinson's arch. Source: Warren, Charles, Underground Jerusalem, 1876.

Reconstruction of Robinson's Arch and the flight of steps leading up to the Temple Mount. Courtesy of Israel Exploration Society.

has survived, and no archaeological excavations have ever been conducted where it stood. In fact, it is doubtful whether anything of the Temple will ever be found, because its destruction was massive, and the Dome of the Rock was built many years later on the spot where it once stood.

As is common with holy edifices, there were gradations of holiness in the compound and in the Temple itself.[30] The Temple Mount compound was open to all, Jews and non-Jews alike. The first boundary delineated an

area of about 16 acres, into which only Jews were allowed to enter. This boundary was marked by a high fence in which were inserted large stone slabs carrying inscriptions in Greek and Latin warning non-Jews not to proceed further. The inscription states: "A non-Jew shall not enter beyond the fence surrounding the Temple and the courtyard around it. He who is caught will be killed." One intact slab and the central section of another, both in Greek,[31] were found on the eastern slopes of the Temple Mount. These slabs are the only objects relating to the Temple that survived its catastrophic destruction.

Beyond this fence, steps led to the Temple and its inner courts, enclosed within protective walls. The Temple was in fact an inner fortress within the strong walls of the Temple Mount enclosure. Those who were allowed to enter the Temple proceeded through a gate into the first courtyard, which had rooms in its four corners, used for various Temple activities. In this courtyard, activities not related to sacrifices were performed. Women could not proceed beyond this Women's Court. The men went up a flight of steps and entered the narrow Court of the Israelites through the ornate Nicanor Gate, named after the benefactor who donated the doors. Beyond the Court of the Israelites was the Priest's Court, entered only by the priests who officiated in the Temple. Here was the large altar for animal sacrifices and the implements for washing and cutting the sacrificial meat. Another flight of twelve steps led from this courtyard to the Temple proper.

The Temple itself had the same dimensions as the Solomon's Temple and also had a three-story auxiliary structure along three of its sides. Its height of 50 meters, double that of Solomon's Temple, was perhaps intended to confer a sense of majesty to the building. The space between the ceiling of the inner spaces of the Temple and the roof of the building was left empty. The entrance hall was wider than the building itself, protruding on both sides of the main hall. It gave the Temple a shape "narrow in the back and wide in front, resembling a lion" (Mishnah Midot 4:7). As in Solomon's Temple, the inner space was divided into three sections: the entrance hall, the main hall, and the Holy of Holies.

The facade of the Temple was imposing.[32] It was 50 meters wide and 50 meters high. Coins from the time of Bar Kokhba (about sixty years after the destruction of the Temple) depict the Temple's facade with four pillars and a flat roof. The entrance to the Temple was also monumental, and above it was a spectacular decorative arrangement made of alternating wooden beams and rows of stones. The upper beam was wider than the entrance lintel, and the ones below it were gradually narrower, until the lowest beam was the lintel itself. This unique arrangement is unknown in any other contemporary structure. Above the opening King Herod placed a gold eagle, and arousing the anger of the people, who objected to placing an image in such a holy spot. The Temple was not closed by doors but by a fabric curtain. The entrance hall must have been a spectacular space. A vine complete with leaves and bunches of grapes all made of gold and supported on cedar poles decorated its ceiling. Its back wall was gilt, and a gold chandelier hung over the entrance to the main hall.

The opening that separated the entrance hall from the main hall was again immense and was closed by two sets of gilded wooden doors. When the doors were open, a curtain separated the two spaces, and when both this and the outer curtains were lifted, the men in the Court of the Israelites could catch a glimpse of the ritual in the main hall.

The priests conducted most of their ritual work in the main hall, which had gilt walls. In it stood a candelabrum with its cleaning implements, an altar, and a table for the show-bread, all made of gold. The Arch of Titus in Rome, built to commemorate Titus's victory over Judah in 70 C.E., depicts several of the Temple's objects are depicted being carried in

Temple Façade on a coin from the time of the Bar
Kochba Revolt. Courtesy of Kadman Numismatic
Museum, Tel Aviv.

Façade of Herod's Temple in model of Jerusalem in the Second Temple period at
the Holy Land Hotel Model. Courtesy of Holy Land Hotel, Jerusalem.

a triumphal procession. The most important of these objects, the candelabrum with a stepped base, was adopted as the official emblem of the State of Israel, a symbol of the revival of the Jewish people after the disastrous destruction of their Temple and country. It is now believed that the heavy stepped base of the candelabrum on the Arch of Titus was added to facilitate carrying this heavy gold object, for representation of a candelabrum found scratched on the wall of a house in a residential neighborhood of Second Temple Jerusalem has a tripod base. Somewhat different forms of candelabra with tripod bases are depicted on mosaic floors of ancient synagogues around the country.

Two curtains separated the main hall from the Holy of Holies, one opened to the right, the other to the left. When the High Priest entered this space to perform the ritual of the Day of Atonement, he first lifted one curtain, stepped behind it ,and then lifted the other, so no one could see the inside of this holiest of spaces. The Holy of Holies was totally dark and completely empty, because the Ark of the Covenant, the most sacred object of Jewish ritual, had disappeared in the First Temple period. This emptiness was a source of great wonder to the Romans, who were used to placing statues of their gods in their temples. The Roman historian Tacitus reported the great astonishment of Pompey, the Roman general, who entered the Temple to celebrate his victory over Judah and found the Holy of Holies totally empty. The Holy of Holies was the highest point of the Temple Mount compound and of the Temple itself. And in this high point, so relates the Mishnah, an exposed rock protruded three fingers above the floor of the Holy of Holies. It must have been the very same rock on which the Holy of Holies of

Solomon's Temple was founded. The holiness of this rock has been preserved in legends and myths, and in the seventh century this holiness was adopted by the Muslims, who built over it the Dome of the Rock.

The Significance of the Second Temple in Jewish Life

The Temple in Jerusalem was the only place of worship for the Jewish people around the world at that time, and the only Temple in the city of Jerusalem. This phenomenon in itself was unique in the contemporary world, where each pagan god had many temples and each city boasted numerous holy precincts. When the emperor Augustus came to power, he initiated the repair of eighty Temples in Rome.

The Temple Mount, as the pulsing heart of contemporary Judaism, was not a sterile, silent compound but a space teeming with life. It was the meeting place for all segments of the nation, which, during the Second Temple period, was split between various contesting religious and political sects. It was the main stage on which differences between the conflicting opinions were publicly aired, sometimes violently. The Sanhedrin, the Supreme Court that functioned also as the Parliament and highest religious academy of the time, met daily in the Chamber of the Hewn Stones in the Temple courtyard to deliberate, decide, and publicize matters of national importance.

On the Temple Mount were synagogues where people prayed while sacrifices were being made in the Temple courtyards and incense was burned on the altar in the main hall. Here also were places of study where teachers of various opinions—revered rabbis, sages and messianic figures such as Jesus – daily preached and taught their lessons to students and to passers-by who flocked to hear

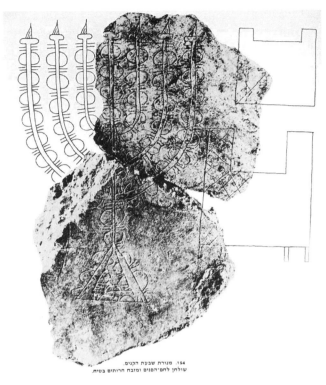

Candelabrum with tripod base. Courtesy of Israel Exploration Society.

The Temple Candelabrum as depicted on the Arch of Titus in Rome.

their words of wisdom. Here economic transactions were carried out; pilgrims from many countries exchanged their foreign currencies for the half-shekel that the every Jew was obliged to contribute to the Temple. People daily brought animals to be sacrificed in the Temple, and the bleating of oxen and sheep and the cooing of doves added to the general atmosphere of vitality. This was the nature of everyday life in the Temple Mount, a mixture of the sublime and the mundane. It was the focal point of Jewish life, a place full of energy, sometimes positive, at other times negative.[33]

All this energy was multiplied many times during the yearly pilgrimages to the Temple. The Torah states that every Jew has to make a pilgrimage to Jerusalem three times a year, on

the three major festivals that have agricultural aspects: Passover, when the first sheaves of grain are cut, Shavuot (Pentecost), when most of the field crops are harvested, and Succot (Tabernacles), when grapes and other fruits ripen.

Of course not everyone made all the pilgrimages yearly, but given the large and expanding Jewish population in the country and in the diaspora, tens of thousands of people congregated in Jerusalem for each of the festivals. They came from Judah, from Babylon and Mesopotamia, from Syria and Antioch, and from many towns in Asia Minor and Cilicia—all in Asia. They also came from Rome, Greece, and Cyprus in Europe and from Cyrene, Egypt, Libya, and Ethiopia in

Africa. The pilgrims would often organize themselves in processions of people from the same settlement headed by the village elder, or of extended families headed by their patriarch. Others would join them on the way, and they arrived in Jerusalem amid the sound of music and singing. The apex of the pilgrimage was a visit to the Temple to bring the sacrificial animals, the tithes of agricultural products, and the half-shekel, and to participate in the rituals.[34]

To accommodate the multitudes of pilgrims, the citizens of Jerusalem opened their homes and housed as many as they could. Others found accommodation in the villages surrounding Jerusalem, while others camped in open spaces in and around the city. Jewish communities in the diaspora established compounds for their own people, as is mentioned in the New Testament. An inscription chiseled on stone that was discovered in Jerusalem reads: "Theodotos son of Vetinus, priest and head of synagogue, son of head of synagogue, and grandson of head of synagogue, built the synagogue for reading the Torah and studying the law, and the hostel and the rooms and water installations for housing the needy who came from abroad." The name Vetinus indicates that the builder was a Roman Jew, and the installation he built was intended to house members of his community.[35]

Objections to the Temple: The Dead Sea Scroll Sect

Despite its centrality in the life of the majority of Jewish people during the Second Temple period, there were those who objected to the Temple on various grounds. For example, Jesus objected to the secular activities conducted in the outer courtyard of the Temple, and prophesied that the Temple would be completely destroyed (Matthew 24:2).

One group of people that objected to the Temple, its priests, and the ritual activities performed in it left Jerusalem and settled in and around the site of Qumran near the Dead Sea. This sect, identified with the Essenes mentioned by Josephus Flavius and other historians, had their own calendar, different from the regular one used by all other Jews. They could therefore not partake in the festivals, which were celebrated, in their view, on the wrong days.[36] They also adhered to very strict rules of ritual purity and objected to the priests, who, according to their belief, were lenient in keeping these rules.

The sect left a hoard of scrolls known as the Dead Sea Scrolls, many of which were discovered in caves around their center. The longest and one of the best preserved scrolls, known as the Temple Scroll, is written in the first person, as if by God himself. It gives a description and plan of the Temple as it should have been built, and also the rules and regulations of the activities to be held in it. A lengthy description is devoted to the three square concentric courtyards where most of the ritual activities, especially the sacrifices, were to be performed. It is interesting that the Temple itself is only briefly described. According to the sect, the Temple they proposed was to operate from the time of its building until the End of Days, when God will build a new Temple by his own hand. The expectation that God will build a new Temple at the End of Days is a recurrent theme of Jewish and Muslim legends and myths, and is brought up against those who make preparations to build the Third Temple.

The Whereabouts of the Temple Treasures

The whereabouts of the Temple treasures was the subject of another scroll, the Copper

Theodotos Inscription. Source: Reinack, T., L'insscriptions de Theodotos, 1920.

Scroll, so called because it is incised on copper sheets. Although it was found hidden with the other Dead Sea Scrolls, its attribution to the Essene sect is doubtful because of its content and the unique material on which it is written. The scroll enumerates sixty-four hoards of large quantities of gold and silver bars, 619 gold and silver vessels, and 608 clay vessels filled with coins. In addition, it mentions units of precious wood and incense, and the vestments of the High Priest. The total weight of the gold and silver was calculated at 200 tons. All this wealth was hidden in various places around Jerusalem, in the Jordan Valley, and in places farther away. However, none of these places can be identified, because the descriptions of the locations are so very vague. The scroll is considered a purely imaginary-legendary document, especially because of the vast quantities of precious metals. However, it

has recently been suggested that it may in fact refer to treasures hidden by Temple priests and attendants in anticipation of the war with the Romans that culminated in the destruction of the Temple.[37] If so, the scroll would have originated in the Jerusalem priesthood rather than the Essene sect.

The Destruction of the Second Temple

The Temple Mount was the largest holy compound in the Roman world of its time, and the Temple was considered one of the most beautiful buildings. The sages of the Mishnah, who had very little sympathy for King Herod, nevertheless appreciated the beauty of the structure he built and proclaimed that he who did not see Herod's Temple did not see a truly beautiful edifice. They compared the marble and gold building to a sparkling mountain of snow lit by the sun.

The Romans too were not blind to the uniqueness, beauty, and holiness of the Temple. The Roman historian Sulpicius Severus tells of a debate held in the headquarters of the Roman general Titus after the fall of Jerusalem on the question of whether to burn the Temple. Several of the participants advised against doing so because it was a holy building more splendid than any built by man. It should be left intact, they said, as evidence to the moderation of the Romans, while its destruction would publicize the cruelty of the Romans conquerors.[38] Despite this sound advice, the Temple was burned down, and no trace of it survived.

The Temple Mount Under Pagans and Christians

The destruction of the Temple on the ninth day of the month of Av (July) in 70 CE ended 1,000 years of almost uninterrupted Jewish presence on the Temple Mount, replaced by pagan Romans and then by Christian Byzantines. The destruction initiated the very long period, still not ended, in which the Temple Mount has been occupied by a succession of pagans, Christians, and Muslims.

Jewish Reaction to the Destruction of Jerusalem and the Temple

During most of this long period Jews were barred from living in Jerusalem and even from visiting it, much less from entering the Temple Mount. Despite this restrictions, there are both Jewish and Christian records testifying to a fairly regular stream of Jewish pilgrims who came to Jerusalem to pray, throughout the year and especially during the three festivals in which pilgrimage to the Temple was obligatory.[39] Prominent sages of the Mishnah such as Rabbi Yohanan ben Zakkai and Rabbi Akiba visited the destroyed Temple Mount.[40] Small groups of pilgrims sneaked through the Roman guards, entered Jerusalem, and went up to the Temple Mount, where they mourned the destruction of the Temple and expressed their hope for its rebuilding.

This type of small-scale pilgrimage, a substitute for the joyous pilgrimages in the days when the Temple was still standing, recurred throughout the following centuries.[41] A document of uncertain date but after the destruction of the Temple instructs pilgrims how to behave during such pilgrimages. It suggests that the pilgrim should first go to Mount Scopus, from where he can get a good view of Jerusalem and the Temple Mount. There he should dismount his donkey, take off his shoes, tear his garment as a sign of mourning, and lament the destruction of the Temple. On arriving in the city he should again tear his garment, pray, and thank God for enabling him to make this pilgrimage. He should then circle the city wall and visit all its gates and corners.

Several pilgrims scratched graffiti on the walls and gates of the Temple Mount. One such inscription, reading "Yonah and his wife Shabtiah from Sicily be strong in life," probably dates to the Byzantine period.[42] Pilgrims used to refrain from eating meat and drinking wine on the day they visited Jerusalem, and some even fasted. The pilgrims not only circled the city but also visited the Temple Mount proper; the Talmud (Yevamot 6:2) decrees that one going up to the Mount should keep a proper decorum and not enter the holy place with his traveling attire—his stick, dusty shoes, and outer garment. An anonymous non-Jewish pilgrim from Bordeaux in France who visited Jerusalem in 333 CE related that the main Jewish pilgrimage to the Temple Mount took place on the ninth of Av, the day of the burning of the Temple. The same pilgrim mentioned the "perforated stone," referring perhaps to the sacred rock on which the Holy of Holies probably once stood. The mourners anointed this stone with oil, then cried, lamented, and tore their cloths as a sign of their deep grief.[43] The rock on the Temple Mount has a round hole in it leading to a subterranean cave, but, interestingly, neither is mentioned either in First Temple or Second Temple accounts.

Despite the destruction Jews continued to live in Jerusalem[44] and viewed themselves as citizens and even legal masters of the city. The main Jewish activity concerning the holy mount during the two millennia since the destruction of the Temple was confined to ongoing prayers for the rebuilding of Jerusalem and the resurrection of the Temple. The daily prayers were designed to coincide with the daily routine of sacrifices that had once taken place on the Temple Mount.

The intense mourning over the destruction of the city and its Temple is manifested throughout the life of Jewish people, as, for example, in the custom of breaking a glass at weddings or in the procedure of leaving a section of a wall in the house unpainted.[45] Another avenue for remembrance was the ongoing creation and elaboration of myths and legends that raised the prestige of the city and the Temple and sustained hopes that they would soon be rebuilt.

The Temple Mount Under the Pagan Romans

After the Roman legions conquered Jerusalem, they remained stationed in the destroyed town, and built a camp for themselves. Most likely the camp was situated next to the southwest corner of the Temple Mount,

where many finds relating to that period have been unearthed in archaeological excavations.[46] The Romans also used the area next to the western gate as their military headquarters, for it was well protected by a Herodian tower that the Romans had left standing as a witness to the strong fortifications of the city they had conquered.[47] Both camp and headquarters were on a small scale, and most of the area of former Jerusalem, including the Temple Mount, was left in ruins.

The destruction wrought by the Roman army in 70 CE in Jerusalem and the exile of many of the inhabitants were followed by the total eradication of Jewish Jerusalem. These severe measures culminated in the establishment of a new town over the ruins of part of former Jerusalem.[48]

This project was undertaken by the Roman emperor Hadrian, who named the new town Aelia Capitolina, Aelia being his family name, and Capitolina in honor of the chief Roman god, Jupiter Capitolinus. The first act that symbolized the building of a new town in Roman custom, comparable to lying a foundation stone, was to plough the boundaries of the designed area with a pair of oxen. For the Jews this act was viewed as a fulfillment of the tragic prophecy of Micah "Zion . . . will be plowed like a field" (3:12).[49] Hadrian populated his new town with retired soldiers from various parts of the Roman Empire and forbade Jews from settling in it.[50]

The extreme unrest caused by these acts erupted in the Bar Kokhba revolt of 132–135 CE. The leader of the revolt was Simon Bar Kosiba, renamed Bar Kokhba by the great Rabbi Akiba. This new name means Son of a Star, expressing the desire and hope that he would be like a messiah and revive the political and religious independence of Israel. The

Fragment of a column found in the Temple Mount Excavations carrying a Latin inscription mentioning the Roman emperors Vespasian and Titus and the commander of the tenth legion. Courtesy of Israel Exploration Society.

revolt was at first successful, and at one point the Jewish army managed to capture Jerusalem and the Temple Mount and hold them for a short time. This victory strengthened the belief that Bar Kokhba was the messiah and aroused strong hopes for the rebuilding of the Temple and a renaissance of Jewish life. These hopes were expressed on the coins that Bar Kokhba struck, which carry on one side the inscription "Year one [or two or three or four] of the freedom of Israel," and on the other "Simon President of Israel." But soon the Romans mobilized legions from distant parts of their empire and had the upper hand. Several Jews who managed to escape to caves overlooking the Dead Sea brought with them,

among other belongings, coins struck during the revolt mixed with Roman coins of Aelia Capitolina.[51]

The basic plan of the Roman city, a square with two main streets, one running north-south and the other east-west, intersecting in the city center, can still be detected in the Old City of today. As in every Roman settlement, temples to the gods were built in the new town. Contemporary historians and travelers relate that an apparently open sacred compound was dedicated to the supreme Roman god, Jupiter, on the Temple Mount.[52]

Ironically, while attempting to erase all signs of former Jewish existence in Jerusalem, Hadrian chose the Temple Mount as the location for the holy compound to a Roman god, thus perpetuating its holiness, albeit in a completely different context. The Bordeaux pilgrim mentioned that in the compound Hadrian had two statues of himself installed, one probably equestrian. Another temple, dedicated to the Roman goddess Venus, was built in the civic center of Aelia Capitolina, in the heart of the Old City of today. While nothing remains of the compound of Jupiter on the Temple Mount, traces of structures related to the Temple of Venus were unearthed in the area where the Church of the Holy Sepulcher was later built. This sacredness of the pagan temple was thus transferred to the holiest Christian site in Jerusalem.

Desolation Under the Byzantine Christians

During the first 300 years of Christianity, after Paul shifted the center of the new religion from Jerusalem to Rome and converted gentiles became the most important group of new Christians, the importance of Jerusalem was greatly reduced. It was no longer regarded a relevant earthly location and was transformed, on the basis of Old Testament prophecies like Isaiah 53–54 and of the Pauline doctrine as expressed in Revelations 20–21, into a spiritual place, a locus of eschatological aspirations. The prophetic words of Jesus, "There shall not be left here one stone upon another that shall not be thrown down" (Matthew 24:2) were fulfilled. This change helped shift the interest of early Christianity from the existing city, now a pagan Roman city, to a heavenly Jerusalem of the future that would "come down from God out of heaven, prepared as a bride adorned for her husband" (Revelations 20:2). Jerusalem thus became a place of spiritual and symbolic value. It remained so in many circles of Christianity in

the ancient world and during the Middle Ages, and to some extent even to this day.[53]

A marked change in the fate of Christianity, and in its wake on the fate of Jerusalem and the Temple Mount, occurred early in the fourth century CE. The eastern part of the Roman Empire, known as the Byzantine Empire after its capital city, Byzantium (today Istanbul), adopted Christianity as its official religion. Soon after the Roman emperor Constantine became Christian in 324 CE, he sent his mother, Helena, on a reconnaissance mission to Jerusalem to locate sites connected with the Passion of Jesus. Helena's success in finding the site of the crucifixion and even the wooden True Cross in a cave under it prompted Constantine to initiate an ambitious project of constructing a series of churches in Jerusalem.[54]

Within a few years Jerusalem was transformed from a small, remote pagan town to the spiritual capital of the Christian Byzantine Empire. As a result of these transformations, Jerusalem, the city where Jesus spent the last days of his life and where he was crucified and buried, now became sacred to Christianity, not just as a spiritual idea, but as a tangible, earthly place.

While transforming Jerusalem, Christianity was faced with a deep contradiction of ideologies regarding its relationship with Judaism and the Jews and with the holiness of Jerusalem and the Temple Mount to the Jews. One way of dealing with this was to move Jewish traditions from the Temple Mount to the new Christian religious center. Thus the pilgrim Arculf wrote in 670 that the place of Isaac's binding was not on the Temple Mount, but "between these two churches [Holy Sepulcher and Golgotha (Calvary), which at that time were separate edifices] is the famous place where the patriarch Abraham built an altar, put on it a pile of wood and stretched his hand to take the knife to sacrifice his only child Isaac." Similarly Adam's tomb was now located at the bottom of a fissure in the rock of Golgotha (Calvary), and so was his place of creation, although in Jewish tradition it was on the holy rock on the Temple Mount.

Since its early days, its centuries of martyrdom when the Romans cruelly put many of its devout followers to death, Christianity had elevated the spirit at the expense of the transient flesh. It now began to view itself as the true Israel of the Spirit, while Judaism was reduced to the defeated Israel of the Flesh. The destruction of Jerusalem was seen as a visible sign of the downfall of Judaism and its religious earthly ideology, a fulfillment of the prophecy of Jesus, and a punishment of the Jews for not recognizing the divinity of Christ. The Jewish holiness of Jerusalem based on an earthly Temple was consequently transformed into a spiritual Jerusalem with a heavenly Temple "made without hands" (Mark 14:58). Christianity now replaced Israel as the People of the Promise.

This ideology, based on the defeated and desolate Jerusalem, was relevant at the time when the city was partly in ruins and partly converted into a pagan place. But within a short time after the triumph of Christianity, ravaged Jerusalem was converted into a flourishing city adorned with spectacular edifices. The gap that was created between the ideology of true Jerusalem as a spiritual city and the earthly Jerusalem built by and for Christians had to be bridged and the discrepancy explained in proper theological argumentation. To achieve this end, various means were used. The destroyed Temple Mount, the most

visual sign of the defeat of Judaism, was left in its ruinous state. Throughout the Byzantine period it remained a field of wreckage, a powerful and visible symbol of Christianity's victory over Judaism.

Another strategy for overcoming theological difficulty centered on the development of the idea of the New Jerusalem. The newly constructed city that replaced the old Jewish city was defined as New Jerusalem in accordance with St. John's vision. Thus its construction was not a plain, earthly action, but a spiritual one, in fulfillment of the prophetic words of both Old and New Testament prophets. In this way, the conflicting ideas were united, the historic and the symbolic becoming one. The Christian historian and theologian Eusebius was the main advocate of this policy, pointing out that the three most important new churches – The Holy Sepulcher, Eleona, and Holy Zion—were built outside the old earthly city of Jerusalem.[55] These churches were to be the cornerstones of a new city, a non-Jewish New Jerusalem.[56]

Indeed, the most important and sacred location to Christianity, the place of the crucifixion and burial of Jesus, on which the Church of the Holy Sepulcher stood, was outside the city in the time of Jesus. This situation was in keeping with the strict Jewish religious law that forbade anything related with death within the city, since death was considered the ultimate cause of ritual defilement. The Eleona Church was built on the Mount of Olives, which overlooks Jerusalem from the east and has always been outside the city. The Church of Holy Zion was constructed on Mount Zion, which was indeed outside the Roman Aelia Capitolina, but perhaps unknowingly to its builders, within the boundaries of the Jerusalem of the time of Jesus. And so a New

Jerusalem holy to Christians replaced the old Jewish Jerusalem, and its churches replaced the destroyed Temple as new locations of holiness, a visible symbols of the superiority of Christianity.

While rulers and commoners wholeheartedly accepted the reality of earthly Byzantine Jerusalem, several high-ranking church authorities, adhering to the Christian Pauline dogma of a Spiritual Jerusalem as it developed during the first 300 years of Christianity, objected.[57] Although they could not deny the existence of the city, they did not see its earthly qualities favorably. Those who held this view tried to discourage pilgrimages to Jerusalem because they strengthened the aspect of the city as an earthly place and also out of fear that they might revive memories of Judaism, but they could not stop the stream of pilgrims that visited it throughout the Byzantine period.[58] Their fear was well grounded. The lady Egeria, a fourth century CE pilgrim, noted that the holy relics she saw in the Church of the Holy Sepulcher were the True Cross, the ring of King Solomon, and the horn with which the kings of Judah were anointed.[59] Even Heronimus, one of the most influential early church fathers (fourth century CE) evoked Jewish associations when he declared that if Jerusalem, where Christ had suffered, was indeed cursed, how was it that the apostle Paul rushed to the city to celebrate Pentecost (the Jewish festival of Shavuot)? Pilgrimage thus not only put the dogma in question, but also brought to life memories of Jewish Jerusalem in the time of its glory. Notwithstanding, numerous bishops, martyrs, church fathers, and other religious Christians came to Jerusalem to strengthen their belief by worshipping Christ in the earthly place of his martyrdom.

To strengthen the Christian hold on the city, important events in early Christian history were also often evoked through celebrations. Thus, shortly after Jerusalem fell to the Persians in 618 and the Holy Cross was taken as a prize of war, the Byzantine emperor Heraclius fought the Persians and managed to defeat them. He recovered the Holy Cross and brought it back to Jerusalem. Heraclius entered the city in a triumphal procession through the newly designed Gate of Mercy in the eastern wall of the city, with its joyous citizens welcoming him with palm fronds. This event was designed to echo memories of the triumphant entry of Jesus to Jerusalem, and at the same time enhance the importance of the Holy Cross as the most important relic of Christianity.

A dramatic episode relating to the Temple Mount occurred not long after Christianity took hold in Jerusalem. One of the first projects undertaken by the Byzantine emperor Julian after he ascended to the throne in 361CE, was to undertake the rebuilding of the Jewish Temple in Jerusalem. Although Julian had been brought up as a Christian, he was early attracted to pagan religions and in particular to their sacrifice of animals, and he tried to revive these religions in his empire at the expense of Christianity.[60] In this context, Julian regarded Judaism as yet another animal-sacrificing religion. In 363 CE, while preparing to fight the Persians, he sent a letter to the Jews declaring his intention to rebuild their Temple so that they could resume sacrificing to their God. Julian sent orders to his officials in Jerusalem to begin work on building the Temple at the expense of the royal treasury. He also ordered the Christians expelled from Jerusalem.

The Jewish world was ecstatic. A slightly distorted quotation of Isaiah 66:14, "And

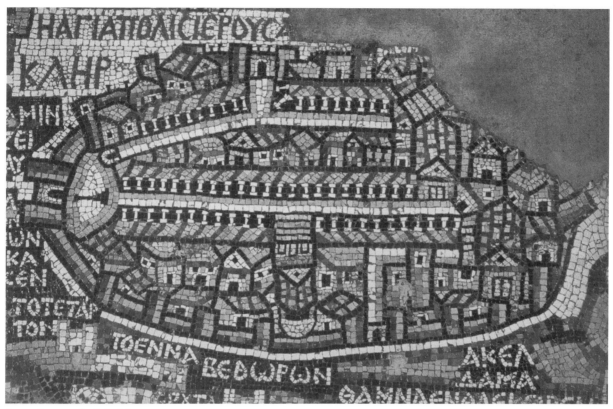

Jerusalem in the Madaba map.

when you see this, your heart shall rejoice and your bones shall flourish like herb," scratched by a pilgrim on one of the stones of the west wall of the Temple Mount may be an expression of these feelings of elation.[61] The Temple Mount was cleared of any ruins of the Jewish Temple as well as of the pagan cultic installation that were there, and the area was prepared for construction.

A series of calamities put an end to the project. On May 18, 363 CE, fire broke out on the construction site and work was halted. Stories of a miraculous fire from heaven began to circulate among the Christians who had not yet been expelled from Jerusalem, and may have started it. About a month later, on June 26, Julian was killed in battle against the

Persians, and his project came to an end. The hopes of the Jews to see their Temple rebuilt were crushed, and the Christians, who must have been in a state of panic lest the project materialize, now tightened their grip on Jerusalem. The Temple Mount, the heart of Jewish existence and of the despised "earthly Jerusalem" was now allocated as a place for disposing of garbage, a visible sign of the fate of the defeated Jewish people.

The 300 or so years of Byzantine Christian rule were the only time in its 3,000-year history that the Temple Mount was robbed of all vestiges of holiness and became an empty and desolate place. The attempts to erase it from memory were so successful that this large and imposing esplanade does not even appear in the sixth-century mosaic map of Jerusalem depicted on the floor of a church in Madaba, Jordan.[62] Nothing was built on it, and apparently no one visited it. The destroyed Temple Mount voiced more clearly the victory of Christianity than any church could do.

The Revival of the Temple Mount in the Early Muslim Period

In 638, two years after the Arabs first appeared in southern Palestine, Jerusalem fell to the Muslim armies that swept out of Arabia under the leadership of Caliph 'Omar ibn al Khatab.[63]

The Jerusalem that the Muslims found was a Byzantine Christian city that had recently known a very stormy time. Twenty years earlier, in 618, the city had fallen to the Persians, but after several years of Persian rule the Byzantine emperor Heraclius defeated the Persians and brought back to Jerusalem the Holy Cross that they had taken. The Christians then held the city for another ten-year period, until it was lost again, this time to the Muslims. This change of hands was to last for a very long period. Some time after the city fell, Caliph `Omar came to visit Jerusalem and presented its inhabitants with a letter of protection, sometimes referred to as an official contract. The people of Jerusalem were designated *dhimmi* (non-Muslim "people of the book"—Jews, Christians, and Zoroastrians), a status that granted them protection of life and property in exchange for a special poll tax (*jisiya*).

Muslims Adopt the Jewish Sanctity of the Temple Mount

The Muslim conquerors, whose religion was influenced to a large extent by the Judaism and Christianity then practiced in Arabia, were aware of the sanctity of Jerusalem to both Jews and Christians, and they adopted it, thus adding a third contender to the holiness of the place. Their main competitors over the specific holiness of the Temple Mount were the Jews, who maintained its sanctity despite many generations of destruction and never gave up their hope for the rebuilding of the Temple on that very space. To the Christians, on the other hand, the significance of the compound was only in its desolate state, a visible sign of the victory of Christianity over Judaism. The Muslims thus inherited the large and virtually empty esplanade, perhaps still strewn with ruins of the former buildings, that carried revered biblical associations of holiness. Two biblical personalities related to the Temple Mount had much meaning for Muslims. One was Solomon,[64] one of the most beloved of the Old Testament personalities adopted by the Muslims, and the other was Abraham, father of Isaac and also of Ishmael, ancestor of the Arab people. Muslims substituted Ishmael for Isaac in the story of the Binding of Isaac, which as mentioned earlier was connected with the Temple Mount, believed to be Mount Moriah.

Judaism was one of the main influences on Islam in its early stages. This influence is clearly witnessed in the fact that when Muhammad was still in Mecca, he used to turn toward the Temple Mount in Jerusalem while praying. Thus Jerusalem was the first Muslim *kibla* (direction of prayer). Only later, after he moved to Medina, and perhaps after realizing that the Jews of Arabia would not accept his teachings, did he change the direction of Muslim prayer toward Mecca.[65]

In addition to the Jewish associations, adopted by the Muslims as their own, Muslim reverence of the Temple Mount is based on chapter 17 verse 1 of the Koran. "I declare the glory of Him who transported His servant by night from the Masjid al-Haram [the mosque at Mecca] to the Masjid al-Aqsa [the Farthest Mosque], the surroundings of which We blessed, so that We could show him some of Our signs; for he is the Hearer and the Seer." The location of the al-Aqsa Mosque is not specified in this verse, and Muslim writers suggested several possibilities, such as a mosque on the outskirts of Mecca or the mosque at Kufa, Iraq. One writer even located the Masjid al-Aqsa in heaven. Later traditions, however, while elaborating on the manner in which Muhammad was transported to this mosque atop the winged animal Burak, set it on the Temple Mount in Jerusalem, holy to the Jews.[66] Another tradition, not mentioned in the Koran, was later added to Muhammad's Night Flight. This is the tradition of the *Ma'raj*, the ascent of Muhammad in the company of the Angel Gabriel from the Temple Mount to the presence of God seated on his throne in heaven. On his way to heaven he saw all the prophets who had preceded him, and also Hell, where the wicked are tormented, as well as Paradise, prepared for the righteous. In heaven he was given the five obligatory Muslim daily prayers. These combined traditions are the essence of the sanctity of the Temple Mount to Muslims, who refer to it by the name *Haram a-Sharif*, The Noble Sanctuary. The power of traditions and legends in influencing events found its utmost expression here.

Several traditions relate to the way in which the Temple Mount and within it, specifically, the place of the former Jewish Temple were rediscovered soon after the Muslim conquest. At the time of the conquest,

the Temple Mount was covered by heaps of garbage, piled there by the Byzantine Christians. Both Muslim and Jewish contemporary sources relate that members of these two communities participated in cleaning the Temple Mount of the garbage accumulated on it. It is told that they did the work under the watchful eye of Caliph 'Omar ibn al-Khatab, and that whenever a piece of a rock was exposed, 'Omar asked the Jews whether it was the rock on which their Temples once stood. As the work continued one of the elders pointed out to 'Omar the edge of the rock they were looking for, and 'Omar stood by until it was all exposed.[67]

The elder may have been Ka'ab al Ahbar, a Jew who had converted to Islam and accompanied 'Omar to Jerusalem. During this visit 'Omar expressed his desire to set a place for the Muslims to pray. Ka'ab suggested a spot to the north of the now fully exposed holy rock, so that the worshipper would face both the rock and Mecca. 'Omar refused, accusing Ka'ab of secretly wishing to revive the Jewish custom of praying toward the rock, and he set the place of prayer to the south of the rock.

The Christian pilgrim Arculf, who visited Jerusalem between 679 and 682, describes a large, simple mosque, seemingly on the southeastern section of the Temple Mount, which could contain some 3,000 people.[68] Tradition attributes the building of this mosque to Caliph 'Omar. The very act of building the mosque was a public declaration that Islam has adopted the sanctity of Jerusalem. Despite 'Omar's recognition of the deep connection between the Jews and Jerusalem, the capitulation treaty signed between him and Sophronius, the Christian patriarch of Jerusalem, forbade Jews from living in the city. This clause in the treaty, the result of strong pressure exerted by the patriarch, seems to have been retracted very shortly after the treaty was signed.

The Jews were now able to establish themselves in the city and, perhaps because of their participation in the original cleaning of the Temple Mount, were granted entrance to the Temple Mount as cleaners of the edifice and producers of glass for the mosque's lamps. In return, those individuals who were thus occupied were exempt from poll tax. Thus, during the early Muslim period Jews not only lived in Jerusalem but were allowed on the Temple Mount, and there are literary indications that they may even have had a synagogue there.

Another synagogue at the Western Wall is mentioned. The Jews managed to purchase the Mount of Olives, or at least part of it, and during the well-attended yearly pilgrimages to Jerusalem on the festival of Tabernacles (Succot) a large-scale assembly took place there. On the occasion of the pilgrimage the pilgrims also circled the city walls and prayed at the Gate of Mercy in the eastern wall.[69]

The Rise of the Umayyad Dynasty and Its Activities on the Temple Mount

The first Muslim ruling dynasty, the Umayyad Dynasty, founded in 658, declared Damascus the capital of its huge empire,

Mosaic inscription on the interior of the Dome of the Rock. Photographer: A. van der Heyden, 1989. Courtesy of The Jerusalem Publishing House.

which spread from the borders of India in the east through the Middle East and North Africa to Spain in the west. The decision to rule the empire from Damascus placed Jerusalem close to the center of Muslim power. Its geographical proximity to the source of power, combined with the high religious prestige already recognized by the Muslims, promised the city a central place in the building plans of the rulers. A series of palatial buildings, probably the local seat of power, were built along the western and southern walls of the Temple Mount.[70]

A rebellion that broke out in Mecca against the Umayyad rulers was believed to be the trigger that brought about the rebuilding of the Temple Mount. It has been suggested that the Umayyads offered the sumptuous new structures in Jerusalem—the Dome of the Rock, or *Kubat el Sahra* in Arabic (erroneously sometimes called 'Omar's Mosque) and the al-Aqsa Mosque—because they hoped to create a substitute for Mecca. The beauty and attractiveness of the Jerusalem edifices was designed to lure pilgrims and dissuade them from going to Mecca on the yearly prescribed pilgrimage, the *hajj*. However, it is now believed that the Umayyad rulers centered on the Temple Mount and adorned it with two magnificent structures because of their desire to compete with the lavish Christian churches of Jerusalem, especially with the Church of the Holy Sepulcher.[71]

No doubt these new structures were designed to demonstrate both to their own people and to the Christian world the power and wealth of Islam. The 734-foot-long mosaic inscriptions that surrounds the base of the dome inside the Dome of the Rock lends support to this view. This inscription, part of the original scheme of the building, includes quo-

tations from the Koran that proclaim three major declarations of the Islamic creed: (1) that God is one, implying that God does not have a co-partner; (2) that God's messenger is Muhammad; and (3) that Jesus, son of Mary, was also a messenger of God and should be honored because he brought his divine revelations to mankind. The inscription also quotes other koranic verses that refute the virgin birth and states that it is not for God to take for himself an offspring. The inscription ends with a call to the People of the Book to adopt Islam.[72] It is perhaps surprising that the many inscriptions on the walls of the Dome of the Rock do not include the Night Flight of the Prophet Muhammad to the Temple Mount, a story that lies at the heart of Muslim sanctification of Jerusalem. The inscriptions were set high on the uppermost section of the wall and were therefore almost illegible to the visitor. Perhaps they were set up there more as an evocation, not actually meant to be read.

The Dome of the Rock

The second Muslim building on the Temple Mount (following 'Omar's early mosque) was the Dome of the Rock, brainchild of Caliph 'Abd el-Malik of the Umayyad dynasty. It was built between 688 and 691 and stands to this day in its original form, although, because of earthquakes and the ravages of time, its dome has been replaced as a result of the earthquake of 1016,[73] as were several sections of the inner and outer decorations. It is considered the undisputed masterpiece of early Islamic architecture. Its name and plan indicate that this was not a mosque, but a rather a commemorative structure honoring and protecting the holy rock at its center, the rock from which, according to one tra-

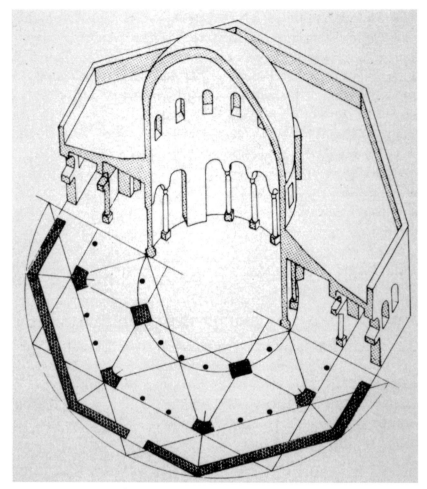

Plan and section of the Dome of the Rock according to Creswell.

dition, Muhammad is believed to have ascended to heaven. The structure is been used to this day for private rather than for communal prayer.[74]

The Dome of the Rock evokes many associations, and meanings for Muslims and indeed for anyone who visits it. Situated on the beautiful esplanade built by King Herod, which at the time of its construction may still have been strewn with architectural elements of the destroyed Temple, the Dome of the Rock evokes historical memories. It also inspires religious associations mainly with the Old Testament, sections of which were incorporated into the Koran and therefore known to the Muslims. It is also a focus of eschatological beliefs pertaining to the End of Days and the resurrection of the dead. Lastly, it is a strong declaration of victory and power, past and present. It encapsulates memories of the supremacy of Judaism, then of Christianity, and finally, with the building of the Dome of the Rock, the absolute supremacy of Islam. [75]

The Dome is an octagonal concentric building, each of its eight sides measuring 66 feet. Four doors placed at the four points of

Interior of the Dome of the Rock. Photographer: Fritz Cohen, 1976. © 1997–1998, The State of Israel, Government Press Office.

the compass provide entrance to it. This is an interesting scheme, since one could enter from either side of the building and be confronted immediately with the very focus—the holy rock.[76]

There is no lengthy approach to the center of holiness required in such religious buildings as churches and temples. The interior is divided into three concentric circles by two sets of square piers and round pillars that support arches. Four piers with three round pillars between each pier define the inner circle of the structure and support the high drum and dome that soar above the rock. This is the heart of the structure. Between the second and third circles are eight angled piers with two pillars between each pier. These piers hold the sloping roof, which then rests on the outer walls of the structure. The only movement allowed by such a plan is a rotating, circumambulating movement around the rock.

The harmony of the building lies in its perfect symmetry: the measurement of 66 feet of each of the eight sections of the outer walls is repeated in the circumference of the dome, and in its height.[77] The dome is actually constructed of two domes, one inside the other; the space in between is wide enough to allow a person to walk around and make necessary repairs. Both domes were built of wood, and

Interior of the Dome of the Rock with decorated dome. Photographer: Moshe Milner, 1975. © 1997–1998, The State of Israel, Government Press Office.

the outer dome was gilt.[78] In the earliest description of the Dome of the Rock, written by Ibn al Fakih in 903, the dome is described as being covered with red gold, perhaps gilt copper. In 1016 the dome caved in as a result of shocks from a severe earthquake. When it was restored, lead replaced the gold covering, according to Nasir I-Khusru, who wrote a description of the Dome of the Rock in 1047. The lead covering is also mentioned in the long inscription set by Salah a-Din inside the

cupola of the Dome after his victory over the Crusaders. The dome was again gilt by order of the Ottoman sultan Mahmud II in 1808–1839.[79]

As far as is known, the rock was left in its natural state and was surrounded by an ebony balustrade. Curtains woven with gold threads hung between the pillars and piers that surrounded it. Tradition has it that a chain holding a jewel and the pair of horns of the ram that Abraham sacrificed on this rock instead

Detail of mosaic scroll decoration in the Dome of the Rock. Photographer: A. van der Heyden, 1989. Courtesy of The Jerusalem Publishing House.

of his son came down from the center of the dome and dangled above the rock. This tradition echoes the adoption by the Muslims of the Jewish tradition that the place of the Binding was Mount Moriah, identified with the Temple Mount. Another Muslim tradition relates that prior to the building of the Dome of the Rock these horns hung in Mecca. While the Muslims substituted Ishmael for Isaac, the location of the event was still shifting between Mecca and Jerusalem. It ended up in Mecca.

The building is lavishly decorated on both the inside and the outside. In the interior, the mosaics on the drum and on both sides of the arches of the middle octagon as well as on the inner side of the arches have been preserved to this day in their original state.[80] The mosaics show strong Byzantine influence and were perhaps executed by Christian artisans. They are made of innumerable glass cubes, many of them with gold leaf encased between two glass panels. The overall colors of the mosaics are green, blue, and gold, with a scatter of pieces of mother of pearl, lending the mosaics a special luster. Their designs are mostly floral—compositions of leaves, trees, and flowering and fruit-bearing plants. There are also unusual depic-

Exterior of the Dome of the Rock with southern entrance. Photographer: A. van der Heyden, 1989. Courtesy of The Jerusalem Publishing House.

tions of pieces of jewelry—crowns, necklaces, bracelets, and pendants—intertwined in the floral designs.[81] Around the drum and walls are quotations of verses from the Koran, as well as words of praise to the builder of the structure and the date of construction, all executed in mosaic.

A historical irony is witnessed in a mosaic inscription in the inner arcade, in which Ma'amun, one of the later caliphs, who perhaps coveted the honor of building the magnificent Dome of the Rock, replaced the name of 'Abd el Malik by his own.[82] He did not, however, change the date. Ma'amun also added his name to the copper plaques bear-

ing verses from the Koran installed by 'Abd el-Malik above the north and east entrances to the building. In other parts of the interior, such as the ceiling of the arcades, the original decorations have not been preserved because of frequent earthquakes and the weight of the lead-covered dome, and were replaced in a variety of materials and styles.

In the Mamluk period (fifteenth century) the interior of the dome and the ceiling of the arcades were redecorated in the style of the period. The heavy weight of the lead that covered the exterior of the dome kept causing great concern for safety of the entire building. It was not until the early 1970s that major repair work was again undertaken. The dome was covered with anodized aluminum, which gave it its splendid golden appearance, and finally in 1993 Saudi Arabia contributed a $1 million worth of gold foil, which now coats the dome.

The exterior decorations of the building were not preserved. The original marble slabs that covered the lower section of the outer walls were replaced several times, and ceramic tiles were installed soon after the Ottoman Turkish conquest of Jerusalem in 1516, in place of the easily deteriorating delicate glass mosaics that covered their upper part. The glaze of ceramic tiles usually deteriorates when exposed to the weather, so the sixteenth-century Turkish tiles were repaired several times and many individual tiles were replaced.

Both the plan of the Dome of the Rock and its decorative scheme were influenced by the Classical-Hellenistic-Byzantine style that prevailed in the region for almost 1,000 years prior to the Muslim conquest. Into this stylistic scheme were introduced Oriental motifs, especially Persian elements, which the Muslims picked up during their conquest of Persia and the toppling of its Sassanid dynasty. The Muslims, who subjugated diverse populations of various religions while creating their vast empire, did not hesitate to adopt many cultural attributes of the people they defeated. Perhaps ironically, the highest architectural achievement of the first half-century of their rule, the Dome of the Rock, was basically Byzantine in nature, reflecting the architectural and artistic norms of the people they had just defeated.

It has been suggested that the decorative scheme of the Dome of the Rock was intended to reflect the glory and splendor of Solomon's Temple.[83] Islamic imagination, in the wake of Jewish legends, was greatly inspired by the figure of King Solomon, by the wealth he invested in decorating the Temple, and by his power over the demons. Muslim legends elaborate on these themes and relate that the demons helped Solomon by mining gold, marble, rock crystals, and other special rocks, and by collecting precious stones, amber, musk, and pearls for the Temple. Other legends tell that the Temple was built of white, yellow and green marble and its pillars were of rock crystal. The inner and outer walls as well as the ceiling were reputed to have been inlayed with precious stones including pearls and emeralds, and the floor was made of turquoise slabs. Because of the abundance of gold and precious stones the building shone at night like a full moon or like a lamp.

Trees grew spontaneously in the Temple courtyards. Solomon, so the legend relates, would ask them for their special qualities and then planted them in his gardens. The typical motif in the oldest mosaics preserved is a stylized tree growing out of an amphora. Many of these particular trees have multicolored trunks and luxuriant flowers and fruit, sometimes several kinds of fruit on the same tree. Some trees carry old crowns, others gold and bejeweled collars. The many kinds of fruit, the crowns, and the collars indicate fecundity, abundance, and wealth, associating them not only with Solomon's Temple but also with the lush Garden of Eden. The multicolored mosaics, with gold cubes and mother of pearl inlays, that originally covered the outer walls of the Dome of the Rock evoke the richly inlaid, shining walls of Solomon's Temple in Islamic legend. The interpretation of the Dome of the Rock as a structure designed to evoke the memory of Solomon's Temple as

Detail of mosaic decoration in the Dome of the Rock with a crown on an amphora.
Photographer: A. van der Heyden, 1989. Courtesy of The Jerusalem Publishing House.

well as the Garden of Eden, brings to the foreground its functions as a monument of religious, historical, and even prehistorical significance, albeit with a dash of fable and myth.

Another interpretation of the decorative scheme sees in the profusion of rich jewelry mostly in Byzantine style—tiaras, breastplates, bracelets, armlets, anklets, earrings, rings—depicted in the mosaics on the walls of the Dome of the Rock a visual symbol of the victory of Islam over Christianity. Similarly, another conspicuous motif depicted in the mosaics are pairs of symmetrical wings which evoke Persian style, which are thus interpreted as presenting the victory of Islam over the Zoroastrian Sassanid Dynasty, which ruled Iran just prior to its conquest by the Muslims.

This interpretation then emphasizes a political motivation and views the Dome of the Rock as a monument proclaiming victory and conquest.

Alongside the construction of the shrines, the Umayyad rulers developed special religious ceremonies that took place mainly in and around the Dome of the Rock. The building was open to the public only on Mondays and Thursdays, and the other days were reserved for the ritual of the attendants. They would enter the Dome only after purifying themselves and changing their clothes, and then burn incense, rub the rock with perfume, and pray. A point of special significance was a black paving stone embedded in the floor of the Dome, believed to be the entrance to

Paradise, and the eastern gate of the Dome, the Gate of the Angel Israfil.[84]

In recognition of the beauty of the Dome of the Rock, Muqqadasi, a Jerusalem-born Muslim geographer, praised it in 985 with these words: "At dawn, when the light of the sun first strikes the cupola and the drum catches the rays, then is this edifice a marvelous sight to behold and one such that in all Islam I have never seen its equal. Neither have I heard tell of another built in pagan times that could rival in grace this Dome of the Rock." [85]

The al-Aqsa Mosque

In contrast to the Classical-Byzantine style of the Dome of the Rock, the style of the al-Aqsa Mosque, the second early structure built on the *Haram a-Sharif* (Temple Mount), is typical of Islamic mosque architecture.[86] It is a simple large space with rows of pillars that hold the roof and divide the space into several aisles. The new the al-Aqsa Mosque, founded on the south side of the *Haram a-Sharif*, replaced the old mosque built perhaps by Caliph 'Omar many years before. Its construction had already begun in the days of 'Abd el Malik, builder of the Dome of the Rock, and after a series of severe earthquakes that occurred during his reign, it was completed, or perhaps renovated, by his son el-Walid between 705 and 715. It is interesting that the construction of this important mosque is not mentioned in early Muslim sources. It is first described by the Jerusalem geographer al-Mukaddasi in 985, almost 300 years after its construction.[87] Perhaps in preparation for the construction of the new mosque, the southern section of the Temple Mount was leveled on a lower plane than the upper platform on which the Dome of the Rock was constructed.[88] The difference in elevation between the upper and lower sections of the Temple Mount's esplanade is preserved to this day. The name of the mosque recalls the miraculous Night Journey of the Prophet Muhammad as described in the Koran, indicating that by the beginning of the eighth century, tradition had already placed this mystical mosque in Jerusalem.

Since its building, Muslims have considered the al-Aqsa Mosque their third-holiest mosque by Muslims, and Jerusalem their third-holiest city. Jerusalem is sometimes referred to by the name the al-Aqsa Mosque, and since 832 has been called *Al-Kuds*, the Holy One. The dual Jewish-Muslim sanctity of the Temple Mount and of Jerusalem lies at the heart of the conflict between Muslims and Jews. To the Jews the place on which their two destroyed Temples stood is their only holy site, and Jerusalem their one and only holy city. To Muslims the al-Aqsa Mosque is only the third in holiness. In contrast to the Jewish-Muslim competition, there was no conflict between Islam and Christianity over the Temple Mount, because Christians, from whom the city was taken, no longer have any interest in it, believing that it should best be left in ruins.

The al-Aqsa Mosque is the most important site on the *Haram a-Sharif*, being a "Friday mosque," a place for the obligatory communal worship held every Friday, the Muslim holy day. Thus it is the holiest structure on the Mount, holier than the Dome of the Rock, which is a place for personal prayer and meditation. In fact the mosque gave its name to the whole compound, which is thus referred to also as al-Aqsa.

Having been built on Herod's artificial platform, the mosque was completed destroyed in a severe earthquake in 748, and no

Interior of al-Aqsa Mosque. Photographer: Fritz Cohen, 1967. © 1997–1998, The State of Israel, Government Press Office.

trace of it remains.[89] There are also no written records that describe this early mosque. It was rebuilt, probably in 771, again completely destroyed without leaving a material or written trace, and rebuilt again around 780. This is the first building for which there is a written description.[134] It was a large structure with fifteen aisles, the central being higher and wider than the side ones. Each aisle opened to the façade, which thus had fifteen gates. There were also eleven gates in the eastern wall. The space in front of the *kibla* (prayer niche in the southern wall pointing toward Mecca to indicate the direction of prayer) was surmounted by a dome.

The mosque was severely damaged by later earthquakes, the most destructive being in 1033. Further restorations reduced the size of the mosque, until it received its present-day size. A major reconstruction was carried out in 1927 by the British Mandate Department of Antiquities. However, despite its long history of destruction and construction, its original character as a traditional Muslim pillar-mosque with a *mihrab* in its south wall has been preserved.

Smaller Muslim Structures on Haram a-Sharif
Dome of the Chain

The Dome of the Chain, a structure to the east of the Dome of the Rock, may have been built at the same time as its neighbor but certainly before the tenth century, when it is mentioned in writing. The function of this

Façade of al-Aqsa Mosque.
Source: Charles W. Wilson,
Picturesque Palestine, Sinai
and Egypt, 1880.

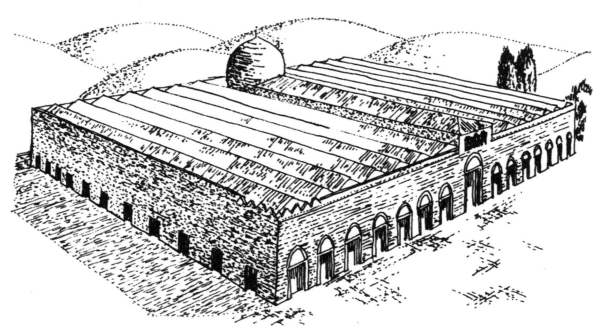

Reconstruction of the 8th century mosque according to Creswell.

small, circular, open structure is unknown. It is believed to have originally been a closed building and served as the treasure house where the riches collected for the construction of the Dome of the Rock were assembled. By the tenth century it is already described as "merely a cupola, supported on marble pillars, being without walls."[91] Because it is similar in plan to the Dome of the Rock, it may have been an architect's model for its illustrious neighbor. The name "Dome of the Chain" derives from a Muslim legend relating that here, in the place where King David used to judge his people, a chain of light would come down from heaven and identify those who spoke the truth and those who were lying. Another tradition says that here Muhammad met the black-eyed young women of Paradise who assembled to delight him on the night of his Night Journey.[92]

Dome of the Prophet

The Dome of the Prophet commemorates the place where the Prophet Muhammad prayed in the company of the angels and the prophets who preceded him before ascending to heaven. It is therefore believed that prayers said in this building will be answered. The structure was destroyed in the fifteenth century and replaced by a *mihrab* (prayer niche) named after the prophet.

Dome of the Ascent

Built around a small outcrop of bedrock to the north of the Dome of the Rock, the Dome of the Ascent is a small, open structure which, according to the prevailing tradition, commemorates the ascent of Muhammad to heaven from this rock. This tradition conflicts with the one that locates his place of ascent on inside the Dome of the rock. The structure that

stands today was built in 1201, replacing an older one that was completely destroyed.

Dome of Gabriel

A small structure surmounted by a dome, the Dome of Gabriel commemorates the archangel Gabriel, who accompanied Muhammad during the Night Journey and the Ascent to Heaven. It is not known when this dome was destroyed.

Early Pilgrimage to the Haram a-Sharif

A pilgrim's itinerary dating to the eleventh century lists thirteen places on the *Haram a-Sharif* that the pilgrim ought to visit.[93] The schedule begins at the Dome of the Rock and the black paving stone inside it, the underground cave and the site where the Prophet prayed, and finally the eastern Gate of Israfil. The pilgrim is then advised to visit the many small domed structures and several of the gates of the compound. He should then proceed to the al-Aqsa Mosque and visit all the *mihrabs* within it, and from there go to the southeastern corner of the Temple Mount for a visit to *mihrab* Maryam, the Cradle of Jesus. After this arduous program, the pilgrim is advised to ascend the Mount of Olives and finally end his pilgrimage at *mihrab* Dawud, the Tower of David, at the western entrance gate to Jerusalem.

The Crusaders on the Temple Mount

In 1099, 460 years of Islamic rule came to an end when the Crusader armies conquered Jerusalem. They had made the arduous journey to the Holy Land in obedience to the call of Pope Urban II to redeem the holy places of Christianity from the hands of the Saracens (as the Muslims were then called).[94] Medieval Christians were well versed in the sanctity of

Jerusalem, a Heavenly Jerusalem rather than an earthly one, through their attendance at church services as well as their awareness of churches named New Jerusalem in many European towns.

The prospect of entering the Heavenly Jerusalem and obtaining eternal salvation spurred thousands of people from various European countries to take part in the Crusades.[95] Religious fervor was coupled, no doubt, with personal ambitions and the dream of plundering the fabled riches of the East. Organized in seven crusading armies according to their country of origin, they were led by their high noblemen.

Full of holy passion, the soldiers of the First Crusade, in 1096, encountered the Jewish communities along the river Rhine in Germany. Here was an opportunity for them to take revenge on the enemies of Christianity even before reaching the Holy Land and fighting the Saracens. The Crusaders brutally massacred these communities as a first installment of the holy and spiritual mission that lay before them. The Jews of the Rhineland towns—for whom the Temple in Jerusalem was a living reality funneled by daily prayers, and who looked forward to the resumption of the sacrifices in the future Temple—commemorated these terrible events in poetry and prose. They used the Temple sacrifices as a ready metaphor for their terrible ordeals, describing themselves as "splendid offerings in the sanctuary of the Temple, as one poet put it. The rabbi of one community was reported as urging his followers to "let us offer ourselves as a sacrifice to the Lord, like a whole burnt offering to the Most High offered on the altar of the Lord."[96]

Those Crusaders who survived the four harsh years on the road reached Jerusalem and camped in military formation around the city. They besieged the city for two months before finally managing to break into it on July 15, 1099. That morning the Flemish army under the leadership of Godfrey de Bouillon breached the city wall near its northeastern corner, and the first soldiers swarmed into the city. This section of the wall was defended by the Jews who lived in that quarter of the city, as well as by Muslim neighbors.[97]

While the soldiers busied themselves with massacring the people of the city and robbing their homes, the noble Tancred the Norman turned toward the Temple Mount and its treasures, about which he had heard fabulous stories. Being the first Crusader to reach this destination, Tancred entered the Muslim shrines and stripped them of their riches. It was told that six camels were needed to carry the loot, which included gold and silver vessels and many other valuables. The soldiers who followed Tancred to the Temple Mount found the place stripped of treasures, but, having withstood terrible thirst during the two-month-long parched summer siege, welcomed the cool water stored in its many subterranean cisterns. During the first day of the conquest, the entire Jewish and Muslim populations of the Jerusalem were systematically massacred. Only a handful managed to escape.

After things calmed down, the Crusaders turned to the affairs of the city and the Temple Mount. Since the middle of the ninth century, Western Christianity had identified the Muslim shrines on the Temple Mount with the fabled Temple of Solomon known to them from the Bible. Of the actual structures on the Mount they had only a very vague knowledge embroidered with legendary stories. The Crusaders were the first Western Christians who actually saw the two shrines, and no doubt they were astounded by their beauty.

One of their first acts in Jerusalem was to "baptize" them. They converted the Dome of the Rock into Templum Domini (the Lord's Temple), believing that it was the actual Temple built by Solomon on the threshing floor of Aravna, and converted the al-Aqsa Mosque into Templum Solomonis (Solomon's Temple), or rather Palatium Solomonis— Solomon's palace.[98]

The layout of the Temple Mount enclosure was well understood by medieval Christians from Western Europe. It reminded them of a cathedral compound or cloister, with a major basilica (al-Aqsa Mosque) and a commemorative octagonal church (the Dome of the Rock), as well as an episcopal chapel and palace, and auxiliary structures.[99] The Crusaders did not hesitate to accept the sanctity of the Dome of the Rock and convert it into a church, since its plan was ecumenical, without an obvious sacred sign or emblem of any other religion. Moreover, by identifying it with Solomon's Temple they enhanced its sacredness and gave it historical depth and value.

Despite the conversion of the Muslim shrines into Christian edifices, a contemporary source relates that the Crusaders showed surprising consideration for the feelings of the Muslims and allowed them to pray on the Temple Mount, between the Dome of the Rock and the al-Aqsa Mosque. Muslim dignitaries were even permitted to enter the Dome of the Rock, despite the fact that it had been converted into a church.

The Lord's Temple

Now there were two holy Christian centers in Jerusalem. One was the old and revered Church of the Holy Sepulcher, which the Crusaders rebuilt and incorporated into it the Rock of Golgotha (Calvary), which until then had been a separate edifice. The other center was the newly designated Lord's Temple on the Temple Mount, on top of which the Crusaders placed a huge gold cross to announce the Christian victory over Islam. In converting it into a church, the Crusaders did not modify the general outline or the exterior of the Dome of the Rock, but they introduced changes on the inside.

The special holiness of the rock was known to Christians of this period through transference and adaptation of Jewish stories and legends, and the many enthusiastic pilgrims who followed the Crusaders began chopping pieces of the rock as souvenirs to take back home. The church authorities surrounded the rock with an ornamental iron grill and covered it with marble slabs, on which they built an altar dedicated to St. Nicolas. In the 1960s the Jordanian authorities removed the iron grill and placed it in the Islamic Museum on the southwestern side of the Temple Mount.

Auxiliary altars were built to the north of the rock. One altar was dedicated to Jesus. On another Mary is believed to have redeemed her son Jesus when he was thirty days old, according to the Jewish custom of *Pidyon ha-Ben*, and on another the Crusader kings placed their crowns as a symbol of their submission to Jesus. The Crusaders converted the cave under the rock into a confessional. They plastered the walls of the Dome of the Rock, covering the splendid mosaics and the Muslim inscriptions, and then had verses of Christian significance written on them. Monks of the Augustinian Order were allotted the honor of serving in this new church, and a house was built for them north of Templum Domini.

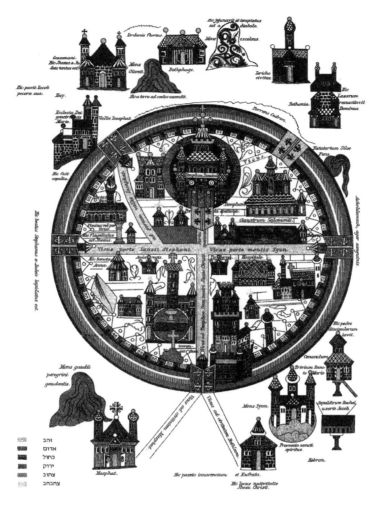

Crusader map of Jerusalem, probably of the 14th century. In the upper center—Lord's Temple, in the upper right: Claustrum Solomonis. Source: Roehrich R., Karten und Plane zur Palastina-kunde, III, 1891.

To give the Lord's Temple an equal standing with the Church of the Holy Sepulcher, several Jewish and Christian traditions now became connected with it, such as that Jacob had a dream on the rock inside the edifice, or that the footsteps of Jesus could be detected on it. Significant ceremonies were devised to enhance the importance of this newly created church, and others were transferred to it. The Crusaders identified the Lord's Temple not only with the Temple of Solomon but also with the Temple built by the Babylonian returnees, with Herod's Temple, and even with an imaginary Byzantine edifice which they believed had once stood there. Because this disregarded the Muslim origin of the building, the Lord's Temple acquired a purely Judeo-Christian lineage. The Crusaders even claimed that the original Arabic mosaic inscriptions on the walls of the Dome of the Rock mentioned its illustrious Judeo-Christian lineage.

The Christian religious establishment of Jerusalem helped raise the prestige of the Lord's Temple by decreeing that important religious ceremonies were to proceed from the Church of the Holy Sepulcher to this new holy edifice.[100] The procession marking the day Mary went to the Temple to be purified from the ritual defilement of being a new mother now began at the Church of the Holy Sepulcher and ended at Templum Domini. A similar route was taken by the procession held on the day the thirty-day-old baby Jesus, first-born to his mother, was presented in the Temple to be redeemed by a priest according to Jewish law (*Pidyon ha-Ben*).

The procession of Palm Sunday, in the course of which the Holy Cross was taken out of the Church of the Holy Sepulcher and carried around the streets, began in Bethany, a village to the east of Jerusalem where Jesus stayed before embarking on his journey to Jerusalem. The procession then entered the Temple Mount through the Gate of Mercy (the Golden Gate in Christian tradition) in the eastern wall of the Temple Mount and proceeded to the Lord's Temple. This was the only time of year when this gate was open. The triumphal procession on the day Jerusalem fell to the Crusaders (July 15) began in the Church of the Holy Sepulcher, passed through the Lord's Temple, and ended at the point at the northeast corner of the city where its wall was breached. The Crusader kings were crowned in the Church of the Holy Sepulcher; the coronation procession then went up to the Lord's Temple, and from there proceeded to the king's palace.

The Crusader identification of the domed Dome of the Rock with Solomon's Temple was adopted in both Christian and Jewish visual depictions as the authentic shape of the ancient Temple.

Solomon's Temple (or Palace)

The al-Aqsa Mosque had a different fate. Renamed Solomon's Temple, or rather Palace, it served secular purposes throughout the Crusader period. The secular use was in accordance with the Crusaders' identification of the Temple Mount with a West European cathedral compound, which included a bishop's palace in the corner. For the first nineteen years of the Crusader period, the al-Aqsa Mosque served as the palace of the Crusader kings, until a new royal palace was built in the vicinity of the citadel (known as David's Tower) near the western city gate.

In 1118 the building was turned over to the newly formed Order of the Knights Templars, their name deriving from their headquarters—Solomon's Temple. The Knights Templars modified the huge interior of the mosque by subdividing it into small living rooms. They blocked the *mihrab*, the niche in the southern wall of the mosque that pointed toward Mecca, with a thick wall and added chapels in the eastern wall of the mosque where various saints were revered.[101] The southern part of the Temple Mount thus lost its exclusively holy function and reverted to civilian-military use, as perhaps was the case when occupied by King Solomon's original palace. The Templars added several structures to the east and west of their headquarters. To the east of the mosque, they built a large structure that served as the church of the knightly order.

This church was preserved intact and was later joined to the mosque, and it is now part of it. The niches inside the building have also survived intact to this day. Their marble pillars, decorated capitals, and the six-petal rose window of the Chapel of Zechariah are considered good examples of Crusader period art and architecture. Other Crusader architectural elements were used in later restorations of the mosque, such as the *dikah* (the small platform on which the leader of the Muslim prayers sits) located west of the dome. A row of rooms built by the Crusaders along the eastern wall of the Temple Mount and used for storage were badly damaged by earthquakes and removed during restoration work carried out in 1938–43.

For their armory the Crusaders added a structure on the western side of their headquarters, well preserved to this day and at some point converted into the Women's Mosque. Recently it was turned into a Muslim religious school. Farther to the west they added another building, perhaps a granary, that now houses the Islamic Museum.[102] The Crusaders used the subterranean structures under the Temple Mount as stables for their horses, hence the popular name "Solomon's Stables," still used today. To facilitate entry to the stables, the Crusaders opened a gate close to the eastern corner of the southern wall of the Temple Mount. This gate, known as the Single Gate, was later blocked. The subterranean structures, originally part of the arches that held up the Herodian plaza, were repaired and rebuilt in the early Muslim period when the long-destroyed Temple Mount was repaired. They were later used by the Crusaders as stables and in 2000–2001 were converted into a mosque (see chapter 7).

The Impact of Crusader Jerusalem on the Christian World

The impact of the Crusader conquest of Jerusalem on medieval Christianity was immense. The early Byzantine Christian idea that the Temple Mount should be left in ruins to signify the supremacy of Christianity over Judaism was no longer valid. Not only was Jerusalem again a Christian city, but the Temple Mount itself had become a holy Christian site through the conversion of its Muslim shrines into Christian edifices. By declaring the Muslim structures the Lord's Temple and Solomon's Temple, the Crusaders skipped over 2,000 years of history and without hesitation associated themselves with the glory of the former Jewish Jerusalem. They identified the rock in the center of the Dome of the Rock as the place where David had built his altar, and the Holy of Holies of Solomon's Temple became the place where Solomon had placed the Ark of the Covenant.

While Christian domination of Jerusalem was justified in the Byzantine period by the claim that the Christians were in fact the true Israel, the Crusaders connected themselves directly to biblical traditions. To them Jerusalem was not only the city of the New Testament but also the city of the Jewish Bible, and they referred to it by names that evoke the Jewish Temple. They called Jerusalem by names such as "The Holy of Holies" and "God's Sanctuary."[103] Baldwin I, the first Crusader king of Jerusalem, was viewed as the successor of the dynasty of King David; and his city, as the City of David. The numerous pilgrims who visited Jerusalem spread these views in Europe, where they were written down by laymen and clergy, and sung by troubadours.

The fall of Jerusalem and the Crusader Kingdom to the Muslim general Salah a-Din in 1187 was a deeply felt blow to the entire Christian world. It was equated to the fall of Jerusalem to the Babylonians, and appropriate biblical verses from the Book of Lamentations were used to describe it. It is interesting that despite the strong connection the Crusaders had to the Old Testament, and despite their belief that their kingdom was the true successor of the kingdom of David and Solomon, their laments when their kingdom failed centered almost exclusively on the loss of the tomb of Jesus. All other holy places, including the Temple Mount, were now ignored.[104]

With its fall Jerusalem again lost its position as the biblical city and reverted to what it had been prior to the First Crusade— the city of the Holy Tomb. Moreover, certain circles in the Church, especially the strong monastic movements, now preached that believers should turn again from the earthly Jerusalem to the Heavenly Jerusalem represented by the Church and substitute prayer for pilgrimage.

This idea is best represented by Bernard of Clairvaux, one of the most influential medieval Christian clergymen, who declared, using the image of Revelations 21:2, that "You have two from heaven, both Jesus the Bridegroom and the Bride Jerusalem. . . . The visible image and beautiful appearance of that heavenly Jerusalem, which is our mother, became known and revealed to us in and through Christ." Heavenly Jerusalem and Christ were united to become the Church.[105] For Bernard they became specifically his own monastery, where he and his monks dwelled in heavenly Jerusalem. He and other clergymen discouraged pilgrims from going to Jerusalem, as did several church fathers in the early Byzantine period. They preached that the true holy city, the city free from worldly woes and conquering infidels, was in heaven, and the believer could ensure his soul's salvation by living a pious Christian life according to the doctrines of the Church.[106]

The Return of the Muslims

The expulsion of the Crusaders from the Holy Land in 1187 was a tremendous Muslim victory, and the name of Salah e-Din (Saladin) is remembered to this day as a symbol of Muslim valor and military success. The conquest opened a period of 730 years of Muslim dominance over Palestine, Jerusalem, and the Temple Mount that ended in 1917 with the British conquest of the area.

The Late Muslim period is subdivided into several subperiods, according to the ruling dynasty that dominated the area.

The Ayyubids

It is perhaps surprising that the fall of Jerusalem to the Crusaders in 1099 did not cause deep despair in the Muslim world. Except for three writers—one far away in Spain, one far away in Samarkand in Central Asia, who lamented the fall of the al-Aqsa Mosque, and the third in nearby Syria, who called for a holy war (*jihad*) against the Crusaders—none of the other writers of the period mentioned the event. About fifty years after the Crusader conquest, Zengi, the strong and ambitious ruler of northern Syria, voiced his intention to capture Jerusalem and declared a holy war on the Crusaders. Wisely clothing his political ambitions with strong religious undercurrents, he gained the support of rulers, religious functionaries, and simple people alike. His successors reaped the fruit of his policy, which culminated in the capitulation of the Crusader kingdom to Salah e-Din. The *jihad* waged against Christianity, and the great victory over the "infidels" who by force had taken over the third-holiest compound of Islam, strengthened and solidified the sanctity of Jerusalem and especially of the *Haram a-Sharif* in Muslim consciousness. The increased awareness of the holiness of city and holy compound gave birth to an extreme Islamic ideological attachment to Jerusalem that has not diminished to this day.[107]

Shortly after the fatal Battle of Hattin (August 1187) in which the Crusaders lost most of their mounted knighthood and with it their Kingdom of Jerusalem, Salah a-Din entered Jerusalem. He ordered all vestiges of Christian ritual removed from the *Haram a-Sharif* and the structures returned to their original Muslim function. The large golden cross that topped the Crusader Lord's Temple, now again the Dome of the Rock, was taken down and dragged along the streets of Jerusalem in order to shame Christianity. It was replaced by a crescent, the symbol of Islam, which is there to this day. The altar that stood on the holy rock inside the Dome of the Rock and the marble paving that covered it were removed, as was the iron grill that surrounded it. The icons and holy pictures were taken down, and the plaster was removed from the walls. The original mosaics again shone in splendor.

In the al-Aqsa Mosque the walls that divided the space into small rooms were removed, as was the wall that blocked the *mihrab* (prayer niche) facing Mecca. Salah e-Din imported mosaics from Constantinople to decorate the *mihrab* and the entire south wall (*kibla*) He also installed in the mosque a splendid new *minbar* (preacher's pulpit) of Damascus work with inlays of mother-of-pearl and multicolored wood which he brought from Aleppo. Both the *Haram a-Sharif* and the al-Aqsa Mosque resumed their original functions, which they retain to this day. Salah e-Din's descendants repaired the central facade of the al-Aqsa Mosque and razed the house of the Augustine monks to the ground,

leaving no trace of it.[108] The Muslims now did as the Crusaders had done before them, and converted many churches and monasteries in Jerusalem and elsewhere into mosques and other Muslim buildings. Salah a-Din prohibited the entry of Christians to the Temple Mount; any Christian entering would be killed unless he converted.[109]

With the return of Muslim rule over Jerusalem, a number of Jews were allowed to settle in the city, and a small community began to organize, with new settlers being added over time. Because of recurring political upheavals and invasions of various warring groups, these communities did not survive in Jerusalem for long. And yet, between one conquest and disturbance in the city and the next, Jews made renewed attempts to settle in Jerusalem. It is possible that Jews settled on the southwestern hill of Jerusalem, where they formed the kernel of what was to develop in the following centuries into the Jewish Quarter.

The Christian world, shocked by the fall of Jerusalem, reacted by organizing several additional Crusades that recaptured the Coastal Plain and parts of the Galilee. These conquests enabled the Crusader Kingdom to survive for another century. None of the Crusades, however, managed to recapture Jerusalem by force, although Frederick II, emperor of the Holy Roman Empire, was able, in the course of the Sixth Crusade, to regain Jerusalem for Christianity by negotiating with the Muslim ruler of Egypt. Between 1229 and 1239 Jerusalem was again in Christian hands. The Temple Mount with its mosques, however, remained in a Muslim compound.

The Rule of the Mamluks

After a turbulent period marked by violent competition between the descendants of

Salah a-Din and a number of unsuccessful crusades aimed at bringing the area back to Christian domination, a group of ambitious officers in the Egyptian army rebelled and ousted the last of Salah e-Din's heirs from the throne. These officers were all foreigners, having been purchased or kidnapped in their childhood from their homes, especially in the Balkans, and brought to Egypt where they were educated as soldiers and officers in the Egyptian army. Within a short period these officers, known as Mamluks, managed in 1250 to gain victory over the Mongol army and avert the danger of the Mongol invasion of the country. They then established their rule over a huge territory, from the Nile cataracts in the south to the Euphrates River in the north, and ensured a period of over 250 years of peace for the entire area.

In their new administrative subdivision of this vast territory, the Mamluks did not confer upon Jerusalem a status of political importance. Having suffered greatly in the previous turbulent periods, the city was devastated, its walls demolished, and its population small and poor. And yet, now that it was under absolute and undisputed Muslim rule, this desolate town resumed its holiness in the eyes of the Muslims. Under the Mamluks it became a place of temporary or permanent exile for dignitaries who had lost favor in the eyes of the sultan in Egypt. These exiles devoted their resources and time to erecting in and around the Temple Mount religious schools of higher learning, monasteries for Muslim mystics who now flocked to Jerusalem, libraries, shelters and soup kitchens for the poor, inns for pilgrims and other buildings of religious significance.[110] The entrances of many of these buildings were profusely decorated in elaborate Mamluk style stone carvings. The

Mamluk sultans contributed profusely to the repair and beautification of the *Haram a-Sharif*.[111] With these contributions the mosaics on the outer walls of the Dome of the Rock were renewed, the dome and ceiling of the al-Aqsa Mosque was repaired, and its southern *kibla* wall was reinforced and lined with marble slabs. Its doors were covered with wooden tiles. Other contributions were made toward the repair, or rather the rebuilding, of the dome of the Dome of the Rock. They again constructed two domes: an inner, round one built of wooden ribs and covered with intricately carved and painted stucco, and an outer, slightly elliptical one, also built of wooden ribs and covered with lead sheets. The Mamluk sultans also contributed toward the replacement of the mosaics on the exterior of the building, since the original ones had deteriorated with time. A spectacular set of arches was erected on top of the northern flight of stairs leading to the upper platform of the *Haram a-Sharif* on which the Dome of the Rock stands. A marble pulpit, known as the Summer *Minbar* because it is used in the summer, when the al-Aqsa Mosque overflows with worshippers, was installed immediately to the west of the southern set of arches. The sultans also erected on the Temple Mount watering fountains (*sebils*) for the comfort of the worshippers, the most spectacular being the one built by Sultan Kayyat Bey, and they built other small domed structures for solitary prayer and for rest. The Mamluks gave the Temple Mount the shape it retains to this day.

During the Mamluk period many books praising Jerusalem were published. These served as guidebooks for pilgrims, who were encouraged to visit Jerusalem on the way back home from the major pilgrimage to Mecca. Many pilgrims indeed visited the *Haram a-*

Sharif and spread its name throughout the Muslim world.

All these activities were aimed at enhancing the glory of Jerusalem and the *Haram a-Sharif* as a major religious Muslim center, and at the same time at erasing all traces of Crusader activities. With the Crusaders having been overcome, the prestige of Jerusalem as a holy city to Islam and of the *Haram a-Sharif* as the third most important mosque in the Muslim world was unequivocally established.

The Days of the Ottomans

In 1516 the Mamluks were ousted by the Ottoman Turks, who established a vast empire which they ruled from Istanbul. At first the Ottoman sultan Suleiman the Magnificent rebuilt the walls and gates of Jerusalem, but soon after his death the city began its long descent into the status of a small, insignificant town removed from all political and economic activities. This was its position during most of the 400 years of Ottoman rule The Ottomans added very little to the *Haram a-Sharif* as it was left by the Mamluks; the most important of their additions was the Mosque of 'Omar to the east of the al-Aqsa Mosque. Several repair projects were carried out in the Dome of the Rock and the al-Aqsa Mosque. The most impressive project replaced the worn-out Mamluk mosaics on the outer walls of the Dome of the Rock with glazed tiles painted in Turkish style. The Summer *Minbar* on the south side of the upper plaza of the *Haram a-Sharif* was also repaired. Most of these repairs were cosmetic rather than constructional, and so the condition of the structures on the *Haram* gradually deteriorated. No major program of reinforcing them was undertaken until the British Mandate period.

Perhaps more important than the repair work was the reluctance to open up the Temple Mount, which had been closed to Christians since the expulsion of the Crusaders, and to Jews since the Temple Mount had been taken over by the Crusaders. The prohibition was so severe that it reached bizarre proportions. J. T. Barclay wrote in the mid-nineteenth century that "when the clock of the Mosque needed repairing, they are compelled, however reluctantly, to employ a Frank [European Christian]. But in order to have a clean conscience in the commission of such an abominable piece of sacrilege as the admission upon the sacred premises, they adopt the following expedient . . . a certain formula of prayer and incantation is sung over him at the gate. This being satisfactorily concluded, he is considered as exorcised not only of Christianity, but of humanity also and is declared to be no longer a man but a donkey. He is then mounted upon the shoulders of the faithful . . . and being carried to the spot where his labors are required, he is set down upon matting within certain prescribed limits."[112] The same procedure was carried out when he left the site. In the middle of the nineteenth century, under pressure from European countries, which were having more and more influence on the Ottoman Empire, Christian dignitaries were sometimes allowed to visit the Mount. Adventurous, travelers and eventually scholars ventured—sometimes in clandestine ways, sometimes with full permission—to measure, sketch, and study the Temple Mount and its surroundings, and they contributed much to our knowledge of the holy enclosure. Jews were not included in any visiting arrangements and were barred from entering the Mount until 1967.

The small Jewish community of earlier centuries grew with time, as people migrated from the Ottoman Empire as well as from Europe. Because of the proximity of the Jewish Quarter to the west wall of the Temple Mount, one of the few exposed remnants of the retaining walls King Herod built when he enlarged the Temple Mount compound, this section of the wall became a place of Jewish prayer and mourning. This section of the wall, known as the Western Wall to the Jews and Wailing Wall to the Christians, was the closest Jews could get to the holy compound of the Temple Mount, The Western Wall became, and still is, the holiest place for the Jews, and with time also a place of contention and strife with the Muslims. The Western Wall, with two cypress trees growing beyond it, became a visual symbol of Jerusalem in Jewish folk art of the Ottoman period. Similarly, the Dome of the Rock, under the name Solomon's Temple introduced in the Crusader period, became a recognized image depicting Jerusalem in many items of popular art produced in Jerusalem. These images, printed on pages or embroidered on coverlets for the Sabbath bread, were purchased as souvenirs by tourists or sent abroad as gifts to prospective donors toward the upkeep of the small, poor Jewish community in Jerusalem.

Investigating the Temple Mount in the Ottoman Period

Until the beginning of the nineteenth century very little was known about the Temple Mount, because the Muslim authorities did not allow Europeans to enter the *Haram a-Sharif* and investigate its layout and structures. As early as 1807 a Spaniard, probably a spy in the service of Napoleon, managed to enter the site in Muslim disguise and under a Muslim name. He stayed in Jerusalem for quite a while and visited the Temple Mount several times, and later he published quite accurate plans and sections of the site.

Some twenty-five years later, in 1833, three Englishmen, headed by Frederick Catherwood, presented to the Muslim authorities of the Temple Mount a *firman* (document of authorization) stating that they were architects in the service of then ruler of Palestine, Muhammad Ali. Disguised as Egyptian army officers, the team worked on the Temple Mount for six consecutive weeks, measuring the entire site and studying in greater detail the Dome of the Rock, the al-Aqsa Mosque, and the Gate of Mercy. They did not find a publisher for their work, which was later incorporated in books by others.

The American explorer Edward Robinson visited Jerusalem in 1838 and noted a section of an arch springing from the west wall of the Temple Mount. The arch is appropriately named after him and has proved to be the topmost arch of a series of arches, all destroyed, that gave access to the Herodian Temple Mount. The Swiss physician Titus Tobler visited Jerusalem several times in the 1830s–1850s and discovered a complete arch springing out of the west wall of the Temple Mount, to the north of Robinson's Arch. The arch he discovered is known as Wilson's Arch.

After the Crimean War (1853–1856) and the increasing involvement of European powers in the affairs of the area, it became easier for researchers to enter the Temple Mount even without disguises. The first distinguished visitors to visit the Temple Mount were the duke and duchess of Brabant, who later were crowned king and queen of Belgium. They were accompanied by several dignitaries, including James Finn, the British consul in Jerusalem, who wrote a detailed description of the Mount. Scientific research on the Temple Mount began in the 1860s with the work of Marquis de Vogue, who in 1864 published a volume entitled *The Temple in Jerusalem* and also discovered remnants of the Roman town of Aelia Capitolina. Pierotti, the Italian city-engineer of Jerusalem, who had free access to the Mount, continued his work.

The foundation of the British Palestine Exploration Fund in 1865 gave a push to the scientific work on the Temple Mount. That same year, the engineering officer Charles Wilson published an exact map of the original topography of the Mount, as well as an exact plan and photographs of the site. His work is still the cornerstone for any work on the Temple Mount. His colleague Charles Warren carried out excavations along the west wall of the Temple Mount despite the strong resentment of the Ottoman authorities. Because of their refusal to let him dig openly, Warren resorted to digging deep shafts at several points next to the wall, and from their bottom he cut tunnels that joined them into one system. In this way he discovered the contour of the bedrock around the Temple Mount.

An important addition to the study of Jerusalem was made by the German architect Conrad Schick, a resident of Jerusalem, who in 1887 published a comprehensive study titled *The Temple Mount as It Is Today*, the result of his meticulous ongoing studies. This work is still a basic compendium of information for any study carried out since.

While archaeological research was going on, there were a few adventurers whose aim was to discover, not the reality of the Temple Mount, but hidden treasures. The best-known

of these was the Swedish officer Montague Parker, who between 1909 and 1911 dug in the City of David in an attempt to discover the Temple treasures. He declared that the place where the treasures were hidden had been revealed to him by a London spiritualist who gave him a secret document. He found nothing and turned his attention to the Temple Mount proper. He spent money on bribing Ottoman officials, who turned a blind eye to the work he did inside the Dome of the rock for nine nights in April 1911.[113]

However, rumors spread in Jerusalem, and the expedition was in danger when thousands of Muslim pilgrims congregated in Jerusalem for the yearly Nebi Musa festivities. The authorities then issued an order to imprison Parker, who managed to escape at the last moment, empty-handed, and boarded a ship waiting for him in Jaffa port. Nevertheless, rumors spread among the Muslims that Christians had stolen the King David's crown, Solomon's sword, the Ark of the Covenant with the Tablets of the Law, and many other holy items from the Dome of the Rock. These rumors strengthened the feeling among Muslims that the real aim of Christian research on the Temple Mount was to loot treasures, and since then they have banned all scientific activities on the Mount.

It should be noted that despite the efforts of so many people, work on the Temple Mount is to this day based only on measuring, observing, and sketching. Orderly archaeological excavation to reveal the exact location of the ancient structures and perhaps to find some remnants of them has never been allowed by the Muslim authorities, and it is doubtful that it ever will be allowed in the future.

Notes

[1] Mazar B. 1975b: 29.

[2] Cogan 2000: 70–71; Eliav 2001: 28.

[3] Horovitz 2000: 144–147; Herzog 2000: 155–171.

[4] A cubit is an ancient measurement unit based on the average length of the arm. It varies between 48 and 52 cm depending on the time and place. An average of 1 cubit = 50 cm is accepted, and hereafter the biblical measurement will be converted into meters.

[5] Andrews 2000: 39–40.

[6] Horovitz 2000: 149–150.

[7] Herzog 2000: 160.

[8] Horovitz 2000: 151.

[9] Mazar B. 1975a: 99.

[10] Ussishkin 1973: 78–105.

[11] Ginzberg Vol. IV 1913: 149–154.

[12] Soucek 1976: 83–84.

[13] Horovitz 2000: 147.

[14] Avi–Yonah and Yadin 1986: 293–265, figs d74; d107–110; d112; Milstein 1999:25–27.

[15] Horovitz 2000: 135.

[16] Horovitz 2000: 135.

[17] Ginzberg Vol. IV 1913: 320–321.

[18] Ginzberg Vol. IV 1913: 320–321.

[19] Gutmann 1976.

[20] Lazarus–Yafeh 1999: 228; Horovitz 2000: 136–137; Uffenheimer 2000: 179–185.

[21] Levine 1987: 211–212.

[22] ibid 1987: 215.

[23] Ginzberg Vol. IV 1913: 353–354.

[24] Japhet 2000: 345–382.

[25] Herr 1980: 9–10.

[26] Mazar B. 1975a: 65–66

[27]71 Ibid 131–135.

[28] Ibid 140–148.

[29] Ibid 124–125.

[30] Levine B. 1987: 213–214.

[31] Schwabe 1956: 358–361.

[32] Avi–Yonah 1956: 392–418.

[33] Mazar B. 1975a: 106–111.

[34] Safrai 1965: 42–87.

[35] Schwabe 1956: 362–365.

[36] Yadin 1985.

[37] Lefkovitz 2000: 455–470.

[38] Stern 1980: 268.

[39] Safrai 1999: 15–16.

[40] ibid 384.

[41] Isaac 1999:11.

[42] Safrai 1980.

[43] Limor 1999: 401–404.

[44] Safrai 1999: 16–20.

[45] Lazarus–Yafeh 1999: 292.

[46] Mazar E, 1999: 52–61; Steibel 1999: 68–96.

[47] Tsafrir 1999: 124–132.

[48] Isaac 1999: 6–7.

[49] Mazar B. 1975a: 235.

[50] Safrai 1999: 26–28.

[51] Meshorer 1999: 182–183.

[52] Mazar B. 1975a: 242.

[53] Sanders 1999: 90–103; Stroumsa 1999: 352–353.

[54] Linder 1979: 18–22.

[55] Prawer 1968: 186; Perrone 1999: 228–229.

[56] Prawer 1981: 105–106.

[57] Limor 1999: 391–416; Peronne 1999: 228–236; Prawer 1981:103–104.

[58] Bitton–Ashkelony 1999: 188–203.

[59] Limor 1999: 407–410.

[60] Linder 1979: 11–12.

[61] Mazar 1986: 37–39.

[62] Avi–Yonah 1954: 50–60, Pl. 7.

[63] Gil 1996:1–8.

[64] Soucek 1976: 87–88.

[65] Hirschberg 1951–52: 112–113.

[66] Soucek 1976: 89–106.

[67] Hirschberg 1951–52: 114–118.

[68] Rosen–Ayalon 1996: 386.

[69] Braslavi 1968: 120–144.

[70] Bahat 1996: 70–73.

[71] Eldad 2001: 73–77.

[72] Grabar 1996: 56–71; Nuseibeh and Grabar 1996: 48–49.

[73] Le Strange 1965: 101.

[74] Rosen–Ayalon 1996: 389–390.

[75] Nuseibeh and Grabar 1996: 37.

[76] Grabar 1996:52–56; 104–110; Nuseibeh and Grabar 1996: 55–70.

[77] Rosen–Ayalon 1996: 390.

[78] Allen 1999: 206–208.

[79] Le Strange 1965:134–135.

[80] Nuseibeh and Grabar 1996: 74–118.

[81] Grabar 1996: 71–104.

[82] Eldad 2001: 70–77.

[83] Soucek 1976: 73–123.

[84] Eldad 1999: 300–303; Eldad 2001: 82–84.

[85] Nuseibeh and Grabar 1996: 147.

[86] Grabar 1996: 117–122.

[87] Le Strange 19 65: 91.

[88] Wilson and Warren 1871: 172; Bahat 1996: 82; 84.

[89] Eldad 2001: 63–70.

[90] Le Strange 1965:98.

[91] ibid 152–153

[92] Eldad 2001: 77–78.

[93] Ibid 87–89.

[94] Prawer 1968: 186–188; Prawer 1981:99–100.

[95] Schein 1991:241–242.

[96] Chazan 1999: 282–292.

[97] Prawer 1991: 22–23.

[98] ibid 32; Bahat 1991:101–106.

[99] Cahn 1976: 48.

[100] Schein 1991: 239.

[101] Benvenisti 1970: 64–68.

[102] Le Grange 1965: 107.

[103] Schein 1991: 237–238.

[104] Ibid 240.

[105] Stroumsa 1999: 360.

[106] Schein 1991: 246–251.

[107] Sivan 1991:287–301.

[108] Prawer 1991: 47; Bahat 1991: 129–131.

[109] Prawer 1991: 45.

[110] Drori 1981: 131–143.

[111] Heyd 1968: 197.

[112] Barclay 1858:482–483.

[113] Andrews 2000:234–239.

Chapter 5
Legends, Beliefs, and Aspirations Regarding the Temple Mount

The Temple Mount as a Locus of Legends

Although we do not have any clear and explicit knowledge regarding the significance of the hill that later became known as the Temple Mount in pre-Israelite times, some ideas can be formulated out of what is recorded in written sources as well as in mute, archaeological data. The hill may have been a burial place for a group of seminomadic people who roamed the area around 2000 BCE. This suggestion, by no means proven, is based on the similarity of the shaft leading to the cave under the holy rock to common shafts of burial caves in cemeteries of the period that are scattered up and down the central hilly ridge of the country. Moreover, much later Jewish sources of the Mishnah and the Talmud hint at an uneasy feeling that the Temple Mount may be ritually unclean because of the existence of tombs under it.

The notion that the hill may have been a holy site to the pre-Israelites is further strengthened by the reference to the threshing floor on the hill, which David purchased from Aravna, the last Jebusite king of Jerusalem. It is perhaps indicative that in order to stop the plague that infested the people in those days, David appealed to God by means of the altar

he was ordered to build on the threshing floor, and not by means of the Holy Ark, which at that time was already in Jerusalem. This hints at some special qualities of the threshing floor, always an important installation in a rural society. Threshing floors were often also places where the dead were mourned, perhaps because agriculture was conceived as a cycle of death, burial and revival, a cycle manifested in the mythologies of many peoples, such as the ancient Egyptians, Babylonians, and Greeks.

Thus the Israelite Temple was built on a place that may have been revered from time immemorial, and whose sanctity is perhaps one of the oldest ever recorded. As time went by and the holiness of the two Jewish Temples became firmly established, and even more so after they were destroyed, numerous legends and myths were drawn to it, increasing its religious significance. These legends, not part of the basic religious dogmas and the teachings and law, were born out of popular imagination and aspirations.[1]

They emphasize the deep need of the Jewish people, whose earthly sanctuary was destroyed, to endow the destroyed site with intense transcendental qualities that would preserve its stolen holiness and carry on the hope that one day the earthly sanctuary would be built again.

The need to add traditions of holiness to the holy Mount was especially felt after the destruction of the Second Temple and, with it, the loss of both the political and the religious independence of the Jewish people. The loss was so great that it had worldwide repercussions. Rabbi Joshua said that from the day the Temple was destroyed there has been no day without a curse, the dew has not condensed, and the flavor has left the fruit. Rabbi Jose added that the fullness of the fruit (its nourishing qualities) was removed (Sotah 48a). Another sage added that since the destruction of the Temple the gates of prayers have been sealed (Berakhot 32.b).

The transformation of the Jewish people from a proud, independent nation into a beaten and scattered group was so dramatic that some means had to be devised to heal and comfort them. Weaving legends that intensified the sanctity of the Temple Mount, symbol of all that was unique and admirable in the Jewish religion, was one way of doing so. Indeed, new traditions are often born out of crisis—when a group of people consolidate into a tribe or a nation, when social upheaval disrupt the fabric of a society, or, as in this case, when a nation has to rebuild itself after a major catastrophe.[2] The destruction of the Temple in 70 CE did not crush the spirit of the Jewish people but became the trigger transforming it from a nation centered on a Temple to scattered groups of people whose religious identity was preserved through prayers, observance of the Law, longings, and legends.

Now that the Temple Mount, the core of Jewish sanctity, had lost its practical function as a place of sacrifice and pilgrimage, the peo-ple increased its holiness by redefining it as the location of world-shaking occurrences. Their reverence for it only grew, and in the absence of the Temple where religious activities could be performed, it expressed itself in declaring its universal centrality. Furthermore, the Temple became the locus of crucial events that were supposed to have taken place on it, and of events that will take place there in the future. Significant mythical occurrences with only a vague geographic definition also came to be attached to this place of recognized holiness. Even some events that occurred in well-defined other places were transferred to the Temple Mount. This process of magnifying the destroyed Temple Mount and the rock in its center was probably a lengthy one, and on the whole it is not known when, how, or by whom the legends and myths were born. We can only record, then, when they first appear in writing. But once written down, they added to the recognized sanctity of the Temple Mount and magnified it.

Since Judaism is the oldest of the three religions that have a stake in the Temple Mount, many of the legends that were born out of the Jewish need to broaden the sanctity of the place were absorbed by the other two. When Christianity and then Islam took over the domination of the Temple Mount, they recognized its holiness and adopted many of the miraculous events that became attached to it. However, because of their ambiguous relation to this site of entrenched Jewish association, in many cases they transferred the location of these events to other places, more sacred and central to them. At the same time they introduced their own legends and stories that enhanced the sanctity of their own holy sites. The Christians moved most of the stories and legends from the rock on the Temple

Mount to the rock of Golgotha (Calvary) in the nearby Church of the Holy Sepulcher. The Muslims in their turn transferred many of them to their holy Ka'ba in faraway Mecca in Arabia. Many momentous events, from the Creation of the World to the Last Judgment, that were originally centered on the Temple Mount dispersed to other holy places, and are now believed by the Christians and Muslims to be located in places other than where they were born.

Jewish Myths and Legends
On the Creation of Jewish Legends Relating to the Temple Mount

The kernel of the myths relating to the Temple is found already in the prophetic books of the Bible. In their visions, proclaimed when the First Temple was still standing, several prophets foresaw "The Day of the Lord" (Amos 5:18–20), when God will take revenge on humanity for its sins, and in which darkness will prevail (e.g., Amos 8–9). However, following this catastrophic upheaval Israel will be restored and a new large and spectacular Temple will be built, which will draw to it many believers from the non-Israelite nations.

Shortly after the destruction of the First Temple, the prophet Ezekiel, a priest in the Temple who was exiled to Babylon alongside his fellow countrymen, drew up a plan for a new, visionary Temple that would be part of the eventual salvation scheme of Israel. Ezekiel's Temple, the Temple of the End of Days, is very formal and is described in great details, with exact measurements (Ezekiel 40–48). The outer perimeter is an exact square inside of which are three courtyards, and in the inner courtyard, which is reserved exclusively for the priests, is the Temple itself.

The importance of the Temple at the End of Days is stressed by Second Isaiah, who envisions that on that day the Temple will obtain a universal position: "For my house shall be called a house of prayer for all people" (Isaiah 56:7). This Temple is also the subject of the Temple Scroll, the longest of the Dead Sea Scrolls, which relates the beliefs of the Essenes, members of a Second Temple–period Jewish sect that disputed the rites and rituals carried on in the Temple. Because of their extreme views, they left Jerusalem and settled on the shores of the Dead Sea, where their library, known as the Dead Sea Scrolls, was found. The Temple Scroll sketches the plan of the Temple that should have been built in Jerusalem in place of the defiled one that existed in their time. According to the Essenes and other Jewish sects of the time, this Temple would be only temporary, for at the End of Days God would built a new and permanent Temple with his own hand.

After the Destruction of the Second Temple and the loss of national sovereignty, popular imagination found some comfort for its loss by dwelling on the mythical connections between the Temple and where it stood. These legends span a period of about a thousand years, more or less from shortly after the destruction of the Second Temple to early in the second millennium. Some are attributed to known sages and rabbis, others are anonymous. They are intertwined in the Mishnah and in the Babylonian and Jerusalem Talmud, as well as in collections of explanations and elaboration on these sacred texts, and in compilations of legends. Although several legends are attributed to specific personalities, they may have originated many years before they were written down and were transmitted verbally over many generations. Since these legends are scattered in such a vast body of written material and extend over such a long time, there sometimes are conflicting points of view between the various traditions. Some legends are unique, quoted only once; others appear and reappear in various forms. It is perhaps to the credit of the compilers of the various texts that they did not try to systematically edit the material but left it as a collection of thoughts, visions, and points of view.

The Jewish legends and myths surrounding the Temple Mount are of a cryptic nature, not developed into a mythology of epic dimensions, as, for example, is Greek mythology. The short, cryptic sayings are scattered through the vast body of literature, and most are based on creative interpretation of biblical texts.

The Navel of the Earth and the Foundation Stone

The holiest spot on the Temple Mount is a bare rock, covered since the seventh century CE by the Muslim Dome of the Rock (*Kubbat a-Sahra*). This rock, which according to the most prevalent belief was incorporated into both Solomon's Temple and the Second Temple, became the locus of events relating to the very beginning of the world,[3] as well as to the prehistory of mankind. It is identified in Jewish lore with the navel of the world and the center of the universe, the place where creation actually began.[4]

The notion that a certain place is the center or navel of the earth is not exclusive to Judaism; it is known in many religions around the world.[5] The center of the earth, a notion of mythic geography,[6] is the place where the most direct contact with the divine can be made. It is described metaphorically in many ways, such as the womb of the universal

mother, the meeting point of the spokes of the wheel of the universe that never stops rotating, or the hearth where the fire of life is kept. It is manifested in different forms, such as a mountain, a tree, a ladder, a pole, and a Temple.[7]

In Jewish lore, the navel of the world is the center of holiness, a place that connects all three worlds—heaven, earth, and the netherworld. It takes the specific form of the rock located on top of Mount Zion (the poetic biblical name of the Temple Mount) in the city of Jerusalem. On the basis of interpretation of biblical and postbiblical verses,[8] these three locations—the rock itself, the mountain on which it is located, and Jerusalem—represent three levels of holiness in diminishing order. The verse "This is Jerusalem: I have set it in the midst of the nations and countries that are round about her" (Ezekiel 5:5) is expanded to refer to the city of Jerusalem as the center of the world. In the same vein, Isaiah's verse "Therefore, thus saith the Lord God, Behold, I lay in Zion a foundation, a stone, a tried stone, a precious corner stone, a sure foundation" (Isaiah 28:16) is interpreted as referring to the rock, the cornerstone of the world, situated on Mount Zion. The notion of the centrality of Mount Zion in the epic event of the creation of the world is further expressed in early postbiblical literature of the Hellenistic period. The Book of Jubilees states that "He [Noah] knew that . . . Mount Zion [is] in the center of the navel of the earth" (8:19).

The sages of the Mishnah provide a figurative description of the process of creation by a stone by expounding on the verse "The Lord by wisdom hath founded the earth" (Proverbs 3:19). One sage expressed the surprising and very figurative notion that "God threw a stone in the sea, and from this the world was founded" (Tractate Yoma 5:2). Other sages claimed: "God created the world as a human fetus. As a fetus begins with the navel and from there begins and expands, so the world began from its navel and from it stretched here and there. And where is its navel? It is Jerusalem. Its navel itself is the altar. And why did he call it Foundation Stone [*Even Shetiyya* in Hebrew]? Because the entire world was founded from it" (Beit Hamidrash 5:63–70). This stone of foundation is none other than the sacred rock on the Temple Mount. The centrality of this rock is expressed in another rabbinical text, which envisions the world as a series of concentric circles: "The Land of Israel is located in the center of the world, Jerusalem in the center of the Land of Israel, the Temple in the center of Jerusalem, the *heikhal* [sanctuary] in the center of the Temple, the ark in the center of the *heikhal*, and in front of the *heikhal* is the *Even Shetiyya* from which the world was founded" (Kohelet Raba 3:7).

The idea of pointing to the exact place from which God began the act of creation is a world-wide notion.[9]

It is a rather materialistic description of the event, in contrast with the spiritual biblical description according to which the world was created by God's utterance. The stone of creation may be a vestige of pre-Israelite, pagan cosmological ideas about the process of creation. Such notions may have been adopted by the Israelites who sanctified this stone by building on it the Israelite Temples and then further expanding its sanctity by attaching to it significant acts performed by the patriarchs of humanity, and specifically by the patriarchs of the Jewish nation.

According to one Talmudic opinion, it was not only the entire universe that evolved from *Even Shetiyya*; the human race, too, originated

in it. Adam—the first human being—was created from a ladle full of earth that God took from the place of the altar (Jerusalem Talmud, Nazir 7:2). Thereafter God had a special liking for Adam because of the purity of the earth from which he was fashioned, the earth on which the Temple was later built. Adam was also buried under the rock.[10]

The choice of place for the creation of humankind was not random but very purposeful, as expressed by the saying: "Out of the place where atonement is made for him, man has been created" (Breishit Raba 17:6).

Even Shetiyya as an Altar

The significance of *Even Shetiyya* both in the Temples and after their destruction lies in its being an altar. The sages of the Mishnah suggested that the altar was a very ancient one, created at the same time the world was created. The sages seriously debated the question of how exactly the rock functioned as an altar. One point of view (Tractate Yoma 5:2) was that this rock was located inside Solomon's Temple, within the Holy of Holies, and served as the base for the Ark of the Covenant. When the Temple was destroyed, the rock became exposed. In the Second Temple, which had no Ark, the rock remained exposed and bare, and the High Priest burned incense on it.

Another point of view, based on Ezekiel 43:13–17, claims that the large altar on which animals were sacrificed to atone for the sins of the people was built over *Even Shetiyya*. According to this view, the rock was located, not inside the Temple, but outside, in the courtyard, and it was in fact the sacrificial altar that David, on the orders of the prophet Gad, built on the threshing floor of Aravna the Jebusite, and on which he sacrificed to God.

Moreover, this altar, that part of the original scheme of the creation of the world, was the same altar on which Adam sacrificed, and after him his sons Cain and Abel, and Noah[11] and his sons (Pesikta Rabati 43, Breishit Raba 34 9). When Abraham was ordered to sacrifice his son Isaac on one of the hills in the Land of Moriah, which was identified in II Chronicles 3:1 as the hill on which Solomon built the Temple, God showed him this same altar.[12] God also told him that his illustrious ancestors had also sacrificed on it.

The Binding of Isaac, a momentous event that sealed the bond between Abraham and his seed and God, and deeply influenced Jewish thought, literature, and legend, took place on the same primeval altar that was also the navel of the earth, giving the event cosmic dimensions. The episode of the Binding of Isaac ended when a ram replaced the sacrificial human, implying that God preferred animal rather than human sacrifices.

Even Shetiyya and Jacob's Dream

Another outstanding event involving one of the patriarchs became connected with *Even Shetiyya*. At some point this rock was identified with the stone on which Jacob slept when he left his father's home to go to Haran,[13] and on which he dreamed his fabulous dream of a ladder connecting heaven and earth (Genesis 28:11–22). When Jacob woke from his sleep, he named the place Beit-El. The identification of Beit-El with the Temple Mount was made despite the fact that the location of Beit-El, north of Jerusalem, is clearly specified in the Bible. Beit-El, meaning "House of God," and the Temple, also the House of God, became one. It may be of interest that in a lecture on the Israeli-Arab dispute over the Temple Mount given recently in Jerusalem by a

Muslim scholar, the lecturer insisted that the Jewish Temples were never built in Jerusalem but rather in Beit-El.

In the identification of Beit-El with the bare rock on the Temple Mount, the rock acquired an additional cosmic dimension as a link between the celestial and the earthly worlds. Moreover, this same rock connected the earth with the netherworld. A late legend expounding on the biblical narration relates that after Jacob took the stone on which he slept and placed it as a standing stone (*masseba*), God stamped the stone with his right foot and sank it to *tehom*,[14] the depths of the earth (Pirkei Rabbi Eliezer). The stone thus connects the three cosmic realms: earth, heaven, and the netherworld.

Even Shetiyya, Tehom and Subterranean Water

The connection of *Even Shetiyya* with the *tehom*, or netherworld, is expressed in other ways as well. The altar was connected to the netherworld (*tehom*) by channels that conducted the blood of the sacrifices and the water used to wash the blood to *tehom*. This idea is expressed in the statement that "A way was made for these channels which descended unto tehom" (Tractate Succah 49a). Another type of connection is given by another sage, who said, "When David dug the channels, *tehom* rose and threatened to submerge the world" (ibid. 53a). The rock—the navel of the earth—is thus the entrance to *tehom*, and the rock in fact guards the world from the frightening and threatening netherworld and makes sure it is kept in its proper place and does not burst out to destroy the world.

The statement that the opening of *tehom* is under the stone expresses another aspect of the connection between *Even Shetiyya* and water, both threatening primeval water and beneficial spring water. This connection perhaps is based on the fact that the Hebrew word *shetiyya* derives not only from the root "to lay foundation" but also from the root "to drink." The stone that tightly seals the opening of *tehom* and prevents its water from coming up and submerging the earth has another cosmic function of regulating all the waters of the world. This idea is based on Psalm 87:7, which praises Jerusalem and ends with a statement that "all my fountains are in thee." Interestingly, it has been suggested that the notion of the connection between *Even Shetiyya* and water led to the ceremony of Pouring of Water that was performed in the Temple on the feast of Tabernacles. Its purpose, so this suggestion claims, was to induce nature to imitate what the celebrants did, namely, increase the amount of water under the navel of the earth and create an abundant supply of water for the whole world.

Another legend attributes medicinal properties to the subterranean water that issues from *Even Shetiyya*. It is related that "A watercourse issues forth from the Holy of Holies. At first it is thin like the feelers of a locust, but as soon as it reaches the entrance of the House of David it turns into a mighty stream, in which flux-affected men and women bathe" (Tractate Yoma 77b–78a).

The Celestial Temple

The sanctity of the destroyed terrestrial Temple was greatly enhanced by the notion, developed mainly after the destruction of the Second Temple, that the terrestrial Temple was but a reflection of a celestial Temple, built in heaven right over it. This celestial Temple is eternal and will remain forever in its place, even though its mirror image, the terrestrial Temple, has been destroyed. This notion

bestowed upon the earthy Temple a high spiritual dimension, an aura that may have been feared removed when the structure was destroyed. Several legends were born, claiming that the celestial Temple preceded the terrestrial one, in fact that it was created even before the creation of the world.[15] This idea is expressed in rabbinical literature several times, such as in the saying that "Seven things were created before the world: the Torah, Repentance, the Garden of Eden, Gehenom (hell), the Divine Throne, the Temple, and the Name of the Messiah" (Pesahim 54a). The notion that whatever existed on earth preexisted in heaven is an ancient one, already expressed by the Sumerians of the third millennium BCE, and passed on to the Babylonians and Assyrians. Thus the Sumerians claimed that the gods in heaven did not at first have enough to eat, and so their chief god, Anu, created the goddesses of grain and of sheep and goats, who provided food for the gods. Only when the gods were satisfied did Anu place these two goddesses on earth and give them to humankind, and this is how civilization began.

A Talmudic story tells that when God told Moses to build the Tabernacle, God announced that actually he did not need the Tabernacle for himself, because his Temple in heaven had already been built before the world was created. However, because of his love for his people, God consented to leave his Upper Temple and come down to dwell among them. A legend that expands on Exodus 25:9–40 relates that the plan of the terrestrial Tabernacle was shown to Moses by God, and later, when the time came to build the Temple, God showed its plan to David, who passed it on to Solomon (I Chronicles 28:11–21). Thus, the terrestrial Temples reflect the celestial one. Isaiah 6:1–6, where the prophet described his encounter with God, who was sitting on his throne surrounded by angels, supplies details of either the terrestrial Temple, as claimed by several sages, or the celestial one, according to others. God's high throne in Isaiah's vision is believed by the latter sages to have been the celestial throne, placed exactly above God's throne in the terrestrial Temple, that is, above the Ark of the Covenant (Tanhuma Vayakhel 7).

The Talmud quotes a discussion between the sages concerning the relationship between the two Temples. It is ordained that when a Jew recites his prayers he turns toward Jerusalem, when he is in Jerusalem he turns toward the Temple, and when he is on the Temple Mount he turns toward the Holy of Holies. Now the sages ask toward which Holy of Holies? One sage said the celestial one, another, the terrestrial one. A third sage said that these two interpretations do not conflict, since the terrestrial Holy of Holies was placed exactly below the celestial one. It was also stated that "Anyone who prays at this place in Jerusalem [the Temple] prays, as it were, opposite the Heavenly Throne" (Pirkei Rabbi Eliezer 35). The sages contemplated also on the distance between the two Temples. Rabbi Simon bar Yohai estimates it at 18 miles—the numerical value of the letters of the Hebrew words which mean "and this is," in the verse "And this is the Gate of Heaven" (Genesis 18:17).

Thus the rock on the summit of the Temple Mount was transformed into the Foundation Stone from which began the whole process of the creation of the world and the formation of humanity. It is the center of the universe, a link between heaven, earth, and the netherworld. Its cosmic functions include also guarding the universe against returning into chaos by preventing *tehom* to overflow, and regulating all the fresh water of the world. It is a place of atonement, being at the foundation of the altar on which the first humans and then the patriarchs sacrificed, and then, when the Temple was built over it, all the Israelites did the same. It was also a place of appeasement, where Abraham, following the traumatic event of the Binding of Isaac received a blessing and a promise to his progeny.

Legends Relating to the Gate of Mercy

The holy rock and the Temple built on it were not the only location on the Temple Mount that drew the creative imagination of the Jews. Another site that attracted attention and storytelling was the eastern gate of the Temple Mount, known to the Jews and Muslims as the Gate of Mercy and to the Christians as the Golden Gate. In its present form it dates to the early Muslim period. This is a large, ornate gate overlooking the deep Kidron Valley and the Mount of Olives on the east. From the west, from the Temple Mount esplanade, one goes down several steps to enter the gate. Inside the gatehouse are two pillars surmounted by capitals of different styles, which divide it in two and hold its domed roof. From the other side of the wall, outside the city, are two blocked entrances, which became the focus of many legends, since it is not known why and when they were blocked. During the Middle Ages Jews used to pray in front of the blocked double gate, believing that it was built by King Solomon and thus was a remnant of the First Temple. Others identified one of the blocked gates as a gate through which bridegrooms entered the Temple Mount during the Second Temple

The Gate of Mercy in the Eastern Wall of the Temple Mount.
Photographer: Moshe Milner, 1995. © 1997–1998, The State of
Israel, Government Press Office.

Interior of the Gate of Mercy. Etching by E. Finden, 1835.

period, and the other as the gate through which mourners entered.

A medieval Jewish legend imposes upon the Gate of Mercy an important role in the End of Days that will precede the coming of the final messiah, Messiah ben David. According to this legend "Amarilus [the Jewish 'Antichrist'] will kill Messiah ben Joseph, alias Nehemiah ben Husiel, . . . and Hefsi-bah, mother of Menahem, will stand at the Eastern Gate so that the Evil One may not enter it. . . . Menahem ben 'Amiel [Messiah ben David], Nehemiah ben Husiel [Messiah ben Yoseph], Elijah, and all the resuscitated dead will proceed to Jerusalem in the month of Av. They will stand outside the gates of Jerusalem, opposite the Mount of Olives . . . and those who had been exiled from Jerusalem will ascend the Mount of Olives" (Book of Zerubbabel, Beit ha-Midrash I, pp. 56–57). This is a version of the more prevalent belief that the messiah will enter Jerusalem through the Gate of Mercy. It is expected that when the messiah comes, he will descend on the Mount of Olives and will be preceded by the Prophet Elijah, who will blow the horn to proclaim his arrival. The messiah, riding a donkey (Zechariah 9:9), will descend the slope of the Mount of Olives and ride up to the Gate of Mercy, through which he will enter Jerusalem. Jewish tradition claims that the Muslims blocked the Gate of Mercy in order to prevent this entry, which will proclaim the End of the Days, and furthermore located their cemetery in front of it. The Prophet Elijah, who is a *kohen*, will not be able to pass through the cemetery, and thus neither he nor the messiah will be able to enter Jerusalem.

The expectation that the messiah will descend on the Mount of Olives derives from the prophecy of Zechariah that "his feet shall stand in that day upon the mount of Olives which is before Jerusalem on the east, and the mount of Olives shall cleave in the midst thereof" (Zechariah 14:4). The entry to Jerusalem through the Gate of Mercy was added after the days of Zechariah, since this gate was built much later, most likely in the early Muslim period although there was probably an earlier, Second Temple period gate under it. Its name, the Gate of Mercy, is even later.

The role Zechariah allotted to the Mount of Olives on the Day of the Lord when the messiah will appear was taken up by the Christian tradition of the entry of Jesus into Jerusalem. According to this tradition, when Jesus approached Jerusalem, he came down the Mount of Olives, spent time in the Garden of Gethsemane at the foot of the Mount, and from there entered Jerusalem through its eastern gate. A crowd carrying palm branches greeted him. The role of the eastern gate in momentous events was carried over to the Byzantine period, when, so it is claimed, the victorious Byzantine emperor Heraclius entered the city through the same gate after reclaiming the country from the Persians, who had conquered it in 614 CE. Heraclius brought back to Jerusalem the cross on which Jesus was crucified, which had been taken as booty by the Persians. His entry through the gate was thus both a political and a religious act. The Crusaders opened the gates once a year, on Palm Sunday, and since their days it has never again been opened.

For Muslims the Gate of Mercy is also related to the events of the End of Days, when Muhammad will judge all the inhabitants of the world, past and present, on the Temple Mount.[16]

Christian Myths and Legends

The basic attitude of Christianity toward Jerusalem and the Temple Mount is based on Revelations 21:1–2: "And I saw a new heaven and a new earth: for the first heaven and the first earth were passed away; and there was no more to see. And I John saw the holy city, the New Jerusalem, coming down from God out of heaven, prepared as a bride adorned for her husband. And I heard a great voice out of heaven saying, Behold, the tabernacle of God is with men, and he will dwell with them." With Christianity a new world order began, and a New Jerusalem replaced the old. There would be no need for a Temple, since God would dwell in the hearts of the people. Thus at first Christianity tried to erase any vestiges of the holiness of Jerusalem and of the Temple Mount. But because the place, and especially the holy rock, was laden with so much sacredness and promise, adorned with motifs of creation, sacrifice, and atonement, it was not easy to accomplish this mission.

Transference of Legends to the Rock of Golgotha (Calvary)

With time Christianity adopted the notion of a holy rock, but because it strove to detach itself from Judaism and its holy places, viewing their destruction as a proof of its own success, it transported the sacred rock from the Temple Mount to the hill of Golgotha (Calvary). This hill, the site of the crucifixion of Jesus and the rock on which it is based, are now incorporated into the Church of the Holy Sepulcher. A visible crack that runs from the top of the rock downward is believed to have been chiseled by the blood of Jesus on the cross. The blood dripped all the way down to the deep recesses of the earth and onto the skull of Adam, who is buried under the rock.

Thus a mystical connection was made between Golgotha and various Jewish notions relating to the *Even Shetiyya*. The act of creation of the world and of humanity, represented by Adam, was transferred to Golgotha, and the detail that Adam was also buried there was added. This idea could not have been born in a Jewish mind, which clearly separates holiness from defilement caused by burial. The sacrifice of Jesus on the rock transformed the rock into an altar. But in contrast to the altar on the Temple Mount on which animals were sacrificed to atone for sins, and to the Binding of Isaac, which ended with an animal replacing a human sacrifice, on the altar of Golgotha a human was sacrificed to atone for the sins of all the world.

Christian Stories Relating to the Temple Mount

Most of the crucial cosmic events were transferred from the Temple Mount to the Church of the Holy Sepulcher, from one rock to another.[17] Yet the Temple Mount still preserved some holiness for the early Christians because it was the scene of several events in the life of Jesus, of his brother Jacob (James), and of other personalities of his era. When Mary, the mother of Jesus, went to the Temple to offer the obligatory new mother's offering, she brought her baby son Jesus along with her. She put him in a cradle, which she placed in the southeastern corner of the Temple Mount. The place of the Cradle of Jesus is still revered.[18] On that occasion Simon (Peter) saw Jesus and recognized his special destiny (Luke 2:22–34). As an adolescent, Jesus excelled among the pupils who studied on the Temple Mount (Luke 2:46), and as an adult, he preached to the people gathered there and upturned the tables of the moneychangers (Mark 11:15–19). It has been suggested that this act of Jesus reflected his eschatological view that the Temple would be destroyed (Matthew 24:2, Mark 13:2, Luke 21:6). Indeed, when he was brought to trial the High Priest accused him of threatening to destroy the Temple. When he was on the cross, passers-by mockingly called to him, "You that destroy the Temple and build it in three days, save thyself" (Matthew 27:40). It is also told that Satan tried to tempt Jesus near the Temple, and that Zechariah son of Berachia, a contemporary of Jesus, was assassinated between the Temple and the altar. This incident may be a reflection of the story of the assassination of the First Temple period priest Zechariah son of Yehoiada in the court of the Temple by order of King Joash (II Chronicles 24:20–22).

After the death of Jesus, his brother Jacob became a dominant figure among the Jews who followed the message of Jesus.[19] Their church came to be known as the Church of the Circumcised in Jerusalem, and Jacob was appointed its first bishop. According to the creed of this group, as reported by Eusebius who lived in the fourth century, many years after this church no longer existed, Jacob was killed while preaching his religious message on the Temple Mount. It is told that a priest pushed Jacob from one of the towers of the walls that surrounded the Temple onto the pavement of the Temple Mount esplanade, and the crowd that gathered there stoned him. This tradition also claims that Jacob was buried on the Temple Mount, close to the Temple itself.

This is quite unlikely, because a tomb would ritually defile the Temple Mount. However, it is interesting to note that Jewish rabbinical literature contains vestiges of an awareness that tombs indeed once existed on the precinct of the Temple Mount. The meaning of these references is rather enigmatic, because tombs are considered the ultimate source of ritual defilement. Be that as it may, it is said that Jacob's tomb became a holy place for members of the Church of the Circumcised in Jerusalem, who continued to visit it as late as the early second century, some fifty years after the destruction of the Temple. The Church of the Circumcised of Jerusalem dispersed in the course of the second century CE when more and more non-Jews converted to Christianity and the Church of the Gentiles became dominant. The holiness of the Temple Mount did not mean much to these new converts and it was soon forgotten, or rather it became visible evidence to the victory of Christianity over Judaism.

Muslim Myths and Legends
The Adoption of Jewish Legends by Muslims

While the Christians adopted many Jewish myths and legends relating to the Temple Mount. they moved them to the Church of the Holy Sepulcher. Islam, on the other hand, adopted the sanctity and many of the legends centered on Jerusalem, which they named *Bait al-Makdis* (Temple), and especially on the Temple Mount named *Haram a-Sharif* (the Noble Sanctuary).[20] They moved some of the legends to Mecca, maintained many in their original Jewish location, and added new ones. Jews believe in the exclusivity of the Jewish legends relating to the Temple Mount, whereas Muslims believe in the exclusivity of their legends relating to the same place, and herein lies the root of the conflict over the Temple Mount between the two religions.

Why did the Muslims, who, when they took Jerusalem, already had two holy sites in Arabia, Mecca and Medina, adopt the sanctity of Jerusalem and make it their own? Why did they attach themselves to the holy rock on the Mount, the Jewish *Even Shetiyya*, which Muslims call the *sakhra* (rock)? Did they see it as the rock of David, Solomon, and Herod, or as the rock of Muhammad? Why did Caliph 'Omar ibn al-Khattab, conqueror of Jerusalem, clear away the dump and refuse heaped on the site of the former Jewish Temple during centuries of Christian rule? It is, of course, impossible to answer these questions with any degree of certainty. It is not unreasonable to attribute the transfer of the Jewish significance of the site to Muslim identification to Ka'b al-Ahbar, the learned Jew from Yemen who converted to Islam and was guide and counselor to Caliph 'Omar in Jerusalem. If so, the unique position of Jerusalem and the Temple Mount in Islam may have been a continuation of its centrality in Judeo-Christian tradition. In this regard it is interesting to note that Muqqadasi, a notable Muslim writer, admitted that the sanctity of Jerusalem preceded that of Mecca.[21]

Be this as it may, with the adoption of the holiness of the site, the Muslims adopted many of the myths and legends related to it and added some of their own. They also adopted several Christian traditions.[22]

A vast body of Muslim legends and myths relating to the *Haram a-Sharif* and the holy rock is scattered in several volumes of "Praises of Jerusalem" compiled by various writers between the tenth and sixteenth centuries.[23]

Based on earlier collections that include materials dating back to the second half of the seventh century CE, shortly after the advent of Islam, they contain numerous legends and myths, many adopted from Jewish lore, others from Christian lore. The origin of most of these legends is specified. Each legend is pre-

ceded by a long list of people who transmitted the story, often beginning with a known personality who belonged to Muhammad's inner circle. The list of names has great importance in authenticating the material, which was transmitted orally for many generations until it was written down.[24] These important compilations, known by the generic term "Praises of Jerusalem," are supplemented by anthologies, encyclopedic and geographic literature, and other works that are not exclusively devoted to Jerusalem and the *Haram a-Sharif*. Because we are dealing here not with historical fact but with myths, legends, and reflections of imagination, the exact origin of each tradition and its date will not be cited.

It is possible that many of the traditions relating to the sanctity of Jerusalem and the *Haram a-Sharif* can be attributed to the Ummayad period (640–750). This dynasty of Muslim caliphs, which ruled its vast empire from Damascus, aimed at elevating the holiness of Jerusalem and through it the supremacy of Syria over Arabia. Their efforts included the construction of the major projects on the *Haram a-Sharif* and of a series of six huge buildings, one of them undoubtedly a palace, at the foot of the southern wall of the Temple Mount. The legends and myths about the sanctity of the rock, developed perhaps by Muslim sages who were close to Ummayad circles, were a major spiritual supplement to the efforts of the caliphs to raise the status of their own rule though elevating the holiness of Jerusalem.

The large and diverse collection of Muslim legends relating to the Temple Mount can be divided into two major subjects: the flight of the Prophet Muhammad to the rock and from it to heaven, and the rock and its role at the End of Days. While the Night Flight of

Muhammad is an original Muslim tradition, perhaps based on Christian beliefs about the ascent of Jesus to heaven after his crucifixion, the belief in the End of Days and its relationship to the rock owes much to Jewish myths and legends. Having adopted the Jewish traditions, the Muslims embellished them with events and details. They transferred other legends relating to the rock and the Temple Mount from Jerusalem to Mecca. But before examining these two sets of legends, we should consider the *kibla*, the cornerstone of Muslim reverence of Jerusalem.

The Kibla

In the very early days of the formation of Islam, Muhammad turned in his prayer toward Jerusalem, thus making it the first Muslim *kibla* (direction of prayer).[25] No doubt Muhammad was aware of the holiness of Jerusalem to both Jews and Christians, but he never visited the city while awake. It is reported that Muhammad was heard saying: "He who worships in Jerusalem is likened to him who worships in heaven." But when he realized that he would not win the Jews over to his new religion, he changed the direction of prayer to Mecca. Notwithstanding, Jerusalem remained an important place of pilgrimage for the Muslims, following Muhammad's declaration that "There was no nobler purpose than a visit to three mosques: the Mosque of Mecca, his own mosque [in Medina], and the Mosque of *Bait al-Makdis* [Jerusalem]." A story aimed at enhancing the importance of the Temple Mount tells that a woman who donated a skein of wool for *Bait al-Makdis* was admitted to Paradise. However, with the transference of the *kibla* to Mecca, the main Muslim *hajj* (pilgrimage) was also diverted there. Muslim pilgrimage to Jerusalem did not stop, however,

although its importance was greatly reduced and it became only secondary to the *hajj* to Mecca.

The Night Flight and the Ascent to Heaven

The most important Muslim legends relating to the rock connect it with Muhammad's Night Flight (*al Isra'*). In the words of the Koran: "Praise be to him who transported his servant by night from the sacred Mosque of Mecca to the Furthermost Mosque [*al-masjid al-Aqsa*], the precinct of which we have blessed" (Sura 17:1). The meaning of the expression "the Furthermost Mosque" has been disputed since the early days of Islam, and two options were suggested. In the early period, close to the time of Muhammad himself, it was believed that this mosque was the Celestial Temple. Later, after the construction of the Dome of the Rock, Muslim tradition transferred the miraculous journey to Jerusalem, and claimed that the farthest mosque is on the *Haram a-Sharif*.[26] Tradition elaborated on the koranic verse and claimed that the miraculous Night Flight was made on back of the winged animal Burak. After Muhammad reached the *Bait al-Makdis*, he is said to have prayed in the company of the prophets and apostles. The Gates of Heaven were then opened to him, and, aided by the Archangel Gabriel, he ascended to the Seven Heavens, and also to the highest Heaven of Heavens, known only to Allah (*al Ma'raj*). There he received the five prayers every Muslim is commanded to pray every day. The footprints of al-Burak are shown on the southwestern corner of the rock, but the place where he was tied has long been subject to debate. One tradition points to the southwestern corner of the Temple Mount, another to the entrance to the Double Gate in its south wall. In the late nineteenth century,

Ascent of Mohammad to heaven from the Temple Mount.
Persian miniature of the 15th century.

no doubt in reaction to the developing conflict between Jews and Muslims over the use of the Western Wall, a new tradition was invented claiming that the winged animal was tied to the Western Wall holy to the Jews. The combined stories of Muhammad's Night Flight and his Ascent to Heaven are the basis for Muslim reverence of Jerusalem, and the crux of their claim to exclusivity on the Temple Mount / *Haram as-Sharif*.

Several scholars have suggested that the story of the Night Flight and the Ascension is a compilation of two separate traditions. They claim that the original event was the ascent to heaven, which occurred in Mecca and refers to the consecration of Muhammad as prophet. The Night Flight to the Furthermost Mosque, identified with Jerusalem, is a later tradition, dating to the Ummayad period, and especially to the scholarly circles that surrounded 'Abd al-Malik, who built the Dome of the Rock. According to this reconstruction of events, the story of the Night Flight had political intentions, aimed at glorifying Jerusalem and the Temple Mount, on which the Ummayad Dynasty had built magnificent structures, and through it glorifying the dynasty.

To accentuate the importance of the rock as a place from which ascent to heaven could be accomplished, one story relates that when Allah came up to the mountain on which the Temple was standing, the rock showed humility and offered itself to Allah. Allah rewarded it by ascending from it to heaven and at other times by sitting on it as long as he wished. Another story accentuates other qualities of the rock: when Allah ascended to heaven, He said to the Temple rock: "This is my place and the place of my seat, and the place of the assembly of my servants."

The Navel of the Earth and the Transference of Jewish Traditions to Mecca[27]

Having adopted the holiness of the rock, Islam also embraced the Jewish notion that it was the navel of the world. This idea is expressed in various ways, such as in the saying "When Allah created the world, he started from the site of the Temple," which is so similar to Jewish sayings. Another saying is: "Jerusalem is the center of the world," and yet another: "The Mosque is called the Furthermost [al-Aqsa] because it marks the exact center of the world." It has been suggested that the design of the Dome of the Rock built over the rock—a circle surrounded by two octagons–was intended to reflect the notion that the rock was the Navel of the Earth. Despite the great reverence for the navel in Jerusalem, it was later transferred to Mecca, and an Islamic tradition claims that the Ka'ba, the holy shrine in Mecca, is located in the highest place on earth, right beneath the North Star, and therefore is the very center of the earth.

Alongside the transference of the navel, the figure of Abraham was also transferred to Mecca, where Abraham is said to have built the Ka'ba. Moreover, according to Islam it was Ishmael rather than Isaac who was the favorite son of Abraham, and his mother, Hagar, was Abraham's first wife. It was Ishmael who should have been sacrificed, not Isaac, and this event took place in Mecca. The covenant between God and Abraham was sealed over the primordial altar on which generations of his ancestors sacrificed, and which is also the navel of the world. On the occasion of the Binding of Isaac, God promised Abraham that his descendants would be very numerous, and with the transfer to Mecca this promise was transferred from the sons of Isaac, the Jews, to the sons of Ishmael, the Arabs. The Arabs greatly revere Abraham as their ancestor and view themselves as the legitimate sons of Abraham, a fact reflected in their claim to the tombs of the patriarchs in Hebron. This change of characters and locations also implies that Islam preceded Judaism as a monotheistic religion, thus overruling the Jewish claim for greater antiquity.

Another Jewish belief transferred to Mecca is the great antiquity of the Temple in Jerusalem, which was created, so it was related, even before the creation of the universe. One Muslim tradition claims that "Forty years before Allah created the heavens and earth, the Ka'ba was a dry spot floating on the water, and from it the world has been spread out." Thus it was regarded as the navel of the earth. Another tradition relates that "Allah created the spot of this House [the Ka'ba] two thousand years before he created an atom of the earth." The creation of Adam was also transferred from Jerusalem, and Muslims believe that he was not formed from the earth of the rock but from all the elements of the earth gathered in the vicinity of Mecca. But not only

Adam was thus created in Mecca, the Muslim center of the world, so was Muhammad, for a Muslim tradition claims that "the origin of the clay of the apostle of Allah is from the navel of the earth in Mecca." Muslim tradition also places the burial places of Adam and Muhammad at the center of the earth, since it is expected that the substance of the body should return to its place of origin.

The Last Judgment and Resurrection

Even after the transference of the *kibla* and the centrality of the navel of the earth to Mecca, the importance of the holy rock did not diminish. On the contrary, it assumed a new role, becoming the site where events related to the end of the world will unfold.[28] When the *kibla* was transferred from Jerusalem to Mecca, the rock is said to have appealed to Allah, saying that it had never ceased to serve God's servants as *kibla*, and now this task had been taken from it. Allah replied, "Rejoice! For on thee shall I establish My seat, unto thee shall I gather My creatures, on thee shall I bring My judgment unto light, and here shall I resuscitate the dead." Thus, in Muslim tradition many conclusive future cosmic events will occur on the holy rock.

One such momentous event is the Day of Judgment, which will take place on the *Haram a-Sharif.* Allah will sit on his throne, placed on the holy rock that will be converted on that day into a white pearl, and he will pass the Last Judgment. Next to him will stand the scales on which Allah will weigh the souls of the deceased. The angel Israfil will blow the ram's horn to summon all the people of the world to assemble to the Judgment. All the souls of the believers will assemble in the cave under the rock, called the Cave of the Spirits. On that day they will cross the bridge (*sirat*),[29]

which will span the Valley of Jehosaphat (Kidron Valley) to the east of the Temple Mount. The bridge will begin at the still visible pillar stuck in the eastern wall of the Temple Mount, known as the Pillar of Muhammad, and will end on the Mount of Olives. The *sirat* will be long and slippery, narrower than a hair, sharper than a sword, and blacker than the night. Only the virtuous will be able to cross it.

After the Last Judgment, the dead will resurrect, but not before Allah has rebuilt Jerusalem with his own hands and surrounded it with seven walls of precious stones, gold and silver, clouds, and light. He will cover Jerusalem with a dome that will descend from heaven and shine on her like a sun. Then the righteous will go to Paradise, which lies to the right of the holy rock, while the evil people will go to Hell, identified, in the wake of Jewish legends, in the Josaphat Valley. It is told of one of the early Islamic sages that he was seen standing on the eastern wall of Jerusalem and crying. When asked why he was crying, he announced that he saw Hell (Gehenom) and an angel kindling its ashes. Tradition later transferred the place of hell to the valley to the west of Jerusalem, known to this day as Hinnom Valley (*Gehenom* = hell in Hebrew and in Arabic).

The Rock and the Primeval Waters

The connection between the holy rock and Paradise, on the one hand, and between the rock and the subterranean realms of the earth, on the other, is reflected in the notion that the rock has strong connections with the primeval waters. It is said that the first place from which the water of the flood began to recede was the rock. Another tradition claims that the rock was the only spot in the universe left dry

Mohammad's pillar in the south wall of the Temple Mount.
Photographer: Rivka Gonen.

during the flood, and so in a way it was the place where the world began again after the catastrophe of the flood. The Garden of Eden is located not only in the sky or to the right of the rock, but also in the rock itself, which is the source of the four rivers of Paradise, known in Islamic tradition as Sayhun, Gayhun, Euphrates, and Nile. Likewise, "there is no sweet water of which the source does not originate under the holy rock at Jerusalem" and "all rivers and clouds and

vapors and winds come from under the holy rock in Jerusalem." It is also said that he who comes to Jerusalem shall bathe in the source of the Silwan (Siloam), which springs from the Garden of Eden.[30]

Celestial and Terrestrial Temples

Other aspects of the connection between the holy rock and heaven as reflected in Islamic lore are expressed in the saying, "Allah said to the rock: Thou art my nearest seat, from thee did I ascend to heaven, and under thee did I spread the earth like a carpet." This saying combines three notions, two adopted from Jewish traditions. The rock is *Even Shetiyya*, from which the whole creation began, and is also close to the seat of God in heaven, as the celestial Temple is to the terrestrial one.[31]

According to Muslim tradition, the heavens opened up above the rock in Jerusalem, and Paradise, which is called "The House of Peace" in Muslim tradition, is believed to be located in the Seventh Heaven above Jerusalem, so that if a stone fell from Paradise it would fall on the rock. However, the idea of the existence of a celestial temple against a terrestrial one was transferred to Mecca. In Muslim tradition, the upper temple, surrounded by 70,000 angels, floats above the Ka'ba. As for the terrestrial temple, Islamic tradition claimed that the Ka'ba in Mecca was first built by angels before the creation of the world, and then by Abraham, who is a central figure among Muslim prophets.

Muslim tradition accepts the fact that Solomon's Temple was in Jerusalem and that it was built on a very early foundation. Like the Ka'ba it was first built by the angels, after which it was restored by Adam, then by Shem son of Noah, then by Isaac son of Abraham, and eventually by David and Solomon. The Dome of the Rock built by 'Abd el-Malik is, in Muslim tradition, considered a unit in the long chain of temples built over the holy rock.[32]

Muslim tradition has never abandoned the sanctity of Jerusalem, despite its definite preference for Mecca. It claims that at the End of Days, on the Day of Resurrection, Jerusalem and Mecca will be joined together and the Ka'ba in Mecca will be transferred to Jerusalem as a bride is transferred to her husband's home. The Ka'ba will be accompanied by all the pilgrims who had visited it, and by all the mosques where Allah worshipped. The meaning of this very surprising saying is that on that day the old sanctity of Jerusalem will have the upper hand over the newer sanctity of Mecca, and the Jewish holy rock, the *Even Shetiyya*, will replace the Muslim shrine, the Ka'ba.

Jews and Muslims share the central myths of the beginning of the universe and its end in the day of ultimate judgment and also the location of these events—the Temple Mount/*Haram a-Sharif*. This sharing has not promoted understanding between the two religions. On the contrary, the heavy burden of these and many other myths, and the desire of both Jews and Muslims for exclusivity over the place where they occurred or where they will eventually occur, has only helped fuel the competition between them. When combined with national feelings and aspirations, these myths and traditions have enflamed the hostility and violence between them for the last hundred years. The history and present-day situation of this conflict is the subject of chapter 7.

Notes

[1] Campbell 1973: 3–4.

[2] Hobschawn 1997: 4–6.

[3] Ginzberg Vol. 1 1913: 12; Noy 1968.

[4] Eliav 2001: 45–47.

[5] Wensink 1916; Eliade 1961: 36–47.

[6] Townsend 1987: 508–512.

[7] Eliade and Sullivan 1987: 166–171.

[8] Gafni 1999:39–40.

[9] Wensink 1916; Long 1987: 94–100.

[10] Ginzberg Vol V 1913: 125–127.

[11] Ibid 166.

[12] Ibid 285.

[13] Ibid 350.

[14] Ibid 352.

[15] Optovitzer 1930.

[16] Elad 2001: 80–82.

[17] Eliav 2001: 52–53.

[18] Le Strange 1965: 166–167.

[19] Eliav 2001: 40–42.

[20] Hirschberg 1951–52.

[21] Le Strange 1965:85.

[22] Livne–Kafri 2000: 8–12.

[23] Hasson 1996: 365–377; Elad 2001:58–59.

[24] Livne–Kafri 2000: 1–6.

[25] Hasson 1996: 352.

[26] Ibid 335–359.

[27] Livne–Kafri 2000: 17–18.

[28] Milstein 1999: 43–46.

[29] Livne–Kafri 2000: 18; 47–48.

[30] Ibid: 25–28.

[31] Ibid: 35–38.

[32] Ibid 2000: 102.

Chapter 6
A Century of National-Religious Conflict Between Jews and Arabs

The ongoing conflict over the Temple Mount between Jews and Arabs lies at the heart of a hundred-year conflict between these two people in the small piece of land known as the Holy Land, Israel, or Palestine. At present, although the Temple Mount compound, being part of Jerusalem, is under Israeli rule, the internal autonomy is in the hands of the Muslim authorities. The weekly communal prayers of the multitude of Muslims who flock to the al-Aqsa Mosque on the *Haram a-Sharif* every Friday is always feared because it carries the potential of a violent outbreak. Stones thrown from the esplanade have fallen on Jews who congregate at the Western Wall at the foot of the Temple Mount to pray. Arson, shooting, and killing have occurred on the Temple Mount, causing the spread of violence on both sides. Both Jews and Muslims declare their exclusive right to the area and are unwilling to share it. How did the situation deteriorate to what it is today? To answer this question, one has to go back in time and describe the birth and development of national-religious sentiments and movements in both contesting parties.

The Conflict in the Ottoman Period

Until the end of World War I, the entire Middle East was under Ottoman rule for 400 years. During the hundreds of years of its rule, the Ottoman authorities neglected their territorial holdings, which sank into poverty and apathy. The situation changed dramatically in the nineteenth century, when in 1832 Ibrahim Pasha, son of Muhammad Ali, the ruler of Egypt, conquered Palestine and introduced a firm control over it, which brought about the lessening of disorder. This situation did not last long, and in 1841 Ottoman rule was resumed with all its woes and mismanagement. Shortly afterwards, in the wake of the Crimean War (1853–1856), several European countries demanded and received a position of influence in the affairs of the Ottoman Empire in general, and of Palestine, holy to the Christian world, in particular. The Ottoman Empire was made to introduce changes in its constitution and to establish a firmer hand in local matters.

The Nascence of Arab National Feelings

Toward the end of the century, winds of modernization and western trends began to influence even this remote corner of the empire, bringing about major changes in public as well as in the everyday lives of its citizens. In order to hold on to their power despite these changes, and especially after the

1908 Young Turk Revolution in Turkey, the Ottomans did not allow local Arabs, some of whom were educated in religious Christian institutions, to occupy civilian or military positions. These were held exclusively by personnel sent from Turkey,[1] who to some extent perpetuated the policy of inefficiency and corruption. The misrule of the Ottomans, the policy of barring locals from high positions, as well as the influence of growing national sentiment in various parts of the empire, especially in the Balkans, influenced several Arab intellectuals, who began to harbor a nascent local Arab identity. Urban intellectuals began to cultivate anti-Ottoman sentiments, which slowly increased and spread.

Arab nationalist organizations were formed and gradually gained support. Among the early supporters of these organizations were urban Greek Orthodox Christians, the largest group of Christians in the country. The majority of the local Greek Orthodox community were Arabs, for generations converted to Christianity. The clergy, however, was always Greek, born and educated in Greece. This situation caused growing distress among the local Christian Arabs, who demanded that they too be ordained and serve their community. These feelings of deprivation among the local Christian Arabs, along with anti-Ottoman political feelings, led to the formation of an early national Arab secular organization.

At this early stage, adherents of this and other organizations had not yet established an overall local national Arab movement and expressed themselves mainly in private meetings. Yet they could be considered the kernel of a growing local Arab national identity, in which Muslim Arabs and Christian Arabs cooperated.[2] From its early days, the nascent movement was confronted with conflicting views on the question of its relations with the Arab world. Some of its members supported a pan-Arabic ideology, which claimed that the local Arabs were an integral part of the larger Arab world and should join forces with general Arab causes. Others upheld a local Arab ideology, encouraging locals to concentrate on the situation in Palestine, take their destiny in their own hands, and not become involved in outside issues.

The Effect of Jewish Immigration on the Palestinian Arabs

In addition to the discontent with the Ottoman rule and the growing objection to the massive interference of foreign powers in local affairs, there was another important source of growing dissatisfaction—the gradual increase in the number of Jews and in their activities in the country. Despite the destruction of the Jewish Temples and their loss of political domination over the land, Jews were always present in the country in larger or smaller numbers. Since the Mamluk period, and more so during the Ottoman period, the small local community grew, and in the nineteenth century the trickle of Jews who immigrated into the country gradually increased. By the middle of the century there was already a substantial Jewish population in the country, centered mainly in Jerusalem, where by the 1860s they were the largest population group.

Among the Jewish immigrants who came to the country in the 1880s and later, some were of a different, hitherto unknown type. Rather than joining their Orthodox brothers in the holy towns of Jerusalem, Hebron, Safed, and Tiberias and live a religious life of poverty and dependency on foreign alms, these new immigrants came with the express intention of becoming become farmers and establishing agricultural settlements. For this they needed land, which they purchased from Arab property owners. The growth in the number of Jews in the country, coupled with the purchase of land for the establishment of new settlements, began to cause alarm among the Arab population.[3] The peasants of the countryside, more or less indifferent to the stresses of Ottoman rule and not yet influenced by the new notion of Arab national sentiment, which was urban in nature, felt the gradual loss of the land they had cultivated as shareholders. They developed anti-Jewish feelings that expressed themselves in occasional localized attacks on the tiny new settlements and the killing of settlers. The confrontation with the Jewish settlement movement added yet another aspect to the growth of local Arab national sentiment.

Another issue that was to flare up in the succeeding period was the issue of the Western Wall. The Ottomans recognized the sanctity to the Jews of the Western Wall (or the Wailing Wall, as it is known to Christians), the section of the ancient Herodian wall surrounding the Temple Mount that is closest to the Jewish Quarter of the Old City. It is possible that official recognition of the right of Jews to pray by the Wall was granted already in the second half of the sixteenth century by a *firman* (official decree) issued by Sultan Suleiman the Magnificent. This *firman* may have been related to the efforts of the Ottoman ruler to lure Jews to Palestine as a counterbalance to the Arab population, which had rebelled against the new rulers, who were Turkish rather than Arabs.[4] In 1320 the area in front of the Western Wall was declared by the Abu

Maydan family a *waqf* (property donated by families or organizations to secure income for specific charitable purposes) to support North African pilgrims to the *Haram a-Sharif*. While allowing the Jews to pray at the Wall, the Ottomans forbade them from bringing chairs, benches, and prayer tables, or a partition to divide the area into men's and women's sections. The Jerusalem Jews of the Ottoman period, who for many centuries were few and without any power to thwart them, kept these regulations. When the regulations were later endorsed by the British Mandate, at a time when the Jews began claiming their rights in this holy place, they became the source of many of the Western Wall clashes that occurred in that period.

As against the sporadic actions of the local urban and rural Arabs, the Zionist Movement, which began officially in 1899 as an organized secular Jewish political organization, was gaining power and increasing its membership both locally and among the Jews of the diaspora. The aim of Zionism was to recruit more and more Jews to settle in Palestine and to build new settlements, with the hope of eventually establishing a national home for the scattered Jews. It worked toward this goal by collecting Jewish contributions and establishing funds allocated to the purchase of land and the building of settlements. The example of this national Jewish organization was eventually to trigger the creation of an Arab national movement, during World War I.

Jews and Arabs under British Mandate, 1919–1948

Early British Attitudes Toward Jewish National Aspirations

The total defeat of the Ottomans in World War I (1914–1919) brought about the collapse of the 400-year-old empire. While the war was still raging, Britain, which was about to receive the Mandate over Palestine, issued the Balfour Declaration on November 2, 1917. This declaration, which some view as the most outstanding political act in the modern history of England, while others consider it an ominous British mistake, promised the Jews a national home in Palestine. The declaration was motivated both by pragmatic reasons, such as the continuing Arab opposition to Jewish settlement in the country, and also presumably by fundamentalist Protestant sentiment in England. For English people, educated as they all were on the Bible, the return of the Jews to their homeland was viewed as an act dictated by God. Giving God a helping hand in fulfilling his scheme for his people was considered a major privilege for Britain. The declaration was approved on October 31, 1917 by the British cabinet, and was publicized two days later in the form of a letter written by the British foreign minister, Lord Balfour, to Lord Lionel de Rothschild. While many high British officials viewed Zionist aspirations favorably, many military officers stationed in Palestine during and after the war were, under the influence of the deeds of Lawrence of Arabia, more pro-Arab.[5] They opposed Zionism, and strove to tip the balance of the British rule toward the local Palestinians, thus arousing strife between Jews and Arabs.

Chaim Weizmann, the head of the Zionist Organization, who had been instrumental in persuading the British government to issue the Balfour Declaration, tried to persuade the military rulers of Palestine during the war years to support Zionist activities. At the same time he attempted to reach an understanding with the national Arab movement, established during the war. Weizmann negotiated with Emir Faisal, whom the British crowned king of Syria, and on January 3, 1919 the two men signed an agreement of cooperation between "two people with ancient blood relations." Neither leader was aware of the conflict within the Arab national movement between pan-Arabic desires to unite the local Arabs and their Middle Eastern brothers, and the aspirations of the local Arabs to separate themselves from the rest of the Arab world and build a new national entity. In the last minute before the agreement was signed, Faisal added a handwritten sentence declaring that cooperation with the Zionists would materialize only when Arab national aspirations were totally fulfilled. These aspirations were not specified, and the reasons why Faisal added this sentence are not clear. The local Arabs immediately published an objection to the legality of this agreement.[6]

At the same time the French obtained a mandate over Syria, and Faisal found himself a king without a kingdom. Thus the agreement not only was annihilated but caused the heightening of the national conflict between the Jews and the Arabs.

The overthrow of Faisal put an end to the aspirations of those Arabs who wanted to join with Syria and form a large kingdom of Syria, in which Palestine would be Southern Syria. They turned their efforts to strengthening the local National Palestinian Movement, which, still being a novel idea in Arab society, only added to its fragmentation between the forward-looking urban and the traditional rural segments.[7] The movement did not reach its full bloom during the British Mandate period. This happened only in the later period, after the establishment of the State of Israel.

The Issue of the Western Wall

In July 1920 the military rule established by the victorious British at the end of World War I ended and the period of the British Mandate over Palestine began. The first Jewish-Arab dispute over the Western Wall occurred early in 1920, before the period of military rule ended. The Muslim authorities made minor repairs to the upper courses of the Western Wall. The Jews objected to these activities and appealed to the British military authorities, saying that the repairs were necessary, but, because the Wall was an ancient relic, they had to be made under the supervision of the newly formed Department of Antiquities.[8] Thus Herbert Samuel, the first British high commissioner of Palestine, inherited an atmosphere of conflict. Optimistically, he hoped to bridge over the deteriorating relations between Jews and Arabs. Being a Jew himself, he had the confidence of the Jewish population, and in order to win the Arab side

Jews praying by the Western Wall. Photographer: Eric Matson, 1910.
© 1997–1998, The State of Israel, Government Press Office.

he appointed Hajj Amin al-Husayni, a known supporter of Arab nationalism, to the post of *mufti* (highest legal authority on religious matters) of Jerusalem. Shortly afterwards al-Husayni was also elected head of the Supreme Muslim Council.

As *mufti*, Hajj Amin al-Husayni had at his disposal ample resources obtained from income derived from property donated to the *waqf* of the *Haram a-Sharif*, established in 1432 to manage assets and real estate donated to the *Haram* and use their proceeds for its upkeep. He first initiated a project of restoration of the al-Aqsa Mosque, which had fallen into a deplorable condition because of recurrent earthquakes and poor maintenance during the Ottoman period. But at the same time, and with the same resources, he began to play an important role in enflaming the already tense relations between Jews and Muslims in Jerusalem. To do this he made use of the holiness of the Temple Mount as well as of other holy Muslim sites, converting them into symbols of the conflict.

He began with the yearly pilgrimage to Nebi Musa, the site in the Judean Desert where the Muslims believe Moses was buried. The Nebi Musa pilgrimage, the most important Muslim pilgrimage in Palestine at the time, began in Jerusalem, marched to Nebi Musa, and then returned to Jerusalem. It always coincided with the Greek Orthodox Easter, and was therefore always a source of Muslim-Christian tension in the city. In April 1920 the Nebi Musa pilgrimage coincided both with the Orthodox Easter and with the Jewish Passover.

Hajj Amin al-Husayni used this occasion to deliver a fiercely incendiary speech against Jewish prayer at the Western Wall to the thousands of Arab pilgrims who congregated at

the *Haram a-Sharif* on their way back from Nebi Musa. During a retaliatory anti-Arab demonstration organized by the Revisionist Jewish Movement, riots began. The Arab participants, armed with sticks, stones, and daggers, attacked the Jews of the Old City of Jerusalem and then in other places. Five Jews and four Arabs were killed, and many were wounded. Husayni escaped to Jordan, and the British sentenced him in absentia to ten years in prison. Ze'ev Jabotinski, head of the Revisionist Jewish Movement, was sentenced to fifteen years in prison. They were both pardoned shortly afterwards.[9]

The 1920 Nebi Musa incident raised the prestige of this yearly pilgrimage and of the person who had used it for anti-Jewish propaganda. While up till then the main participants in the pilgrimage had been Arabs from Jerusalem and vicinity, now more and more pilgrims from other parts of the country joined it. The Nebi Musa pilgrimage became a national Palestinian event, and Hajj Amin al-Husayni became the recognized leader of the local Arab population. He instantly used his growing prestige and, on November 2, 1921, the anniversary of the Balfour Declaration, incited crowds assembled at the *Haram a-Sharif* to act. The crowds rushed out of the gates of the *Haram* and attacked Jews in both the Old City and the new suburbs of Jerusalem.

Because of the age-old conflicts between the numerous Muslim, Christian, and Jewish sects and groups over the ownership and ways to regulate the numerous holy sites in Jerusalem and in Palestine, the British authorities, in 1924, published a King's Order in Council concerning the Holy Places. This was an official proclamation of freedom of worship in the holy places for all people. The

Order in Council was a reconfirmation of an internationally recognized status quo relating to Christian places of worship that had existed in the Ottoman period, with the addition of two Jewish holy sites, the Western Wall and Rachel's Tomb near Bethlehem. The order is still valid. The Temple Mount, for centuries under sole Muslim control and therefore not contested, was not included in the act.

The King's Act of 1924 recognized the ownership of the Muslim *waqf* over the Western Wall and the narrow alley in front of it, but at the same time specifically acclaimed the sanctity of the site to Jews and gave them the right to pray there.[10]

Despite this official act, the budding National Palestinian Movement was afraid the Jews would use the Western Wall as a springboard to eventually control the Temple Mount. In the newspaper *El-Yarmuk* of October 18, 1925, Hajj Amin al Husayni claimed that Jewish devotion at the Western Wall was a disguise of "their desired aspiration to gain control over the *Haram a-Sharif*, which is well known to all." Indeed the Jews approached the Muslim *waqf* several times with a proposal that they purchase the Western Wall and were refused.[11] The *waqf* did not even allow the Jews to repair the pavement in front of the Wall at their own expense. In accordance with the Ottoman *firman* and the King's Order in Council of 1924, the Muslims objected to the temporary arrangements the Jews made in preparation for the Sabbath and holiday services. The temporary partition between men and women, temporary benches, portable Holy Ark, and Torah scrolls that the Jews kept placing at the Western Wall despite Arab and British opposition were viewed by the Arabs as signs of the Jewish desire to win the place for themselves.

The great importance of the Western Wall as a remnant of the Temple Mount for Jews and as a sacred place for Muslims is exemplified by Jewish words and by Muslim actions. Jews relate to the Western Wall in a very personal way. To them, when a person dies his family mourns him for a year or two, after which the tears dry out and the deceased is gradually forgotten. Jews have been mourning the destruction of the Temple for thousands of years, and their tears are still flowing. If they still have the strength to cry over it, it is a sign that for them the Temple is not dead.

The Muslims, on the other hand, did not cry but resorted to activity. During the Middle Ages the Jews used to pray by the Gate of Mercy on the eastern wall of the Temple Mount. At that time the Muslims disregarded the Western Wall and, in fact, used to throw dirt and dung next to it. To prevent Jewish prayer at the Gate of Mercy, the Muslims sanctified it by declaring it the place where Muhammad had tethered his winged beast al-Burak when he arrived in Jerusalem on his Night Flight, despite the Muslim historian Ibn al Fakih, who wrote in 903 that Muhammad tied al-Burak "under the corner of the al-Aqsa Mosque."[12]

The Jews then forsook the Gate of Mercy and, after settling in the Jewish Quarter of the Old City, began to pray at the Western Wall and obtained the official permission of the Ottoman rulers to do so. This permit protected Jewish interests at the Western Wall until the middle of the nineteenth century, when the influx of Jews into the country and the growing number of visitors to the Western Wall alarmed the Muslim authorities. They now proclaimed that the location of the tethering of al-Burak was not the Gate of Mercy but the Western Wall.[13] They also established a mosque in honor of the fabled beast in the subterranean passage behind Barclay's Gate, south of the Western Wall. This transference, which sanctified the Western Wall for Muslims, was one of the first documented religious-national political acts designed to prevent the Jews from praying at their holy place. Others were to follow.

Thus the rights of use of the Western Wall became the one of the major bones of contention between Jews and Arabs during the British Mandate period.

Arab-Jewish Armed Conflicts in the 1920s and 1930s

The issue flared on the eve of the Day of Atonement (September 23) in 1928, while Jews were deep in prayer near the Western Wall.

The British police, responding to a complaint filed by the Arabs, insisted that the temporary partition between the men's and the women's section be immediately removed although prayers were still going on. The Jews promised that it would be removed at the end of the next day. But when a British officer visited the place during the day, the Day of Atonement itself, he found the partition still there. He called for British police officers, who entered the area and cleared it of its furniture. A riot ensued, and several people were wounded.[14] Hajj Amin al-Husayni immediately made use of this incident to incite the Arab public. He sent bulletins to Muslim newspapers around the world in which he denounced the alleged defilement of Muslim holy sites, declared that the Jews were plan-

British soldiers bar entry to the Temple Mount. Photographer: Eric Matson, 1938. © 1997–1998, The State of Israel, Government Press Office.

The narrow alley in front of the Western Wall. Photographer: Hans Pinn, 1947. © 1997–1998, The State of Israel, Government Press Office.

ning to take control of the entire Temple Mount, and called for a holy war to protect Muslim sanctity. The Jewish National Committee published a counter-statement expressing its respect for the religious feelings of Muslims and calling them to respect the rights of the Jews. It also clarified that the attempt to attribute to the Jews a desire to use the Western Wall as a base for an attack on the Temple Mount was completely false.[15]

On November 1 of that year the *mufti* organized a large demonstration in which he called on the British authorities to stop the Jews from bringing ritual items to the Western Wall. To further obstruct Jewish prayers at that site so holy to them, the *mufti* ordered a breach opened in the wall at the edge of the alley adjacent to the Western Wall. The cul-de-sac alley now became a two-way thorough-fare, through which people and donkeys would pass and disturb the praying Jews.[16] To further disrupt Jewish prayers, he placed an announcer on a nearby Muslim prayer tower, who five times a day called out loudly to the Muslims to come to pray. He also estab-lished a place for Muslim mystics who held wild ceremonies in the Mughrabi neighbor-hood adjacent to the Western Wall, and encouraged the residents of the neighborhood to harm the Jews on their way to the Wall. As a result of all these events, the Jews and the Arabs established separate committees for the protection of the Western Wall and the *Haram a-Sharif.*

In early August 1929 the *mufti* incited Arabs to hit Jews who prayed at the Western Wall and break their ritual objects. Shortly afterwards, on the ninth day of Av, the anniversary of the burning of the First as well as the Second Jewish Temple, a large Jewish demonstration organized by the Revisionist Movement marched toward the Western Wall carrying the Jewish national flag. The *mufti* again assembled a large Arab demonstration that passed by the Western Wall calling for the slaughter of Jews.[17] Rumors were circulated by the *mufti* that the Jews had attacked Arabs, were about to attack the *Haram a-Sharif*, and had cursed Muhammad. A large crowd of Arabs from Jerusalem and vicinity gathered on the Temple Mount, burst out of the gates, attacked Jews praying by the Wall with stones, sticks, knives, and daggers, and tore and burned their Torah scrolls.[18] The disturbances spread to the Old City, and eventually the sporadic attacks flared into an all-out offensive against many Jewish neighborhoods in the new sections of Jerusalem, some of which had to be evacuated and were set on fire. The worst violence occurred in Hebron, where many Jews were massacred and those who survived left the town.

A committee appointed by the British to investigate the reasons for the severe clashes concluded that the Western Wall has become a symbol of national pride for both Jews and Muslims, and that the question of the rights of both sides was national rather than just religious. The British forwarded the issue to the League of Nations, which set up an international commission to investigate the subject. The commission recognized, as so many had done before, that the Muslims held the ownership over the Wall, but held, at the same time, that the Jews had the right to pray there. Unlike earlier rulings, it allowed the Jews to bring a few specified ritual objects to the Western Wall, but prohibited them from blowing the *shofar* (ram's horn) on the High Holidays and organizing political demonstrations there.

The Muslims objected to the commission's decisions. In 1930 Hajj Amin al-Hussein wrote a memorandum condemning "The active widespread propaganda undertaken by the Jews with the view of influencing the London government as well as the League of Nations in order to take possession of the Western Wall of the Mosque al-Aqsa, called al-Buraq, or to raise claims over the place." He further noted that "Having realized by bitter experience the unlimited greedy aspirations of the Jews in this respect, Muslims believe that the Jews' aim is to take possession of the Mosque of al-Aqsa gradually on the pretense that it is the Temple, by starting with the Western Wall of this place, which is an inseparable part of the mosque of al-Aqsa."[19]

In retaliation to his objection to the decisions of the committee, the British stripped Hajj Amin al-Husayni of his position as head of the religious Muslim courts and also took away his control of the *waqf* income. The Jews, on the other hand, agreed to most of the commission's decisions, except for the prohibition on blowing the *shofar*. From now on members of Beitar, the youth movement of the Revisionist Movement, would smuggle a *shofar* to the Western Wall every year on the High Holidays and blow it despite the threat of being caught and imprisoned. The entire Jewish population of the country caught its breath on every such occasion to hear whether the *shofar* had indeed been blown and what the consequences of this act were.[20]

The Western Wall incidents of 1928–1929 again established Hajj Amin al-Husayni as the most important leader of the Palestinian Arabs and aroused their political awareness. Making use of his growing prestige, al-Husayni, in December 1931, convened an international Muslim conference in Jerusalem to discuss the issue of the Western Wall. Delegates from various Muslim countries participated, making this the first time Muslims from other countries became involved in the affairs of Palestine. Especially active in support of the local Arabs were the delegates from India, who were themselves under British rule and felt under pressure of the Hindus over the possession of religious sites.

The most severe clashes between Arabs, Jews, and the British government occurred in 1936–1939.[21] These events broke out, not because of the Western Wall, but because of Arab objections to the immigration of Jews, especially from Nazi Germany. They feared that the Jews would soon become the largest and most dominant section of the country's population to the point of obtaining control over it. In fact, the "disturbances," as the bloody events were called by the British authorities, were an Arab revolt against British rule in an attempt to win the country for themselves. This time the events, which included many attacks on Jewish settlements, transportation, and citizens, began in the town of Jaffa and spread to Jerusalem and the rest of the country. The clashes in Jerusalem were particularly fierce.

After the assassination of the British governor of the Galilee, the government took action and imprisoned and then deported several Arab leaders. Hajj Amin al-Husayni himself found refuge on the Temple Mount and continued to enflame events from there. Three months later he scaled the wall of the Temple Mount, escaping to Jaffa and from there to Lebanon. Other members of the Arab leadership took over, and the revolt, which continued for a while, became even fiercer. The combined forces of the British army and police and Jewish defense organizations eventually managed to quell the mutiny, which died out in early 1939 with the collapse of the National Arab Movement in Jerusalem.

It should be noted that in 1937, while the Arab revolt was still in full force, especially in Jerusalem, David Ben-Gurion, the head of the Jewish Agency, wrote that he was prepared to divide Jerusalem into two municipal entities, one Jewish, one Arab. The Arab section was to include the Arab neighborhoods of east Jerusalem, and the Jewish section would include the Jewish neighborhoods in west Jerusalem. The Old City, with the Temple Mount, would be converted into a cultural-spiritual-religious museum for all religions under international protection. Only such a separation, he believed, would encourage the creative powers of the Jewish people and turn their city into a real national magnet.

Behind Ben-Gurion's suggestion was his desire to shake off the burden of holiness from Jerusalem, entrust the Western Wall and the Temple Mount to the hands of the international community, and build a new Jewish secular city.[22] Ben-Gurion repeated these same suggestions in 1947 to a special committee appointed by the United Nations to investigate the situation in Palestine.[23] The report of this committee, presented to the secretary general of the United Nations, included two options for solving the volatile situation in Palestine. The majority of the committee members opted for the suggestion that two states be formed in Palestine, one Jewish, and the other Arab, and that Jerusalem and its vicinity be internationalized under a United Nations trusteeship. This suggestion, so it was believed, would protect the holy places and promise free access to them according to the British Mandate's Order in Council. Behind the suggestion to internationalize Jerusalem stood the Vatican, which presented theological objections to placing the Christian holy sites under Jewish rule.[24] The minority of committee members urged the establishment of a federation consisting of a Jewish state and an Arab state, with Jerusalem as its capital.

The proposal of the majority of committee members was presented to the General Assembly of the United Nations, which endorsed it on November 29, 1947. This decision opened the way to the establishment of the State of Israel in part of the Jewish territory of Palestine, and of an Arab state in the other part, populated by Arabs. The Arabs did not accept the United Nations resolution, and even before the British Mandate ended and the State of Israel was officially declared, they started a war against the Jewish population of the country.

On the whole, the British Mandate, despite its attempts, did not manage to understand the depth of feeling of both the Jews and the Arabs, and the profound differences between their respective characters and modes of behavior. The British were not able to find a common denominator between the national and religious aspirations of the two sides and to form a sustainable cooperation or even a temporary agreement between them. Perhaps it was not possible to find a compromise between Jews and Arabs even then. The events that occurred during the British Mandate period around the Temple Mount and the Western Wall foreshadowed the attitudes of both Jews and Arabs after 1967, which often flared into violent action.

The 1948 War and Its Consequences

Even before the British Mandate ended, the growing conflict between Jews and Arabs flared into a full-fledged war. The war in Jerusalem, a city with a mixed population and with sites of powerfully contesting holiness, was especially fierce. Jewish Jerusalem was cut off from the coastal plain and came under heavy shelling, and the Jewish Quarter in the Old City was besieged. Its population, mainly old with few armed defenders, could not hold on. Eventually, after house-to-house fighting, the Jewish Quarter fell on May 28, 1948 to the Jordanian Arab Legion, which had joined the war to aid the local Palestinian irregular militia.[25]

One last attempt to recapture the Old City was made on July 16, 1948, on the eve of a cease-fire, when Jewish forces attacked the Old City from three sides: from the Jaffa Gate in the west, from the New Gate in the northwest, and from the Zion Gate in the south. The spirit of the attackers was high, the fighters hoping not only to regain control over the Jewish Quarter but also to take over the Temple Mount. This prospect aroused deeply imbedded messianic aspirations even in the hearts of nonreligious soldiers. They were so sure of success, and the capture of the Temple Mount seemed so close at hand, that the secular commander of the operation prepared a lamb to be sacrificed on the Temple Mount.

The head of one of the ultranationalist militias (the so-called Stern Gang) that took part in the attack secretly planned to blow up the Dome of the Rock and eventually replace it with a Third Temple.

Despite the high hopes, the attack failed.[26] No further attempt to take over the Old City was made, as Israel and Jordan, both objecting to the idea of internationalizing Jerusalem, acted in unison to divide the city between their two countries and not let it be put under international mandate. The Old City, with the sites holy to the Jews, remained in Jordanian hands for nineteen years.

The Temple Mount became an Arab national shrine, with the burial at its west wall of Abdul Kader el-Husayni, leader of one of the irregular militias active during the 1948 war in the Jerusalem area.

Now the conflict seemingly subsided. The Muslims had exclusive control not only over the Temple Mount, as they had had for centuries, but also over the Western Wall. Despite a specific clause in the 1949 Armistice Agreement between Israel and the Hashemite kingdom of Jordan to the effect that Jews would have free access to their holy places, they were completely barred from visiting the Western Wall and from the synagogues of the Old City. The local Arab population, found housing in the evacuated Jewish Quarter and, with the aid of the Jordanian authorities, destroyed all of the Quarter's synagogues. The yearning of Jews for their holy places found an outlet on the roof of the combined mosque/church on Mount Zion, allegedly the location of the tomb of King David and site of the Last Supper; from there they could get a glimpse of the Temple Mount.

The Hashemite kingdom of Jordan annexed Jerusalem along with the Arab section of Palestine known as the West Bank. In 1951 King 'Abdullah of Jordan established the post of Guardian of the *Haram a-Sharif* and Supreme Custodian of the Holy Places of all Other Religions; it superseded the Supreme Muslim Council, which had administered the site during the British Mandate period. The Jordanian government now exerted control over the compound through the newly established department. The Guardian of the *Haram a-Sharif* now appointed supporters of Jordan in Jerusalem to the staff of the compound and paid their salaries. The income obtained from the many rich assets accumulated over the centuries and owned by the *waqf* of the *Haram* was used by the Jordanian government to strengthen its position in the West Bank and particularly in Jerusalem. To emphasize Jordanian control over the West Bank and Jerusalem, King 'Abdullah used to regularly pray on the Temple Mount. In July 20, 1951, as he was coming out of the al-Aqsa Mosque after the mid-day prayer, King 'Abdullah was assassinated by a Palestinian extremist, apparently from among the followers of Hajj Amin al-Husayni, now exiled in Cairo.[27]

Notes

[1] Porath 1972:23–24.
[2] Ibid. 1972:293–303.
[3] Ibid 31–39.
[4] Ben–Dov 1983:34.
[5] Porat 1972:258–273
[6] Ibid 1972:134.
[7] Ibid 1972:89
[8] Friedland and Hecht 1991: 31–32.
[9] Schure 1987:763–765.
[10] Berkovitz 2000:31–32.
[11] Ben–Dov 1983: 125–126; Friedlander and Hecht 1991: 33.
[12] Le Strange 1965: 163.
[13] Berkovitz 2001:22–26.
[14] Ben–Dov 1983: 128–130; Friedland and Hecht 1991: 32.
[15] Ben–Dov 1983: 130–131.
[16] Friedland and Hecht 1991: 32.
[17] Schure 1987: 775–780.
[18] Friedland and Hecht 1991: 34.
[19] Ibid 1991: 21.
[20] Ben–Dov 1983: 132–134.
[21] Schure 1987: 804–810.
[22] Berkovitz 200:35
[23] Schure 1987: 821.
[24] Ferrari 1999: 143–165.
[25] Schure 1987: 844–845.
[26] Shragai 1995: 15–17.
[27] Friedland and Hecht 1991: 35.

Chapter 7
The Present Conflict

The Six-Day War and Its Aftermath

On June 4, 1976, the Jordanian army opened artillery fire on Jewish Jerusalem from its positions along the cease-fire line between the two parts of the city. Israel retaliated and began surrounding the Old City from the north, west, south, and east. A historic opportunity to capture the Old City now presented itself, but was hotly debated among politicians and generals, some of whom remembered that David Ben-Gurion had been ready in 1947 to hand over the Old City with all its holy places to international rule. Moshe Dayan, the defense minister, also objected to the attack, but he was overruled, and on June 6 the Old City fell to Israeli paratroopers. The Old City was entered on this occasion from the east, through the Lion's Gate which is adjacent to the Temple Mount, and minutes after entering the city soldiers and officers swarmed into the holy edifice, which had been totally out of bounds to Jews for almost 2,000 years. Some went down to the Western Wall, to which no Jew had access for the nineteen years of Jordanian rule. In a regimental assembly held on the Temple Mount, the commander reminded his men that in ancient times, when the Temple Mount was captured by the Greeks, the Maccabees fought to liberate it.

When the Romans destroyed it, Bar Kokhba and his army fought them. For 2,000 years Jews had been barred from the Temple Mount, and now, he said, the paratroopers had given it back to the nation.[1] In the messianic atmosphere that engulfed the country, several rabbis contemplated blowing up the Temple Mount mosques.[2]

The new situation that put the holy places in Jerusalem and around the country under the jurisdiction of the victorious Israelis created administrative and theological problems for both Christians and Muslims. For Christianity Jewish supremacy reversed the age-old order by which Christianity had replaced the downtrodden Jews as the True Israel. The Muslims too had regarded the Jews, for many centuries, as subordinate to them.

The Western Wall at the foot of the Temple Mount, the source of so much strife in previous generations, was now also in Israeli hands. Upon first coming to the Western Wall Rabbi Goren, the chief military rabbi, blew the *shofar* (ram's horn), raised a Torah scroll, and placed a bench as an act of defiance against the restrictions put on Jewish prayer during the Ottoman and British periods.[3] One of the first actions taken a few days after the end of

The open plaza in front of the Western Wall. Photographer: Moshe Milner, 1992. © 1997–1998, The State of Israel, Government Press Office.

Succot celebration at the Western Wall. Photographer: Rivka Gonen, 2002–10–13.

the Six-Day War was to officially annex the area along the Western Wall to Israel.[4] The Mughrabi Quarter next to the Wall was cleared. Now a wide space replaced the very narrow alley in which Jews had to squeeze when they came to pray at the Wall before 1948. Additional actions were taken in the area next to the Wall. Two more courses of the Herodian wall were exposed, elevating the Wall by some 2 meters. Eight more courses are still buried under the surface. Wilson's Arch, the subterranean vaulted hall to the north of the traditional praying area, was cleaned and converted into an additional place of prayer used especially on rainy days.

The section close to the Wall was divided into men's and women's sections, an act prohibited during the Ottoman and British Mandate periods. Eventually the space opened in front of the Wall was designed as a spacious stepped public plaza, which has been serving since for private and public prayers and ceremonies. Many solemn and joyful events are celebrated at the Wall—Holocaust Day Memorial, Memorial for Fallen Israeli Soldiers, Independence Day, and Jerusalem Day celebrations, and the swearing in of new soldiers. Private celebrations also take place at the Wall, especially bar mitzvahs of thirteen-year-old boys. In addition to its function as the most important Jewish place of prayer, the Western Wall had become the central shrine of Israeli civil religion.

The Status Quo[5]

The day after the end of the war, the question of what to do with the Temple Mount arouse. While the ecstatic government was debating this grave problem under the impact of the great miracle of the victory, Moshe Dayan, aware of the heavy weight that history

had placed on his shoulders, made a cool-headed decision based on his understanding of the age-old relationship between the Muslims and the Jews. Soon after Muhammad initiated his new Muslim religion, he had offered it to the Jews who were living in Arabia. The Jews failed to accept it and as a result came to be regarded as a rejected people that should always and everywhere be subject to Muslims. Indeed, throughout history the situation of Jews in Muslim lands reflected these attitudes. On the whole they were not physically persecuted, as they often were in Christian lands, but they had to pay a humiliating poll tax and were confined to special living quarters and to a limited, often degrading number of occupations.

The outcome of the Six-Day War, with the Jews having the upper hand, toppled the age-old situation. Dayan understood that the creation of the State of Israel on what was believed by the Arabs to be their land, and now the conquest of Jerusalem and especially the *Haram a-Sharif*, was a heavy blow to the Muslim world. The Arabs conceived both events not only as a political but also as an ideological usurpation of the land and of the holy site, and the desecration of its sanctity. Dayan was aware that the Muslims would not come to terms with Jewish rule over such a major holy site. He accepted the fact that for the Muslims the *Haram* had for many generations been an active place of prayer, while for the Jews the Temple Mount had been only a place of historical relevance and the object of messianic aspirations.

Under these weighty considerations, Dayan decided that Israel should acknowledge the existing situation, in which the *Haram a-Sharif* was regulated by Palestinian religious functionaries serving under the

Jordanian Department of Holy Sites. Dayan agreed that these officials would go on managing the affairs of the *Haram* as they had done prior to the Israeli conquest. They would continue to maintain order and internal security on it. and Israel would take care of its overall security. The decision also took into account the age-long Jewish yearning for the Temple Mount and decreed that Jews had the right to visit the Temple Mount unhindered and free of charge as long as they behaved decently and observed the religious feelings of Muslims. This was really a monumental change, since Jews had not been allowed on the Temple Mount for about a thousand years. Dayan also decreed that although Jews could visit the Temple Mount, they would not be allowed to pray there, because the entire area was considered the holy the al-Aqsa Mosque. The Jewish place of prayer would remain at the Western Wall, and in 1984 Israel annulled the *waqf* ownership over it and declared it state property.[6]

On June 17 1976, just a few days after the end of the war, Dayan called the Muslim religious authorities of Jerusalem for a meeting at the al-Aqsa Mosque, and there he proclaimed his decision, which Prime Minister Levi Eshkol officially endorsed.[7]

No document was signed, and many details were left unclear, but this agreement, known as the "status quo," is the basis for the status of the Temple Mount to this day. Dayan hoped that by proclaiming the status quo agreement, by which religious sovereignty over the Temple Mount would remain in the hands of the Muslims, while the overall sovereignty would be in the hands of Israel, national aspirations would be separated from religion. These two potentially volatile aspects had always been intertwined in the Jewish-

Arab conflict. He also hoped that his suggested arrangement would lessen the fervent emotions the Muslims had entertained since the days of Hajj Amin al-Husayni toward the *Haram a-Sharif* as the nucleus of Palestinian Arab religious-nationalism, and ease their adjustment to the new political situation. Most Israelis as well as the international public agreed to Dayan's decree that the *Haram* was exclusively a place of Muslim worship with rights of visitation for non-Muslims, and the Western Wall the exclusive place of Jewish worship. The Muslims, because of their total objection to the Israeli conquest of Jerusalem and the *Haram a-Sharif*, did not accept the status quo arrangement and related themselves to the situation as it was during the British Mandate times.

The actual situation as it developed over the years proved to be complicated and volatile. Joint Jewish-Muslim attempts to separate the religious issue from the national one were jeopardized time and again when extremists on both sides tried to stir up a religious conflict over the Temple Mount/*Haram a-Sharif* in the hope that their actions would lead to their desired solution. An ongoing series of acts and counter-acts by both sides led to an almost continuous conflict that sometimes flared into varying degrees of violence. The Jewish side was more active in trying to break the status quo by initiating actions ranging from attempts to pray on the Temple Mount to conspiring to blow it up in order to pave the way for building the Third Temple. The Muslim authorities, being aware of the dangerous potential of inflaming the conflict, retaliated by filing complaints, arousing Muslim and world opinion against Israel, and by organizing demonstrations that in some cases ended in violence.

Since the mid-1990s the Muslims have taken the initiative and carried out large-scale construction work on the *Haram a-Sharif* designed to greatly increase their prayer area and enhance the Muslim sanctity of the site. No retaliatory violent acts were taken against these activities, as the Israeli government and High Court of Justice continuously attempted to confine the conflict rather than allow it to get out of hand. Protests designed to arouse Jewish and world public opinion were the only reactions to these activities. And yet, from 1967 until 2000 both sides, aware of the volatile potential of the site, met discreetly many times and usually managed to calm the situation. They reached a series of understandings on what can and cannot be done on the Temple Mount.

The situation changed drastically after the visit to the Temple Mount in September 200o of Ariel Sharon, the head of the opposition Likud party, despite warnings from Palestinian leaders that the visit would provoke major disruptions. Indeed, the visit triggered the eruption of the al-Aqsa Intifada, a lengthy violent conflict with many casualties on both sides, through which the Palestinians hope to achieve a state of their own. The attachment of the name al-Aqsa to the national aims of the Intifada has added to it a powerful religious symbol with which every Muslim can identify. Although the Israeli-Palestinian conflict is basically a national rather than a religious conflict, introducing the issue of the sovereignty over the Temple Mount/*Haram a-Sharif* provided it with a very powerful religious symbol.

Jordan's Position on the Temple Mount

After 1967 Israel recognized the special status of the Kingdom of Jordan as the rightful owner of the *Haram a-Sharif*, a status it had obtained in 1948 when it annexed Jerusalem and the entire West Bank. After 1967 Israel endorsed the official position of King Hussein of Jordan as Guardian of the Holy Islamic Sites as a way of curtailing the growing influence of the local Palestinians. Thus Jordan maintained its influence on the affairs of the Mount, but in cases of severe conflict with Israel raised its voice in protest and denunciation alongside the local Palestinians. Under pressure from the Palestinians, Jordan in 1988 annulled the annexation of the West Bank and ended all its legal and administrative relations with that area, but it continued to have some influence in the *Haram a-Sharif*. In 1992 the Jordanian king contributed more than $8 million toward repairing and covering anew the golden dome of the Dome of the Rock.

In the 1994 peace agreement between Israel and Jordan, Prime Minister Itzhak Rabin committed Israel to respect "the present special role of the Hashemite kingdom of Jordan in Muslim holy shrines in Jerusalem. When negotiations on the permanent status take place, Israel will give high priority to Jordan's historic role in these Shrines" (Israel-Jordan Peace Agreement, article 9[2]). But in the following years the Palestinians managed to obtain the support of major Muslim countries and depose Jordan of its position, and in 1997 the *waqf* of the *Haram a-Sharif* came under the jurisdiction of the Palestinian Authority.[8]

In the Israel-Jordan peace agreement, Israel declared officially and publicly that while it maintained its political sovereignty in East Jerusalem, it in fact surrendered the Temple Mount to the Muslim religious authorities. Since then, for all practical purposes, Israel waived its sovereign rights over the Temple Mount and has no control over what goes on there.

The Issue of Jewish Prayer on the Temple Mount

While the Muslim authorities were favorably surprised by Dayan's generous consideration of their situation, many Jews rejected the status quo, especially on the grounds that Jews were not allowed to pray on the Temple Mount. For generations the Western Wall had been the traditional place of prayer for Jews instead of the truly holy site—the Temple Mount itself. Now, for the first time since the destruction of the Second Temple in 70 CE, the Mount was open to Jews. who could, in principle, conduct their worship there. In 1929, when Professor Boris Schatz, founder of the Bezalel Art School in Jerusalem, had appeared before a British inquiry committee studying the policy of the British Mandate regarding the Western Wall, he related: "After father died only the cloak remained, and it is for me a memento." By the father he meant the Temple Mount, by the cloak, the Western Wall. Now that the father was back, the cloak should not continue to be his substitute.[9]

The issue of prayer on the Temple Mount, or even entering it, is not only a political matter but has serious religious aspects connected with the issue of ritual purity.[10] According to biblical law, death is the ultimate source of ritual defilement. Since the destruction of the Second Temple, all Jews have been ritually defiled because they have all been in contact with a dead person or even, since this defilement is contagious, with someone or something that has been in contact with a dead person. In the days of the Temple, anyone so defiled could not enter the Temple. The only way to cleanse a person of this impurity is by a priest sprinkling on him a few drops of pure water mixed with the ashes of a specially cul-

tivated red heifer, a ceremony that has not taken place since the destruction of the Temple. But the sanctity of the Temple did not cease even though it is destroyed and the strict laws of ritual impurity still apply to it.

Thus no Jew living today can enter the holy ground where the Temple once stood. The punishment for transgressing is severe—death at the hand of God. As nobody is quite sure exactly where the Temple stood, the rabbinical authorities declared the entire Temple Mount out of bounds for Jews. These authorities were also apprehensive that if a synagogue were built on the Temple Mount, and even if Jews just prayed there, the nature of Judaism, which developed since the destruction of the Second Temple as a religion without a Temple, would change.

The rabbinical ruling, declared jointly by Orthodox and ultra-Orthodox rabbis, was independent of Dayan's decision not to allow Jews to pray on the Temple Mount. Although declared out of religious motives, this rabbinical ruling, like Dayan's status quo, had the potential to prevent serious clashes between Jews and Arabs over the contested sanctity of the Temple Mount. The reality turned out to be different, however, and ongoing attempts by Jews to pray on the Temple Mount, and counter-attempts by Arabs to prevent them from doing so, have become an important part of the Israeli-Arab conflict.

A small minority of Jews, headed by the chief military rabbi, Shlomo Goren, objected to both Dayan's ruling and that of the rabbinical authority on the grounds that these decisions, in fact, handed the Temple Mount over to the Muslims. This group argued that the Western Wall has no holiness of its own but its importance derives from the Temple Mount, and that it symbolizes the destruction of the

Temple and the expulsion of the Jews from Israel. To them, praying at the Western Wall only perpetuates the condition of exile.

Prayer on the Temple Mount, on the other hand, is a symbol of freedom, of the return of the Jews to their homeland and to their holiest site. To find a proper place where prayers could be conducted, Rabbi Goren measured the Temple Mount and ascertained the universally accepted opinion that the Temple once stood where the Dome of the Rock now stands. The holy area where the laws of ritual purity were strictly observed was, according to the Mishnah, a square around the Temple measuring 250 by 250 meters. The large spaces added by King Herod to the Temple Mount on its southern and northern sides were not sanctified, and therefore Jews could visit these areas and pray without fear of trespassing on holy ground.[11] In the days when the Temple was standing, these spaces were open to everyone, Jews and non-Jews alike. In his published decree, Rabbi Goren also relied on historical documentation that Jews were allowed on the Temple Mount during the early Muslim period and even had a synagogue there.[12]

In the early days following the 1967 victory, Rabbi Goren used to go up to the Temple Mount with a few of his followers and quietly pray there. The Muslim authorities did not at that time view this act as a cause for alarm. However, on the following ninth day of Av, the anniversary of the destruction of the First and Second Temples (August 15 1967), just over two months after the conquest of Jerusalem, Rabbi Goren, accompanied by about fifty people, entered the Temple Mount. He brought with him a *shofar* and a portable Torah Ark, and prayed the afternoon prayers.[13]

This time the Arab ushers were alarmed. They called in the Muslim authorities, who filed a strong protest with the Israeli government. The public uproar that followed this event signaled the beginning of the gradual deterioration of the relations between the two sides. Rabbi Goren persisted in his attempts and declared that on the following Sabbath he would bring thousands to pray on the Temple Mount.

The Israeli government was in turmoil. The prime minister declared that he would send the army to evacuate anyone who attempted to go up to the Temple Mount. The Muslim authorities, on their side, locked the Mughrabi Gate, through which Jews entered the Mount. On that occasion it became known that the Muslim authorities charged an entrance fee to Jewish visitors. Negotiations between the sides succeeded in downgrading the tension. The demonstrative prayer did not take place, the keys to the Mughrabi Gate were retrieved, and a unit of the Israeli military police was stationed at the gate to prevent it from being closed again. The entrance fee was abolished. [14]

Over the years further attempts were made to pray on the Temple Mount, especially by the national-religious Faithful of the Temple Mount group. One very serious incident occurred on May 8, 1975, on the eve of the anniversary of the conquest of Jerusalem. A group of adherents of the nationalist Beitar movement entered the Temple Mount and prayed near the Gate of Mercy on the eastern side of the site. An Arab passer-by called in his friends and they began stoning the worshippers, wounding some. A joint Israeli-Arab police unit demanded that the worshippers evacuate the site and filed a complaint against them. The court judge ruled in favor of the

Beitar members, on the basis of the general ruling of 1967 allowing members of every religion to pray peacefully in holy places, rather than Dayan's status quo.

Since then it has been this ruling that is discussed in the Israeli courts.[15] In the months after the court's decision, the Muslims retaliated by organizing riots in the course of which several Arabs were killed and dozens wounded. The Muslim authorities published a proclamation against the court decision, and as in other cases, Arab states opened a diplomatic offensive against Israel. They demanded that the United Nations convene a special urgent meeting of the Security Council to discuss the situation, while accusing Israel of attempting to harm the Muslim holy shrines. As a measure of prohibiting Jews from praying on the Mount, the Muslim authorities again declared that the entire compound was a mosque— the Temple Mount/*Haram a-Sharif* including its outer walls.

As another tactic in their attempt to pray on the Temple Mount, extremist national and religious Jews filed a series of private and group appeals to the High Court of Justice to force the government to change the status quo policy.[16]

In March 1968 an individual submitted an appeal demanding that the minister of religious affairs appoint Jews to make sure that admittance of Jews to the Temple Mount was free of charge. Another appeal was presented in September 1968, accusing the police of preventing Jews from praying on the Temple Mount. After two years of deliberation, the High Court of Justice rejected the appeal, claiming that the right to pray on the Mount did not come under its jurisdiction and that it was the task of politicians to rule in such a delicate and complicated matter.[17] Despite this

call for an open declaration of its policy, the government never outspokenly declared that Jews were prohibited from praying on the Temple Mount. The Minister of Religious Affairs even announced that there was no legal prohibition against Jewish prayer on the Temple Mount, but because prayer in such a place might impair public safety, it had to come under the jurisdiction of the police.

In 1976 another appeal by an individual was handed to the High Court of Justice, claiming that the police had prevented him from praying in private on the Temple Mount. In March of that year the state advocate declared for the first time, officially and publicly, that private prayers were not forbidden. The president of the High Court of Justice, Aharon Barak, expressed his view on the matter in these words: "The basic principle is that every Jew has the right to enter the Temple Mount, to pray there, and to have communion with his Maker. This is part of the religious freedom of worship; it is part of the freedom of expression. However, as every human right, it is not absolute, but a relative right. The relativity is expressed in that the extent of this right must take into account the rights of others who claim the same right, as well as other human rights. The relativity is expressed in that the realization of this right may be limited by virtue of consideration of the public interest. Indeed, in a case where there is near certainty that injury may be caused to the public interest if a person's rights of religious worship and freedom of expression would be realized, it is possible to limit the rights of the person in order to uphold public interest." [18]

The appeal was rejected, as were all other appeals presented to the High Court of Justice in following years. Based on the High Court of

Justice regulation, the police continued to prevent Jews from praying on the Temple Mount. Even Menahem Begin, who had promised to officially change the status quo when he became prime minister in 1977, was not able to do so. Loyal to his principles, Moshe Dayan, to whom Begin offered a place in his government, put pressure to preserve the 1967 status quo. Benjamin Netanyahu also took it upon himself to open the Temple Mount to Jewish prayers if he was elected prime minister. After being elected, he too was not able to fulfill his promise. So did Prime Minister Ariel Sharon, who has so far failed to stand behind his word.

In October 1986 an agreement between the Faithful of the Temple Mount, the Supreme Muslim Council, and the police made it possible for fifty of the members of the Faithful to visit the Temple Mount in groups of seven, fifteen minutes per group, under heavy police protection. This one-time arrangement, which did not include the right to pray, was never repeated. On October 11, 1987, when the group attempted again to enter the Temple Mount, it was attacked by 2,000 Muslims armed with stones and bottles. The police who rushed to the place were also attacked, and stones were thrown down at the people who were praying at the Western Wall.

In the 1990s a new extreme religious-national group joined the Temple Mount devotees in continually attempting to pray on the Temple Mount. The police stopped both groups, which appealed to the High Court of Justice and were rejected time and again. Every such attempt is followed by protests by the Muslim authorities, who keep declaring that the *Haram a-Sharif* and all of Jerusalem are an occupied area and the Israeli High Court of Justice has no authority over them. They also

keep calling for demonstrations that sometimes flare into violence, and assemble larger and larger crowds of worshippers every Friday, the day holy to the Muslims, to pray in the al-Aqsa Mosque. The hundreds of thousands of worshippers who congregate at the *Haram a-Sharif* every Friday, and especially in the Muslim holy month of Ramadan, cannot be contained in the al-Aqsa. There is a huge spillover of worshippers who fill the large open areas of the compound. Ongoing events at the Temple Mount/*Haram a-Sharif* can be viewed as a religious-national war between Jewish worshippers who continually attempt to pray inside the compound and Muslim worshippers who have the right to do so, and whose numbers increases each year.

Should a Synagogue Be Built on the Temple Mount?

In time Rabbi Goren's claim that Jews had a historic right to pray in certain areas of the Temple Mount that were outside the strictly sacred zone where the Temple once stood began to win support.[19] His persistence was backed by a growing number of prominent rabbis of the more extreme national-religious sector, including the chief Sephardi rabbi of the 1980s, Rabbi Mordechai Eliyahu. Rabbi Eliyahu even called for a synagogue to be built on the southeastern or northeastern corner of the Temple Mount that would be higher than the Muslim shrines.[20] To further this proposal, Rabbi Goren established a Supreme Rabbinical Council, which ruled that Jews could enter certain areas of the Temple Mount. Most other rabbis did not express their views in public for fear of Orthodox and ultra-Orthodox opposition. The rabbinical leaders of the ultra-Orthodox strongly rejected these ideas on the grounds that they would antagonize both the Muslims and the other nations of the world, causing hatred and increasing anti-Semitism. Despite warnings from many Muslim organizations and Arab members of the Knesset (Israeli parliament) that any change in the status quo on the Temple Mount would lead to serious clashes that might develop into a religious war, Rabbi Goren's Rabbinical Council persisted in its view. It even proclaimed that it was the duty of every Jew to pray on the Temple Mount.

In 1992 Rabbi Goren published the exact measurements of the Temple Mount made by expert surveyors, along with the views of the Mishnah and Talmud and other historical sources on this matter. The study, supplemented by a maps, stated that the entire 110-meter-wide southern strip of the Temple Mount, as well as small areas on its northeastern and northwestern corners, are outside the sacred boundaries of the Temple. A synagogue could therefore be built in these areas and Jews could enter them after immersing in a ritual bath.

What Rabbi Goren neglected to mention is the existence of the al-Aqsa Mosque on the very same southern strip of the Temple Mount, and its great sanctity to the Muslim world as its third-most-sacred mosque. The Supreme Rabbinical Council and the Council of Orthodox Rabbis of America published opinions that building a synagogue on the Temple Mount is wrong both according to Jewish law and because it would only inflame hatred and violence. Yet eventually even some Orthodox circles took action on the issue. In 1991 the chief rabbi of the Habad movement ordered his people to celebrate the Pouring of Water on the second day of the festival of Succot on the Temple Mount. The event was canceled because of a very serious incident that occurred two days earlier in which seventeen Muslim worshippers on the Temple Mount were killed.

In recent years the Israeli authorities have begun to favorably consider allowing Jews to pray on the Temple Mount. This change in view is probably the result of growing pressure from many Jewish circles and also from studying the findings of a 1995 survey indicating that the majority of Israeli Jews expressed strong sentiments toward the Temple Mount. Even several rabbis who had previously opposed any visit to the Temple Mount on grounds of ritual defilement now accepted Rabbi Goren's declaration that substantial sections of the Mount are not holy and therefore that Jews not only are allowed to enter it but also should pray there.[21]

Another reason for the change of attitude may be the negative impression created in Israeli public opinion by the building of two additional mosques on the Temple Mount. Several Knesset members and several government ministers have publicly voiced the opinion that the time has come to change Moshe Dayan's status quo and allow Jews to pray on their holiest site. Ariel Sharon, when he was still head of the opposition, claimed that if he became prime minister he would open the Temple Mount to Jewish prayer. As of the summer of 2002, nothing has been officially decided, and the events of the violent Al-Aqsa Intifada prevent any action on the matter.

Attempts to Destroy the Temple Mount

Jewish attempts to pray on the Temple Mount and the Muslim reactions were, on the whole, low-key events that were often calmed by negotiations between the two sides or by the intervention of the police. However, other actions carried out on the Temple Mount were much more violent.

The al-Aqsa Mosque Fire

The most devastating attempt to destroy a religious shrine on the Temple Mount was carried out by a Christian.

The sanctity of the Temple Mount was not simply an issue between Jews and Muslims. Christians, especially members of fundamentalist evangelical sects, were also involved in the conflict. Greatly heightened and invigorated by the Six-Day War of 1967, fervent Christian aspirations for the Second Coming of Christ now centered on the "redeemed" Temple Mount. Fundamentalist Christians believe that the building of a Jewish Temple on the Temple Mount is part of the Great Tribulations that will precede the coming of Christ, a necessary step in hastening his Second Coming.

Realization of these aspirations was tragically attempted on the morning of August 21, 1969, when Denis Michael Rohan, a young Australian member of a fundamentalist Christian sect, set fire to the al-Aqsa Mosque. Rohan did not want to wait until the cataclysmic events unfolded themselves. He wanted to hasten these events and pave the way to the building of the Jewish Third Temple, a necessary step preceding the Second Coming of Christ, by setting fire to the Muslim shrines on the Temple Mount. He believed that God had bestowed the mission of building the Temple upon him. The fire completely burned the spectacular preacher's pulpit (minbar) installed by Salah a-Din, burned the wooden ceiling of the mosque, and damaged parts of its southeastern side. Pillars and arches were cracked, and a wall mosaic was badly damaged.

During the commotion that ensued, Rohan managed to escape, but he was later caught in his lodging in the Old City. It became clear that he was insane. He was sent back to Australia, where he was confined to a mental institution. This did not prevent the Muslim authorities from blaming Israel for the fire. They even accused the Israeli firefighters who rushed in of sprinkling kerosene instead of water in order to set the entire mosque on fire. They called upon the residents of east Jerusalem to declare a strike, organize demonstrations, and close off the Temple Mount. The demonstration flared into riots. The police intervened and declared a curfew. The Muslim authorities demanded an international inquiry commission. Several Muslim countries, such as Egypt, Pakistan, Jordan, Algeria, Tunisia, and Iran, called for a holy war (jihad). The expressions of such deep hatred were alarming.

When the flames and the incitement were extinguished, the Muslim authorities debated whether to leave the mosque damaged and use it for further propaganda or to restore it.[22]

Under pressure of devotees who wanted to pray there, the mosque was eventually restored. The burned ceiling was replaced, the cracks filled, and a new, simpler minbar installed.

As a result of this tragic event, the fear of Muslims that the mosques were in danger of being destroyed by extremists received support, and as a result their fear of any infringement on their right to the Temple Mount heightened. On its side, the Israeli government began to very strictly enforce the status quo that no Jew could pray on the Temple Mount. The Faithful of the Temple Mount extremists saw in the fact that the Muslim world reacted in words rather than deeds evidence that it was irrelevant, and they continued their attempts to enter the Temple Mount. Time proved that their belief that the Muslim world would remain passive was wrong. The conflict over the Temple Mount has only blown up and become more serious since.

Jewish Attempts to Blow Up the Temple Mount

Several Jewish attempts to blow up the Muslim shrines on the Temple Mount were luckily not as devastating as the al-Aqsa fire, since they all failed. While most Jews accepted the fact that the Temple Mount was in Muslim hands, others did not lose hope of gaining control over it and acted both by attempting to enter the Mount to pray and by appealing to the courts to obtain a legal permit to do so. These were more or less peaceful activities. However, more extreme groups were not satisfied with these mild actions and planned to blow up the Muslim shrines. Some moved from planning to action. Their activities proved that the Muslim fear of damage to their shrines and of Jewish attempts to take over control over the *Haram a-Sharif* was not totally imaginary. It became quite clear that aspirations to do just that were harbored by several extreme nationalistic-religious factions born out of the ever growing messianic expectations of post-1967 Israel. When these activities were discovered, they aroused the expected uproar in the Muslim world. The Muslims filed urgent complaints with UNESCO (the United Nations Education, Science, and Culture Organization), which declared the Temple Mount a world monument. A representative of the secretary general of UNESCO was hastily summoned to investigate the incidents. Luckily, all attempts at destroying the shrines had failed.

Alan Goodman, a mentally unstable Israeli soldier, made the first recorded endeavor to blow up the Mount. On April 11, 1982, Goodman entered the Temple Mount with his rifle and began shooting the Arab guards at the Dome of the Rock. He hoped, so he said at his trial, to "redeem" the Temple Mount. A guard was killed and two Israeli police officers who rushed to the scene were injured.[23] The incident aroused violent riots that spread to the Old City. Two days later Yasser Arafat called upon the Arab population of the West Bank and Israel to shed their blood to water the Holy Land of Palestine and start a holy war. He promised that those who died in this war would enter Paradise. Tens of millions of Muslims in Asia and Africa organized a strike. Several Muslim countries convened a meeting of the United Nations Security Council, which expressed its deep concern over the desecration of the holy sites and condemned Israel and its soldiers for shooting, killing ,and wounding Muslims on the *Haram a-Sharif*. Such extreme reactions followed any suspected Israeli activity on the Temple Mount.

At the beginning of 1982, a member of the ultra-national-religious Kach movement formed a youth movement with the aim of taking control of the Temple Mount.[24] At the end of that year, a Kach member and one of the youths of the movement were brought to trial for attempting to ignite a bomb near the walls of the Dome of the Rock. A few months later, several people of questionable reputation known as the Lifta Gang made plans to blow up both the Dome of the Rock and the al-Aqsa Mosque. The police were on their trail while they were still in the planning stages, and on the designated day, while on their way to lay their explosives, they were discovered by the

Muslim guards of the *Haram a-Sharif* and brought to trial.

A more serious and dangerous attempt was discovered at the end of April 1984, when a group of twenty-seven people later known as the Jewish Underground was arrested. This group was responsible for the killing of five Arab students in the Islamic College in Hebron, and for attempting to assassinate and badly wounding Arab mayors of towns in the West Bank. They also put explosives in Arab buses in East Jerusalem and attempted murder by placing hand grenades in two mosques in Hebron. At their trial they confessed that their ultimate action was to blow up of the Dome of the Rock. To do that they had carefully surveyed their target, conducted thorough observations of it, and assembled enough explosives for the task. Luckily, however, at the last minute they abandoned their plan.[25]

And yet, as late as 1996 a member of one of the most extreme organizations did not hide his desire to create a situation in which the golden dome on the Temple Mount could be blown up. He declared that if three people undertook this action, they would be mad, thirty people would be an underground, 300 would be a movement, and 3,000 would start a revolution that might succeed. It was all a matter of numbers.[26]

The attempts to blow up the Muslim shrines on the *Haram a-Sharif* aroused extremely serious fears not only among Muslims but also among Jews who were afraid of the results of such an action. In 1982 participants in a simulation game held at Harvard University predicted that a third world war would start if Jewish extremists blew up the Muslim shrines on the Temple Mount. This scenario exemplifies the extremely volatile situation surrounding the Temple Mount/*Haram a-Sharif*, which could explode even through a small provocation, let alone through any damage or destruction of the Muslim shrines.

Preparations for Building the Third Temple

The ongoing attempts to allow Jews to pray on the Temple Mount, the wish to build a synagogue there, and the several plans to blow up the Muslim shrines were but preliminary activities to the great messianic goal—the building of the Third Temple in place of the Muslim shrines. The group known as the Faithful of the Temple Mount publicly proclaimed this desire for the first time in 1982. It announced that it aimed to expel the Arab conquerors from the Temple Mount and convert it into the center of the Jewish people. It also called on the Israeli government to transfer the Muslim shrines to Mecca and to build the Third Temple in their place. This proclamation, and the annual processions organized on every holiday, ending in attempts to enter the Temple Mount to pray, caused recurring violent clashes with the Muslims. Backed by a High Court of Justice ruling, the police do not allow the devotees near the Mughrabi Gate. Since 1989 the processions organized by the Faithful of the Temple Mount have included a new element. The participants carry a stone that they claim will be the cornerstone of the Third Temple.

The Temple Mount Faithful are not the only group that initiates non-stop activities that , they hope, will eventually lead to the building of the Third Temple. At least ten such activist organizations have been established, each dealing with one or another aspect of the project.[27] Two yeshivas devote their time to studying the regulations and the exact order of the service in the Temple;

another prepares priests to eventually perform these services. Still another yeshiva works on architectural plans for the Temple and has built a model based on its findings.

The Temple Institute is very actively studying in detail the shape and measurements of the various ritual utensils used in the Temple, and employs artists and craftsmen who actually create the utensils, mostly in 1:1 scale and of the proper materials, including silver and gold. The institute had already produced many such utensils, including a gold-plated incense altar, musical instruments, and the large gold-plated Temple candelabrum that was recently put on view in a glass case in one of the central thoroughfares of the Jewish Quarter. This group has the financial and moral backing of evangelical sects in the United States, for whom these activities are yet another step toward the Second Coming of Christ.[28]

Another group weaves fabrics and sews garments like those the High Priest wore when performing the Temple service. All these institutions are based in the Jewish Quarter of the Old City, except one in the Muslim Quarter. In 1997 the newspaper *Yediot Aharonot* reported that a group of workers at the Dead Sea Plant, under the leadership of the director-general, had built the large altar of sacrifices out of scraps from a magnesium plant.

Another group, in a religious agricultural settlement, is working to produce a red heifer, whose ashes are necessary for cleansing all Jews of the ritual impurity resulting from contact with death. Without this purification, no one will be able to go up to the Temple Mount when the time comes to build the Temple and worship in it. In August 1996 a perfect red heifer was born in the religious agricultural

school adjacent to the settlement. She was named Melody and caused great excitement among those who long for the building of the Third Temple.

Many visitors, including distinguished rabbis, came to look at this wonder, but two years later two white hairs were discovered in her tail and she was disqualified. Producing a perfect red heifer is a complicated task, and indeed the Talmud states that throughout the period of the Temple only ten such specimens were born. The Melody incident reached the ears of an evangelical cattle farmer in the United States, who offered to produce by scientific breeding a herd of first-grade red Angus cattle with the hope that one unblemished heifer would be born. He offered the entire herd to Israel, saying that if it fails to produce the expected heifer, Israel would at least have a herd of perfect meat cattle. All attempts to produce the right red heifer have until now failed.[29]

The Third Temple activist groups frequently convene to report on their work related to the future building of the Temple. In October 1989 a 300 rabbis, scientists, archaeologists, and architects met in Jerusalem for the first convention of the newly formed Movement for Founding the Temple. At that time one group was getting ready to cast the gilded Temple candelabrum. The candelabrum was subsequently completed, as was mentioned above. In 1990 all these groups joined forces and formed a movement dedicated to building the Temple, and at the 1997 communal meal there were about a 1,000 paying participants. They were a mixed lot, ranging from moderate religious-national circles to extreme national–ultra-religious ones. All the speakers endorsed the need to pray on the Temple Mount.

The movement puts much emphasis on identifying priests and training them. They secretly planned to assemble ten newborn babies of priestly families and bring them up under strict Jewish religious law until they were thirteen years old, so that when the time comes they will be able to officiate in the Temple and especially deal with the red heifer. It was reported that one mother was ready to dedicate her baby to this experiment.

The 1999 gathering endorsed the suggestion to organize a census of priests and Levites who would be trained to serve in the Temple. At these gatherings, which now take place annually, the accomplishments of its members are brought to the attention of the participants. For example, one meeting presented an animated program of a virtual tour of the Temple, with special emphasis on detailed preparations for a sacrifice; another featured a movie presentation of the gilded candelabrum.[30]

Archaeological Excavations Around the Temple Mount

Archaeological excavations carried out not on the holy site itself but outside it, along its southern and western walls, are another source of conflict between Arabs and Jews pertaining to the Temple Mount/*Haram a-Sharif*.

The Temple Mount Excavations

In February 1968 an archaeological expedition headed by Professor Benjamin Mazar of the Hebrew University began excavations along the southern section of the west wall of the Temple Mount, south of the ramp leading to the Mughrabi Gate, and along the southern wall of the Mount. These areas were empty of any structure except a school, which was con-

verted into the excavation headquarters. As the excavations expanded into more and more areas, and went deeper and deeper, several layers of past occupation were revealed. After debris from recent centuries was removed, a magnificent series of monumental structures from the Ummayad period proved that this area, at the foot of the *Haram a-Sharif*, was the royal quarter of Jerusalem at that time. One of these huge structures may have been the palace of the governor of Jerusalem. These structures and the well-paved streets between them were surprising discoveries, because they are not mentioned in historical records. They added much to the knowledge of the Ummayad period in Jerusalem. Under this level, private residences of the Byzantine period were unearthed, well-stocked with household vessels, and under these, a well-planned public area of the time of King Herod, the builder of the Temple Mount, was revealed. The remnants of this period included monumental steps, partially cut in the rock and partially built, that led to the Hulda Gate in the southern wall of the Mount. The excavations also revealed paved streets lined by shops along the walls of the Temple Mount with sophisticated water conduits under them, as well as remnants of a huge stairway that provided the approach from the foot of the Temple Mount to the level of the Mount itself.[31]

From the moment the excavations began, the *waqf* insisted that they were undermining the walls of the *Haram a-Sharif* and would eventually cause the collapse of the al-Aqsa Mosque.[32]

The *waqf* sent a continuous stream of complaints to UNESCO, which appointed Dr. H. J. Reinink as its delegate to the area in accordance with the Hague Pact on protecting cultural assets in situations of armed conflict. In 1969 Dr. Reinink submitted a report stating that the archaeological excavations did not endanger any existing structure, and, moreover, that they were vital to the study of the history of Jerusalem. Dr. Reinink organized a meeting between Professor Mazar and the head of the Muslim *waqf*, and this eased the tension between the two bodies.

Other delegates were sent to investigate the situation, the most persevering being Professor Lemair. Professor Lemair visited the excavations frequently, sent favorable reports on the importance of the excavations, and stated that they were causing no damage. Despite the complaints and the interference, the excavations were held continuously for nine years, until they ended in 1977.

The *waqf*, aided by representatives of the kingdom of Jordan, approached UNESCO again in 1995, complaining about new excavations on the site. Professor Lemair was again sent to Jerusalem and reported that there were no new excavations threatening the stability of the walls of the *Haram a-Sharif*, but rather a project of reinforcement and restoration of the previously excavated finds. In his final report, Professor Lemair described Professor Mazar's excavations as the most important scientific and spectacular archaeological project taking place in Jerusalem. On the other hand, he voiced criticism that the archaeological excavations were carried out on private land confiscated for the project without permission being obtained from its owner

The Western Wall Tunnel

When it became clear that Jews would not be able to pray on the Temple Mount because of strong Muslim objections, the rabbinical authorities initiated a project to extend the prayer area by clearing the earth and rubble in the underground spaces to the north of the Western Wall. This project, carried out by Ministry of Religious Affairs, began in 1969 when blocked spaces were cleared immediately to the north of the Western Wall, and it developed into a lengthy excavation project that exposed the entire length of the Western Wall.[33] The work, which took the form of tunneling along the wall, created a narrow passage that was reinforced with concrete walls.

The Western Wall tunnel project proved much more harmful to Jewish-Arab relations than the Temple Mount excavations, because the tunnel passed under Muslim religious structures of the Mamluk period, built against the west wall of the Temple Mount. In some cases damage was caused to these old and dilapidated buildings, but it was immediately repaired. In cases where the condition of the building was beyond repair, residents received substantial compensation and were evacuated. After about 240 meters the tunnel hit a rock-cut water tunnel of the Hasmonean period. When the two tunnels were joined, they spanned the entire length of the west wall all the way to the northwestern corner of the Temple Mount, where Herod's Antonia Fortress once stood. The tunnel is now known as the Western Wall Tunnel.[34]

The tunneling did not go unnoticed by the local Arabs or by representatives of the Kingdom of Jordan, which claimed that the west wall was part of the holy compound of the *Haram a-Sharif*.[35]

They also insisted that the work was causing damage to hundreds of medieval structures above the tunnel, including mosques and religious and cultural institutions. Israel was accused of breaching all the decisions of the United Nations and UNESCO regarding

General view of the Western Wall excavations. Photographer: A.van der Heyden, 1989. Courtesy of The Jerusalem Publishing House.

Jerusalem, and of conducting a policy of aggression aimed at destroying the Muslim heritage and holy places. Moreover, the work on the tunnel was described as part of an overall design to take over the Temple Mount and build the Third Temple on it. Several spokesmen even accused Israel of tunneling under the *Haram a-Sharif.*

Israel answered these accusations by reminding the General Assembly of the desecration of Jewish holy places in the Jewish Quarter after it fell to the Jordanians, and it reiterated its policy of keeping free passage and worship to people of all faiths in their holy places. The Western Wall had been recognized as far back as the British Mandate period as a holy site to the Jews, separate from the *Haram a-Sharif,* and work along the outer face of the wall had nothing to do with the al-Aqsa Mosque. Professor Lemair of UNESCO stated that the wide cracks that had appeared in the buildings above the tunnel were not related to the work carried out under them, but were caused by the dilapidated state of the sewage system in the area, and by the heavy winter rains. Israel quickly repaired the damage.

Nevertheless, with the aid of all the Muslim countries and the Soviet bloc, Israel was denounced in 1974 by the United Nations General Assembly for carrying out actions aimed at changing the historical character of Jerusalem and conducting dangerous archaeological excavations. The United Nations also sanctioned Israel for the first time and ordered UNESCO to withhold its yearly contribution. Israel's application to join the regional European chapter of UNESCO was also rejected.[36]

These two acts aroused widespread criticism in many countries around the world, which withheld their yearly subsidies to UNESCO, bringing the organization to the verge of bankruptcy. The decisions were

The Western Wall Tunnel. Photographer: Avi Ohayon, 1998. © 1998, The State of Israel, Government Press Office.

reverted but resumed after only a few days. Professor Lemair was again sent to Jerusalem in December 1977 and July 1978 and reported that all the excavations were completely terminated. Work in the Western Wall Tunnel, however, was resumed shortly afterwards. In 1983, 1984, 1985, and 1986 Professor Lemair was again sent to investigate the accusations of the Arabs that much damage had been caused to historic structures. Israel again repaired all the damage and reinforced the structures.

In 1981, in the course of work on the Western Wall Tunnel, an additional tunnel was discovered branching out of it to the east. This discovery caused great excitement in Jewish religious circles, which hoped that this subterranean tunnel might lead to a place under the Temple, perhaps even under the exact site of the Holy of Holies.[37]

This would have been exceedingly important, not only because it could bring worshippers close to the holiest of Jewish sites, but also because the ritual vessels of Solomon's Temple are believed to be hidden under the Temple.

Rabbi Goren, who had continued his attempts to allow Jews to pray on the Temple Mount, was quick to announce that the tunnel was holier than the Western Wall and should replace it as the place of prayer.[38] Rumors spread among the Arab public that this new tunnel reached under the holy Muslim structures and that clearing it was a new attempt

The Hashmonean Tunnel. Photographer: Avi Ohayon, 1998. © 1998, The State of Israel, Government Press Office.

by the Jews to obtain control over the *Haram a-Sharif*. In order to curtail violence, the police ordered that neither Jew nor Arab enter the tunnel, and its opening was closed. Workers of the *waqf* were later allowed inside, where they built a very thick concrete wall that blocked this enigmatic tunnel.

Work on the Western Wall Tunnel ended in 1987. In his final report, Professor Lemair strongly criticized the project, stating that it had not been carried out under proper archaeological supervision and that its aim had not been scientific but religious. However, he also pointed out that Israel had repaired all the damage caused by the work, and that the reinforcements carried out had prevented the danger of severe damage or collapse in the future.

Projects designed to allow the public to visit the tunnel again caused much unrest on the Muslim side, and Professor Lemair visited the site again several times between 1990 and 1995.

When the entire length of the Western Wall Tunnel was exposed and safety measures taken, it was opened to the public for conducted tours. However, this was a one-way tour, the visitors entering the tunnel next to the Western Wall and then turning around and walking back the entire length of the tunnel to exit through the same opening. This situation allowed only few group visits per day. The Ministry of Religious Affairs therefore decided, in 1988, to open an exit at the northern end of the tunnel, near the Nunnery of the Sisters of Zion, not far from one of the entrances to the *Haram a-Sharif*. Such an exit was also required for safety reasons.

When preparatory work on the exit began, the *waqf* noted it and again spread the rumor that the Jews were tunneling under the al-Aqsa Mosque (synonymous with the *Haram a-Sharif*) in order to weaken its foundations, cause it to collapse, and build the Third Temple. A large crowd of Arabs congregated near the proposed exit and threatened that if work continued blood would be shed to protect the sanctity of the Muslim holy site. Under these threats work stopped, and it was many years before it was resumed.[39]

In 1995 it was reported that everything was ready for the opening of the northern exit. In September of that year, a few members of the government of Israel, headed by Prime Minister Benjamin Netanyahu, decided that the time was ripe for opening the northern exit. The decision was based on a report of a verbal agreement between the chief of Jerusalem's police and the head of the *waqf*, to the effect that in return for permitting Muslims to pray in Solomon's Stables in the coming month of Ramadan, the opening of the exit to the tunnel would proceed quietly. It is not clear whether there really was such an agreement, since the *waqf* published a strong objection to the opening of the tunnel. Several high-ranking Israeli military and political leaders urged the prime minister to postpone the opening, as Israeli-Palestinian negotiations were at a stalemate and the Palestinians were conducting a series of deadly attacks on Israeli civilians and soldiers. Israel retaliated for these attacks with a series of actions that caused numerous Palestinians casualties and by closing off Palestinian settlements, leading to the worsening of their economic situation.

Despite warnings that the desperate Palestinians, incited by their leaders, might react violently to the opening of the tunnel, the thin wall between the tunnel and the street was broken at midnight of September 23 1996, and an iron door was quickly installed in the new opening. In the morning the Arabs of East Jerusalem reacted fiercely, and Yasser Arafat called for a general strike and massive demonstrations. He also called for an international attempt to close the new opening of the tunnel. He referred to it as the al-Aqsa Tunnel and insisted that it be handed over to the Palestinians, thus preventing Israel from further tunneling, as he believed, under the *Haram a-Sharif*. The Arab League too voiced the recurring accusation that Israel was attempting to weaken the foundations of the *Haram a-Sharif* in order to cause it to collapse and be replaced by the Third Temple. Severe disturbances erupted on September 25 and lasted for three days. Thousands of Palestinians, including hundreds of armed soldiers and snipers, attacked Israeli military positions, settlements, and isolated sites. The casualties on both sides were enormous.[40]

The situation was so volatile that President Clinton invited the Israeli, Egyptian, and Jordanian leaders to a summit in Washington. President Mubarak announced that he would not participate unless Prime Minister Netanyahu agreed to close the tunnel, and he sent his foreign minister instead. Netanyahu also rejected King Hussein's demand to close the tunnel and also to let an international group of archaeologists check the accusations that the tunnel affected the *Haram a-Sharif*. The summit ended without an agreement, but in the official closing announcements President Clinton stated that both sides denounced violence and agreed to begin immediate and continuous negotiations to reduce violence and continue implementing the Oslo Agreements. The tunnel was not mentioned. It was left open, and no further violence was recorded. Since then, and despite the al-Aqsa Intifada, which began in September 2000, and the deterioration of Israeli-Palestinian relations, the northern exit of the tunnel has been open. However, there are armed guards at the exit, and they escort visitors back to the Western Wall area.

Muslim Acts on the Temple Mount

In 1990, to protect the *Haram a-Sharif* as a Muslim territory and prevent any presumed Jewish occupation, the Muslim *waqf* began to build several pulpits around the esplanade that defined roofless prayer areas to accommodate the overflow of worshippers from the al-Aqsa Mosque. For the same purpose they also planted gardens in areas that had been empty until then, and eventually they erected a memorial to the victims of the Sabra and Shatila massacre.[41]

The Faithful of the Temple Mount appealed to the High Court of Justice against the police, Jerusalem's mayor, the minister of education and culture, and the director of the Department of Antiquities. It asked to make them enforce the Antiquities Law (1967) and the Law of Planning and Building (1965) and bring the *waqf* to trial for damaging Jewish archaeological relics on the Temple Mount, including ancient walls and cuttings in exposed bedrock that define the line of walls. The Faithful also objected to repair work on the dome of the Dome of the Rock without permission from the planning and building authorities of the Jerusalem municipality. In this case also the High Court of Justice reject-

ed the appeal. Said former Judge Zamir, "Indeed nothing prevents the court—theoretically and practically—from intervening in the case of illegal activity on the Temple Mount. However, such intervention would be an exception from the norm. There must be a strong reason for the court to transcend the norm and to encroach upon the rights of the executive authority in this area."[42]

Creating a New Mosque in Solomon's Stables

Accusations against the *waqf* for intentionally destroying relics of past Jewish occupation of the Mount increased in the 1990s because of a variety of activities it performed on the Temple Mount and in the subterranean spaces. These activities were a response to the "southern option" regarding the location of the Temple (see above, chapter 3), according to which the Temple was said to be located deep under the pavement of the present-day lower platform. The constant attempts of Jews to pray on the Temple Mount and even to build a synagogue, perhaps in one of the underground spaces, also prompted the Muslim activities.

The case of Solomon's Stables was widely publicized. In the winter of 1996, the *waqf* obtained permission to use the underground Solomon's Stables as an alternative place of worship on occasional rainy days in the holy month of Ramadan.[43] Throughout history this extensive space was for the most part left empty, except during the Crusader period, when it was used as stables for the horses of the Order of the Knights Templars stationed in the al-Aqsa Mosque. The reason the *waqf* gave for wanting to use the stables seems to have been only a pretext. The real reason was the Palestinian apprehension that once a final arrangement was reached between Israel and the Palestinians, Israel would convert the sub-terranean space to a place for prayer.

As the *waqf* began preparing the area for its new use, the northern section of the Islamic Movement in Israel joined the project. The *waqf* declared that it aimed to convert Solomon's Stables into a full-fledged mosque that would operate all year round and would contain 10,000 worshippers. In addition to being the time the Stables were used for such a purpose, it would be the largest mosque ever known in the country. The presence of multitudes of worshippers on Fridays was designed to strengthen the Muslim claim over the Mount.

Because the existing entrance to the space was narrow, the Muslims, without obtaining a permit, opened two of the large arches that formed the Crusader entrance to the Stables. To do this they dug a huge hole sloping from the surface of the esplanade to these openings, in which they built a flight of steps and paved the area in front of them. This major act, carried out with tractors and heavy vehicles without any archaeological supervision and without a permit from the municipality, was a gross violation of the status quo. And yet, for fear that the peace negotiations being carried out at the time would be disrupted, the Israeli government did not take any action. Moreover, it tried to conceal these activities from the public and even from the Jerusalem municipality.

When the municipality finally got word of what was going on, it sent inspectors who saw that the workers had built wooden scaffolds inside the Stables in preparation for casting concrete for support or for another purpose. Orders to stop all work were issued and eventually work was suspended, except for laying a pavement. However, the director of the *waqf*

declared that it did not recognize any authority when it comes to construction work in the *Haram a-Sharif*. Eventually the Stables were cleared and paved, the walls plastered, and fluorescent lighting introduced.

In light of these events, Israeli archaeologists and public figures formed a Committee for the Prevention of the Destruction of Antiquities on the Temple Mount. The committee and several national-religious organizations appealed jointly to the High Court of Justice against the *waqf*, the Jerusalem municipality, and the Government of Israel for the breach of the status quo. The High Court of Justice rejected this appeal, claiming that anything to do with the Temple Mount was better decided by the political rather than the legal authorities.[44]

The committee initiated a public campaign against the activities inside Solomon's Stables and on the esplanade to the north of it, claiming that invaluable Jewish relics were being destroyed in the course of the unauthorized digging and building activities. They were not granted permission to inspect the work, but several archaeologists scanned part of the huge quantities of earth and stones extracted from the underground space and dumped on the eastern slope of the Temple Mount and in other dumping sites in Jerusalem. They collected ancient items, mainly pottery shards of various periods. A report published by the Antiquities Authority in 1999 mentioned that 14 percent of the shards dated to the First Temple period, 19 percent to the Second Temple period, 6 percent to the period of Roman occupation, 14 percent to the Byzantine period, 15 percent to the early Muslim and medieval periods, and 32 percent could not be identified. Also collected were fragments of a marble item of the Second

Temple period, a decorated architectural fragment of the early Muslim period, many fragments of shingles and glass of various periods, and many clay tiles of the Ottoman period. It could not, however, be established whether the shards came from the fill or from habitation layers. It would seem that the fairly large proportion of First Temple period shards came from the fill laid as part of the major work carried out in the days of King Herod.

The bloody events relating to the opening the Western Wall Tunnel in September 1996 accelerated the work in Solomon's Stables. Thousands of Arab citizens of Israel volunteered to take part in the work. Others donated money. On December 1996 the mosque was officially inaugurated as the al-Marwani Mosque. It serves not only as a place of prayer but also as a school for religious studies. No non-Muslim is allowed into this new mosque, and Solomon's Stables no longer exist as such.

In a rare interview given to a reporter for the *Jerusalem Post* on June 6, 2000, concerning the work in Solomon's Stables, the chief *waqf* archaeologist disclaimed his responsibility for the work carried out in and around the Stables. He could not say why there had been no archaeological supervision on the site, a part of the Temple Mount which had been declared a World Heritage Site by UNESCO, and he told the reporter that he had not been present during the work carried out there. However, he said, his archeological colleagues had examined the material taken out of the site, "either before or after" the excavation, "and found nothing of special interest."

Another New Mosque in a Subterranean Space

With their success in converting the Stables into a mosque without any intervention or objection from the Israeli government, the *waqf* appealed to the Israeli authorities to clean the underground spaces under the al-Aqsa Mosque, known as al-Aqsa al-Kadima (the ancient al-Aqsa). In actuality this space is the underground passage that led from the City of David through the Hulda Gate (the Double Gate) into the Temple Mount. It dates to the Second Temple period. Shortly after permission was granted, it became obvious that the *waqf*, aided by the Islamic Movement of Israel, had begun repairing and building inside this space with the purpose of converting it too into a huge mosque. Again the *waqf* did not obtain permission, and again archaeologists of the Antiquities Authority were barred from entering the site.

Unlike Solomon's Stables, which in their present shape date probably to the early Muslim period and have no outstanding architectural interest, the spaces now under construction are invaluable remnants of the Herodian period. Part of their domed roof is adorned with exquisite carvings, rare examples of Jewish art of the period. Therefore, careful archaeological inspection was essential, but permission for it was not granted. At some point it was announced that the thick wall separating this space from Solomon's Stables had been removed to enlarge the huge space. It is not quite clear whether this wall was in fact broken through. An inspector on behalf of the Antiquities Authority who managed to enter the area reported that he could not ascertain any breach in the wall. Again the Israeli authorities did not take any action to stop the work and the new mosque was inaugurated in August 1999. [45]

The activities of the Islamic Movement were so successful that its leader issued a public announcement in January 2001 stating that

Scaffolds holding the bulge in the southern wall of the Temple Mount. Photographer: Rivka Gonen.

Jews have no right on the Temple Mount. He claimed that the esplanade, the shrines on it, and the subterranean spaces under it all belonged to the Muslims and to them alone, and Jews have no right even to one particle of earth from this place.

Recently it was noted that a section of the eastern part of the south wall of the Temple Mount was bulging. This is the wall that has served since the time of King Herod as a retaining wall for the Temple Mount esplanade. Work carried out in the spaces behind it without archaeological supervision and perhaps without proper engineering supervision had no doubt caused this bulge. If the wall continues to bulge, as still did in the summer of 2002, the new mosque in

Solomon's Stables, which as built against it, as well as the al-Aqsa Mosque farther to the west, may be in danger of serious damage from a partial collapse.

After the completion of the two mosques, the *waqf* began leveling the area near the Gate of Mercy on the eastern side of the Temple Mount and paving it, again with the aid of heavy machinery that in itself can cause a lot of damage. It is also performing some unknown activities in the water cisterns under the Temple Mount esplanade. The police, the only Israeli force allowed on the Temple Mount, were accused by the Committee for Preventing the Destruction of Antiquities on the Temple Mount of turning a blind eye to what was going on. The committee also claims that under orders from the government, the police have withheld information on the illegal activities of the *waqf*, all in the interest of keeping peace and quiet and avoiding unrest and violence.

Proposals for Solving the Conflict over the Holy Site

All the suggestions for settling the Israeli-Palestinian conflict over the Temple Mount/*Haram a-Sharif* have been part of attempts to settle the wider conflict over Jerusalem. The issue of the Temple Mount /*Haram a-Sharif* within the Jerusalem problem is particularly complicated, the site being such a powerful religious and national symbol to both Jews and Muslims. The various suggestions for solving the problem of joint sanctity all acknowledge that the general status quo should be reserved and that the sanctity and integrity of the site should be protected. They also agree that the site should be maintained by members of the religions that sanctify it, and that those who regard it as holy should have the right of free access and worship. Above all, order and security should be maintained at all times.

Since the establishment of the State of Israel, the question of Jerusalem and its holy places has had high priority in local and international public opinion. In 1948 Jerusalem was divided into two cities. West Jerusalem became Israel's capital, while East Jerusalem, including the Old City with its Muslim, Jewish, and Christian holy sites, was annexed, together with the rest of the Arab territories west of the Jordan River, to the Kingdom of Jordan. Israel could not come to terms with this situation, because, despite an agreement of free access to the Western Wall that was part of the Armistice Agreement signed with Jordan, they were never allowed to visit their

holy place. At the same time, synagogues and places of worship in the Jewish Quarter of the Old City, which had fallen to the Arabs, were destroyed. Neither was the Christian world satisfied with the situation, because they had not been satisfied with the hundreds of years of Muslim control over their holy sites.

Internationalizing Jerusalem and the Holy Sites

Under these circumstances, several suggestions have been brought up at different times to internationalize Jerusalem, that is, to put the city under the rule of an international body. It is interesting that Theodor Herzl, creator of the Zionist Organization, made the first theoretical suggestion to this effect as early as 1902 in his book *Altneuland*,[46] which prophesied the establishment of a Jewish state in Palestine. Herzl agreed to put Jerusalem under international rule when he realized that the European countries would not accept Jewish control over their holy places.

The first time the suggestion to internationalize Jerusalem was brought up officially by the European powers was in 1916, when Palestine was still under Ottoman rule. Shortly afterwards the British Empire obtained the Mandate over Palestine and the suggestion subsided. The best-known scheme to internationalize Jerusalem and put it under international control was a part of the United Nations plan to divide Palestine between the Jews and the Arabs, authorized by the General Assembly on November 29, 1947.[47] The 1948 war that erupted because the Arabs did not accept this decision ended in the division of the country and the establishment of Jordanian rule over Jerusalem. In reaction to the plan to internationalize the entire city, Israel put before the United Nations on May 26, 1950, a proposal to internationalize only the part of

Jerusalem that contained the sites holy to Christians, Muslims, and Jews. Neither proposals ever materialized.

When the international community realized that a territorial internationalization of Jerusalem or only its holy sites was immaterial, it developed a scheme for a functional internationalization. According to this new idea, the nonreligious functions—overall security, supply of water and electricity, and the like—would be supplied by the ruling nation. A special commissioner to be appointed by the United Nations would supervise the religious functions, such as free passage and worship and the upkeep of the edifices.

The idea of a functional rather than a territorial arrangement has come up again in current attempts to solve the issue of Jerusalem and the Temple Mount. One version of this idea was the suggestion to establish a Holy Sites State, modeled on the Vatican in Rome.[48] Again the ruling states—Israel and Jordan, or the Palestinian State when established— would provide the secular functions, while the religious aspects would be governed by the sovereign authorities of the Holy Sites State.

Holy Basin, City of Peace, and Interfaith Rule

After the Six-Day War, Israel proposed that several of the holy sites of Jerusalem be joined under the term "Holy Basin." This basin would include the Old City along with the Temple Mount, the Mount of Olives, the Kidron Valley, and the City of David. The people living and serving there would receive diplomatic status. Jordan would confer this status on the Muslims, and European countries on the Christians. Under such a status, both site and personnel would be immune against all attack or claim. The host country,

namely Israel, would undertake to provide all the services needed to fulfill the special diplomatic status of the area.

In response to this proposal, and perhaps on the basis of several earlier ones, Yaakov Hazan, a Knesset member from the left-wing Mapam party, proposed in 1976 the formation of a "City of Peace." Hazan declared that while united Jerusalem is and will remain the capital of Israel, the city would be divided into self-ruled municipalities according to the ethnic composition of the population. A religious council composed of an equal number of Jews, Muslims, and Christians would administer the Old City, which would be declared the City of Peace of the three major monotheistic religions. Israel would be responsible for maintaining peace and order in the entire city. The major Muslim and Christian sites, including the Temple Mount, would be declared religious extraterritorial ground, and Israel would not have the right to interfere with their internal matters. If, however, the Jewish rabbinical authorities decided that Jews could pray on the southern side of the Temple Mount, an area would be allocated for this purpose and it would be excluded from the Muslim site.[49]

The Muslims also presented proposals calling for joint control over the holy sites. In 1978 and again in 1988, Dr. Walid Halidi proposed that Jerusalem be divided between Israel and the future Palestinian state, and that an interfaith committee with representatives of the three monotheistic religions administer the holy sites. The Jewish sites in the Old City would receive a special extraterritorial status, and free access to them would be promised. 'Adnan abu-'Auda, former prime minister of Jordan, suggested in 1992 that the Old City not belong to any country or religion, but be administered by a committee composed of representatives of the three religions. The Israeli Moshe Amirav and the Palestinian Hanna Seniora proposed in 1991 that Jerusalem be divided into municipalities, and that the Old City have a special status within this arrangement.[50]

Beilin–Abu Mazen Understanding

In February 1996 it became known that after lengthy and secret deliberations between an Israeli team headed by Yossi Beilin and a Palestinian team headed by Abu Mazen, a signed document of understanding had been agreed upon. The Beilin–Abu Mazen document proposed that the area of Jerusalem be greatly enlarged to include surrounding Arab villages and Jewish suburbs. This enlarged area would continue to function as a united municipal entity but would be divided into subareas. Each subarea would be under the sovereignty of Israel or the future Palestinian State according to the ethnic/religious composition of its residents. The status of the Old City would not be decided, but in practice it would come under Israeli sovereignty until an agreement between the sides was reached. The Temple Mount/*Haram a-Sharif* would be declared extraterritorial under exclusive Muslim rule, and the Palestinian flag would be allowed to fly over it.[51]

The Two-Level Division

At the end of 2000, President Bill Clinton put forth his own ideas for solving the Israeli-Palestinian conflict.[52] His proposal contained a specific item intended to find a solution to the problem of the Temple Mount/*Haram a-Sharif*. Clinton believed that the gap between the sides relates, not to the everyday administration of the site, but to its symbolic aspects.

Therefore he proposed leaving the site to the Palestinian authorities, who would be expected to respect the strong Jewish feelings toward it. An international body of inspectors would ensure both these aspects. Israel would have sovereignty over the Western Wall and over the Temple that is assumed to be buried deep under the Temple Mount esplanade, to the east of the Western Wall according to the southern option for the Temple's location. Both sides would agree not to initiate excavations under the *Haram* or beyond the Western Wall. An alternative suggestion gives the sovereignty over the *Haram a-Sharif* to the Muslims and over the Western Wall to the Jews, and proposes joint supervision over any excavations that are jointly agreed upon under the *Haram* and beyond the Wall.

Clinton's suggestion divides the holy edifice horizontally. The upper level would be under the exclusive sovereignty of the Muslims, who have only to respect Jewish feelings toward the Temple Mount. The Western Wall, and behind it an undefined lower level, where a vague, assumed, and mostly unaccepted Temple may be located, would come under Israeli sovereignty. This strange proposal that Israel have control over an underground space was also designed to counteract the Muslim claim that the holiness of the *Haram a-Sharif* extends from the depth of the earth to the highest heaven. However, Israel could not, under this proposal, undertake to uncover what lies buried there, if indeed there is something there, because it would be bound by the requirement to obtain permission to excavate from the Palestinians. They, of course, would never grant it. Thus this proposal is devoid of both practical and symbolic meaning.

The many proposals raised in the attempt to solve the question of sovereignty over the Temple Mount/*Haram a-Sharif* are now arousing the interest of the Israeli public, which until recently was rather indifferent to the fate of this holy site. The realization that most of the proposals tend to grant total sovereignty over the Mount to the Muslim side has brought its fate closer to the heart of more Israelis. The danger to the Jewish claim to the Temple Mount is now more widely appreciated and has spread beyond the extreme national-religious circles that spearheaded the opposition to the present situation, which gives the Muslims actual if not legal control over the Mount. A similar process has occurred on the Palestinian side, where anxiety over the fate of the *Haram a-Sharif* is becoming a concern of widening circles of the population.

Needless to say, none of the suggestions discussed until now has ever reached a state of serious deliberations between the sides, and neither Israel nor the Palestinian Authority has as yet officially accepted any of them. One can only hope that a creative solution to the very serious conflict over the Temple Mount/*Haram a Sharif*, the holiest site to Jews and the third-holiest site to Muslims, will be found sometime in the near future.

Notes

[1] Shragai 1995: 21–22; Ramon 2000: 113.

[2] Shragai 1995: 29–30.

[3] Friedland and Hecht 1991: 39.

[4] Berkovitz 2001:27

[5] Reiter 2001:297–317

[6] Shragai 1995: 24–25; Ramon 2000: 114–115.

[7] Shragai 1995: 25.

[8] Klein 2000: 276–289; Reiter 2000: 160–161.

[9] Shragai 1995: 248.

[10] Ibid 1995: 137.

[11] Goren 1992: 23–24, 177–189; Friedland and Hecht 1991: 39.

[12] Goren 1992: 14–15.

[13] Shragai 1995: 33.

[14] Goren 1992: 15–16.

[15] Shragai 1995: 281–286.

[16] Berkovitz 2000:84–87.

[17] Shragai 1995: 35–37.

[18] Berkovitz 2001:46.

[19] Shragai 1995: 67–71.

[20] Ibid:65.

[21] Ramon 2000: 134–135.

[22] Shragai 1995: 39–44.

[23] Ibid: 161–169.

[24] Ibid: 87–90.

[25] Friedland and Hecht 1991: 40–41.

[26] Shragai 1995: 112–122.

[27] Ibid: 140–141; 152–153; 250–157.

[28] Ibid: 145–146.

[29] Gorenberg 2000: 7–29.

[30] Ramon 2000: 127–130.

[31] Mazar B. 1975: 32–36; Mazar B. 1986: 15–46.

[32] Shragai 1995: 229–230.

[33] Ibid: 214–222.

[34] Bahat 1994: 177–190.

[35] Berkovitz 2000:66–68; Shragai 1995: 230–232.

[36] Shragai 1995: 232,Berkovitz 2000:69.

[37] Shragai 1995: 214; Berkovitz 2000:87.

[38] Berkovitz 2000:87.

[39] Shragai 1995: 239–244.

[40] Berkovitz 2000:74–79–

[41] Friedland and Hecht 1991: 46–47.

[42] Berkovitz 2001:65.

[43] Ibid:103–106.

[44] Ibid 59–69.

[45] Ibid 106–107.

[46] Harel 1989.

[47] No author 1977: 32.

[48] Berkovitz 2000: 404–410.

[49] Ibid 411–412.

[50] Ibid: 414–418.

[51] Ibid:418–420.

[52] Klein: 2000: 291–294.

Postscript

Given the long and extremely complicated issue of the Temple Mount, can some kind of a solution ever be reached? For Jews this site is the one and only holy place on earth, the place on which two Jewish Temples stood in the first millennium BCE. And yet, the Jews have been severed from this place for 2,000 years, in the course of which they developed a religion that survived without an actual and material relation to them and to the site on which they stood. Their memory, however, was kept alive in prayers, longings, and a strong but abstract desire to see a Third Temple built on the spot where the first two stood. Muslims on the other hand, although they have two other, more important holy sites in Mecca and Medina in Saudi Arabia, sanctified the Temple Mount/*Haram a-Sharif* early in the eighth century and have been worshipping in the shrines they built on it ever since. How can one weigh 1,000 years of long-gone Jewish shrines followed by 2,000 years of longing against 1,300 years of actual use of the site? What has more value, a celestial Temple or standing and functioning shrines? This juxtaposition is the essence of the conflict that embitters the lives of Israelis and Palestinians, of Jews and Muslims around the world. This is why groups of zealous Jews try time and again to go up to the Temple Mount and pray there to establish Jewish rights to the site, this is why others are busy preparing themselves for the building of the Third Temple, while still others even attempt to violently clear the site and prepare it for the new Jewish Temple. This is why, on the other side, the Muslims repel every Jewish attempt, real and imaginary, to claim and achieve even the slightest shred of right to the site.

Given these circumstances, it is at this point questionable whether each side will give up some of its feelings of exclusivity and recognize the right of the other side to the site. Would the Jews, who claim that the Temple Mount is their holiest space, sincerely agree that the Muslims can go on worshipping in their shrines? Could the desire, burning in the hearts of a minority of zealous Jews, to see the Third Temple built on the very spot where a Muslim shrine has been standing for centuries upon centuries be relinquished? Would the Muslims, who regard the entire *Haram a-Sharif* as one large the al-Aqsa Mosque, allow the Jews a foothold on one side or the other of the Temple Mount to build there a synagogue—not a Temple—where people could worship their God? Will the huge Muslim world, which extends from Morocco to Indonesia, see favorably the relinquishing of part of its holy space to members of another religion? In short, does one religious worship necessarily negate the other? Can they not live together and worship the same God, the one and only God. who is pure and abstract and not represented by an image?

Unfortunately, a political aspect has been superimposed on the religious conflict in the last hundred years and has embittered it. Now the issue is not only whether Jews or Muslims have a right to the Temple Mount/*Haram a-Sharif* but also who has the right to claim Jerusalem and the country as a whole. The conflict now centers on the question of whether Jerusalem will be the capital of Israel or of an as yet unborn Palestine, and whether the land will be the Jewish state of Israel or the Arab state of Palestine.

Despite what seems an insurmountable conflict, and despite the gradual hardening of positions on both sides, a solution can only come out of a mutual agreement by both sides to relinquish part of their claims to exclusivity. Optimistically, perhaps naively, one can envision the Temple Mount as a unique place where members of two religions can worship two different Gods who in fact are one.

Bibliography

Allen, H.R. Some Observations on the Original Appearance of the Dome of the Rock. In: Johns, Jeremy (ed.). *Bayt el-Maqdis. Jerusalem and Early Islam*. Oxford, Oxford University Press (1999), pp. 197–214.

Andrews, Richard. *Blood on the Mountain*. London, Phoenix (2000).

Ariel, Yaakov. Fundamentalist Christians and the Temple Mount. In: Reiter, Yitzhak (ed.), *Sovereignty of God and Man: Sanctity and Political Centrality on the Temple Mount*. Jerusalem, Jerusalem Institute for Israel Studies (2000), pp.143–154 (Hebrew).

Avi-Yonah, Michael. *The Madaba Mosaic Map*. Jerusalem, Israel Exploration Society (1954).

Avi-Yonah, Michael, The Second Temple. In: Avi-Yonah Michael (ed.), *Sefer Yerushalayim*. Bialik Institute and Dvir Publishing House (1956), pp. 392–418 (Hebrew).

Avi-Yonah, Michael. From Hellenism to Byzantium, In: Avi-Yonah, Michael and Yadin, Yigal (eds.), *6000 Years of Art in the Holy Land*. Jerusalem, Keter Publications (1986), pp. 175–302.

Bahat, Dan. The Physical Layout. In: Prawer, Joshua and Ben-Shammai, Haggai (eds.), *The History of Jerusalem: The Early Muslim Period (638–1009)*. Jerusalem, Yad Izhak Ben-Zvi Publications and New York, New York University Press (1996), pp. 38–100.

Bahat, Dan, Topography and Archaeology. In: Prawer, Joshua and Ben-Shammai, Haggai (eds.), *The History of Jerusalem: Crusaders and Ayyubids (1099–1250)*. Jerusalem, Yad Izhak Ben-Zvi Publications (1991), pp. 68–119 (Hebrew).

Bahat, Dan. The Western Wall Tunnels. In: Geva, Hillel (ed.), *Ancient Jerusalem Revealed*. Jerusalem, Israel Exploration Society (1994), pp. 177–190.

Barclay, J.T. *The City of the Great King.* Philadelphia, James Challen & Sons (1858).

Ben-Dov, Meir; Naor, Mordechai; and Aner, Zeev. *The Western Wall.* Tel Aviv, Ministry of Defence (1983).

Ben-Shalosh, M.H., History in the Times of the First Temple. In: Avi-Yonah Michael (ed.), *Sefer Yerushalayim.* Bialik Institute and Dvir Publishing House (1955), pp. 111–135 (Hebrew).

Benvenisti, Meron. *The Crusaders in the Holy Land.* Jerusalem, Israel University Press (1970).

Berkovitz, Shmuel. *The Struggle over the Holy Sites.* Jerusalem, The Jerusalem Institute for Israel Studies (2000), (Hebrew).

Berkovitz, Shmuel. *The Temple Mount and the Western Wall in Israeli Law.* Jerusalem, Jerusalem Institute for Israel Studies (2001).

Biton-Ashkelony, Brouria. The Attitudes of the Church Fathers toward Pilgrimage to Jerusalem in the Fourth and Fifth Centuries. In: Levine, Lee I. (ed.). *Jerusalem: Its Sanctity and Centrality to Judaism, Christianity and Islam.* New York, Continuum (1999), pp. 188–203.

Braslavi, Joseph. Pilgrimage to the Mount of Olives in the Middle Ages. In: (no ed.), *Jerusalem Through the Ages: The Twenty-fifth Archaeological* Convention, *October 1967.* Jerusalem, Israel Exploration Society (1968), pp. 109–119 (Hebrew).

Brereton, Joel L. Sacred Space. In: Eliade, Mircea (ed.), *The Encyclopedia of Religion*, Vol 12. New York, Macmillan Publishing Company (1987), pp. 526–535.

Cahn, Walter. Solomonic Elements in Romanesque Art. In: Gutmann, Joseph (ed), *The Temple of Solomon.* Missoula, Mont., Scholars Press (1976), pp. 45–72.

Campbell, Joseph. *The Hero with a Thousand Faces.* Princeton, N.J., Princeton University Press (1973).

Chazan, Robert. Jerusalem as Christian Symbol during the First Crusade: Jewish Awareness and Response. In: Levine, Lee I. (ed.). *Jerusalem: Its Sanctity and Centrality to Judaism, Christianity and Islam.* New York, Continuum (1999), pp. 382–407.

Clifford, Richard J. *The Cosmic Mountain in Canaan and the Old Testament.* Cambridge, Mass., Harvard University Press (1972).

Cogan, Mordechai. Royal City and Temple City: The History of Jerusalem from David to Josiah. In: Ahituv, Shmuel, and Mazar, Amihai (eds.), *The History of Jerusalem: The Biblical Period*. *Jerusalem*, Yad Izhak Ben-Zvi (2000), pp. 67–84 (Hebrew).

No author. *Conference on Jerusalem in Jewish, Christian and Islamic Perspectives*. Duke University (1977).

Drory, Joseph. Jerusalem in the Mamluk Period. In: Ben-Arieh, Yehoshua (ed.), *Jerusalem from the Second Temple to the Modern Period*. Jerusalem, Yad Izhak Ben-Zvi, (1981), pp. 129–154 (Hebrew).

Elad, Amikam, Pilgrims and Pilgrimage to Jerusalem in the Early Muslim period. In: Levine, Lee I. (ed.). *Jerusalem: Its Sanctity and Centrality to Judaism, Christianity and Islam*. New York, Continuum, (1999), pp. 300–314.

Elad Amikam. The Temple Mount in the Early Muslim Period. In: Reiter Yitzhak (ed.), *Sovereignty of God and Man: Sanctity and Political Centrality on the Temple Mount*. Jerusalem, Jerusalem Institute for Israel Studies, (2001), pp. 57–110 (Hebrew).

Eliade, Mircea. *The Sacred and the Profane*. New York and London, Harcourt Brace Jovanovich (1959).

Eliade, Mircea, and Sullivan, Laurence L. Center of the World. In: Eliade, Mircea (ed.), *The Encyclopedia of Religion*, Vol 3. New York, Macmillan Publishing Company (1987), pp. 166–171.

Eliav, Yaron-Zvi. The Temple Mount as a Place of Worship and a Political Center in Judaism and Christianity. In: Reiter Yitzhak (ed.), *Sovereignty of God and Man: Sanctity and Political Centrality on the Temple Mount*. Jerusalem, Jerusalem Institute for Israel Studies (2001), pp. 25–56 (Hebrew).

Ferrari, Silvio. The Holy See and the Postwar Palestine Issue: The Internationalization of Jerusalem and the Protection of the Holy Places. In: Levine, Lee I. (ed.). *Jerusalem: Its Sanctity and Centrality to Judaism, Christianity and Islam*. New York, Continuum (1999), pp. 143–165.

Fleming, James. The Undiscovered Gate Beneath Jerusalem's Golden Gate. *Biblical Archaeology Review* IX, no. 1 (1983), pp. 24–37.

Friedland, Roger, and Hecht, Richard D. The Politics of Sacred Places: Jerusalem Temple Mount. In: Scott, Jamie and Simpson-Housley Paul (eds.). *Sacred Places and Profane Spaces*. New York, Greenwood Press (1991), pp. 21–61.

Gafni, Isaiah M. Jerusalem in Rabbinic Literature. In: Tsafrir Yoram, and Safrai, Shmuel (eds.), *The History of Jerusalem: The Roman and Byzantine Periods (70–638 ce)*. Jerusalem, Yad Izhak Ben-Zvi (1999), pp. 35–60 (Hebrew).

Gibson, Shimon and Jacobson, David M. *Below the Temple Mount in Jerusalem*. BAR International Series 637 (1966).

Gil, Moshe. The Political History of Jerusalem During the Early Muslim Period. In: Prawer, Joshua and Ben-Shammai, Haggai (eds.), *The History of Jerusalem: The Early Muslim Period (638–1009)*. Jerusalem, Yad Izhak Ben-Zvi Publications and New York, New York University Press (1996), pp. 1–37.

Ginzberg, Louis. *The Legends of the Jews*. Vols. I, IV, V, IV. Philadelphia, Jewish Publication Society of America (1913).

Gonen, Rivka. Was the Site of the Jerusalem Temple Originally a Cemetery? *Biblical Archaeology Review*, Vol. XI, no. 3 (1985), pp. 44–55.

Goren, Rabbi Shlomo. *Har HaBait*. Jerusalem, Sifrei Hemed (1992), (Hebrew).

Gorenberg, Gershom. *The End of Days: Fundamentalism and the Struggle for the Temple Mount*. New York, Free Press, (2000).

Grabar, Oleg. *The Shape of the Holy: Early Islamic Jerusalem*. Princeton, N.J., Princeton University Press (1996).

Gutmann, Joseph. The Messianic Temple in Spanish Medieval Hebrew Manuscripts. In: Gutmann, Joseph (ed.), *The Temple of Solomon*. Missoula Mont., Scholars Press, (1976), pp. 125–145.

Harel, Chaya. Herzl's Attitude to Jerusalem. In: Lavsky, Hagit (ed.), *Jerusalem in Zionist Vision and Realization*. Jerusalem, Zalman Shazar Center for Jewish History and Center for the Study of Zionism and the Yishuv, Hebrew University of Jerusalem (1989), pp. 75–90 (Hebrew. English summary on p. xii).

Hasson, Izhak, The Muslim View on Jerusalem: The Quran and Hadith. In: Prawer, Joshua, and Ben-Shammai, Haggai (eds.), *The History of Jerusalem: The Early Muslim Period (638–1009)*. Jerusalem, Yad Izhak Ben-Zvi Publications and New York, New York University Press (1996), pp. 349–385.

Herr, Moshe David, Jerusalem, The Temple and Its Cult: Reality and Concepts in Second Temple Times. In: Oppenheimer, Aharon; Rappaport Uri, and Stern Menahem (eds.), *Jerusalem in the Second Temple Period*. Jerusalem, Yad Izhak Ben-Zvi, (1980), pp. 166–177 (Hebrew).

Herzog, Zeev. The Temple of Solomon: Its Plan and Archaeological Background. In: Ahituv, Shmuel, and Mazar, Amihai (eds*.), The History of Jerusalem: The biblical period*. Jerusalem, Yad Izhak Ben-Zvi (2000), pp. 155–175 (Hebrew).

Heyd, Uriel. Jerusalem under the Mamluks and the Turks. In: (no ed.), *Jerusalem Through the Ages: The Twenty-fifth Archaeological* Convention, *October 1967*. Jerusalem, Israel Exploration Society (1968), pp. 193–202 (Hebrew).

Hirschberg, H. Z. The Sources of Moslem Traditions Concerning Jerusalem. *Rosznik Orientalistyczny*, Vol. XVII (1951–1952), pp. 314–350.

Hirschberg, H. Z. The Temple Mount in Jewish and Mohammedan Traditions. In: (no ed.), *Jerusalem Through the Ages: The Twenty-fifth Archaeological Convention, October 1967*. Jerusalem, Israel Exploration Society (1968), pp. 109–119 (Hebrew).

Hobsbawn, Eric, and Ranger, Terence. *The Invention of Tradition*. Cambridge, Cambridge University Press, 1997.

Horovitz, Avigdor. The Temple of Solomon. In: Ahituv, Shmuel, and Mazar, Amihai (eds.), *The History of Jerusalem: The Biblical Period*. Jerusalem, Yad Izhak Ben-Zvi, (2000), pp. 131–155 (Hebrew).

Hubert, Jane. Sacred Beliefs and Beliefs of Sacredness. In: Carmichael, David L; Hubert, Jane; Reeves, Brian; and Schanche, Audhild (eds.), *Sacred Sites, Sacred Places*. London and New York, Routledge (1994), pp. 9–13.

Isaac, Benjamin. Jerusalem from the Great Revolt to the Reign of Constantine, 70–312 CE. In: Tsafrir, Yoram and Safrai, Shmuel (eds.), *The History of Jerusalem: The Roman and Byzantine Periods (70–683 C.E.)*. Jerusalem, Yad Izhak Ben-Zvi (1999), pp. 1–14 (Hebrew).

Japhet, Sara. *The Ideology of the Book of Chronicles and Its Place in Biblical Thought*. Frankfurt am Main, P. Lang (1989).

Japhet, Sara, The Temple of the Restoration Period: Reality and Ideology.
In: Ahituv, Shmuel, and Mazar, Amihai (eds.), *The History of Jerusalem: The Biblical Period*. Jerusalem, Yad Izhak Ben-Zvi (2000), pp. 345–382 (Hebrew).

Kaufman, Asher. Where the Ancient Temple of Jerusalem Stood. Biblical *Archaeology Review* IX, no. 2 (1983), pp. 40–59.

Klein, Menahem. The Temple Mount: Challenge, Threat, and Promise toward a Political Arrangement. In: Reiter, Yitzhak (ed.), *Sovereignty of God and Man: Sanctity and Political Centrality on the Temple Mount.* Jerusalem, Jerusalem Institute for Israel Studies (2000), pp. 269–296 (Hebrew).

Klein, Menahem. *Jerusalem: The Contested City.* London, C. Hurst (2001).

Lamy, Philip. Millennial Myth. In: Landes, Richard (ed.), *Encyclopedia of Millennialism and Millennial Movements.* New York and London, Routledge (2000), pp. 255–257.

Lazarus-Yafeh, Hava. Jerusalem and Mecca. In: Levine, Lee I. (ed.), *Jerusalem: Its Sanctity and Centrality to Judaism, Christianity and Islam.* New York, Continuum (1999), pp. 387–399.

Le Strange, Guy. *Palestine under the Moslems.* Beirut, Khayats Booksellers and Publishers (1965). Reprint from the 1890 original edition.

Lefkovitz, Judah M. *The Copper Scroll.* Leiden-Boston-Cologne, Brill (2000).

Levine, Baruch A. Biblical Temple. In: Eliade, Mircea (ed.), *The Encyclopedia of Religion*, Vol 2. New York, Macmillan Publishing Company (1987), pp. 202–217.

Limor, Ora. Christian Pilgrims in the Byzantine period. In: Tsafrir, Yoram and Safrai, Shmuel, *The History of Jerusalem: The Roman and Byzantine Periods (70–683 C.E.).* Jerusalem, Yad Izhak Ben-Zvi (1999), pp. 391–416 (Hebrew).

Linder, Amnon. Jerusalem as Focal Point in the Conflict Between Judaism and Christianity. In: Kedar, Benjamin Z. (ed.), *Jerusalem in the Middle Ages. Jerusalem,* Yad Izhak Ben-Zvi (1979), pp. 5–27 (Hebrew).

Livne-Kafri, Ofer. *Jerusalem in Early Islam.* Jerusalem, Yad Ben-Zvi Press (2000) (Hebrew).

Long, Charles A. Cosmogony. In: Eliade, Mircea (ed.), *The Encyclopedia of Religion*, Vol 4. New York, Macmillan Publishing Company (1987), pp. 94–100.

Maeir, Aren. Jerusalem Before King David: An Archaeological Survey from Prehistoric Times to the End of the Iron Age. In: Ahituv, Shmuel, and Mazar, Amihai (eds.), *The History of Jerusalem: The Biblical Period.* Jerusalem, Yad Izhak Ben-Zvi (2000), pp. 33–66 (Hebrew).

Malamat, Abraham. The Dawn of Jerusalem. In: Ahituv, Shmuel and Mazar, Amihai (eds.), *The History of Jerusalem: The Biblical Period*. Jerusalem, Yad Izhak Ben-Zvi (2000), pp. 13–23 (Hebrew).

Mazar Benjamin. Royal Shrine and Center of Kingdom. In: Aviram, Joseph (ed.), *Judah and Jerusalem*. Jerusalem, Israel Exploration Society (1969), pp. 25–32 (Hebrew).

Mazar, Benjamin. Assisted by Gedalyah Cornfeld. D.N. Freedman, Consultant. *The Mount of the Lord*. Garden City, N.Y. (1975a).
Mazar, Benjamin. *Towns and Regions in Eretz Israel*. Jerusalem, Mosad Bialik (1975b), (Hebrew).

Mazar, Benjamin. *Excavations and Discoveries*. Jerusalem, Mosad Bialik and the Israel Exploration Society (1986) (Hebrew).

Mazar, Benjamin. *Biblical Israel: State and People*. Magnes Press, Hebrew University and Israel Exploration Society (1992).

Mazar, Eilat. *The Monastery of the Virgins*. Jerusalem, Institute of Archaeology, Hebrew University of Jerusalem, and Ramat Gan, Bar-Ilan University (1998).

Mazar, Eilat. The Camp of the Tenth Legion at the Foot of the South-West Corner of the Temple Mount enclosure Wall in Jerusalem. In: Faust, Avraham, and Baruch, Eyal (eds.), *New Studies on Jerusalem*. Ramat Gan, Bar-Ilan University (1999), pp. 52–67 (Hebrew).

Meshorer, Yaakov. Coins of Aelia Capitolina. In: Tsafrir, Yoram and Safrai, Shmuel (eds.), *The History of Jerusalem: The Roman and Byzantine Periods (70–683 C.E.)*. Jerusalem, Yad Izhak Ben-Zvi (1999), pp. 181–198 (Hebrew).

Milstein, Rachel. The Evolution of a Visual Motif: The Temple and the Ka'ba. *Israel Oriental Studies* XIX (1999), pp. 23–48.

Noy, Dov. The Foundation Stone and the Beginning of Creation. In Elkoshi, Gdali; Tan-Pi, Yehoshua; and Kadari, Shraga (eds.), *And to Jerusalem*. Jerusalem, Yahdav Publications (1968), pp. 60–94 (Hebrew).

Nusaibeh, Said, and Grabar, Oleg. *The Dome of the Rock*. Milan, Rizzoli International Publications (1996).

Optowitzer, Avigdor. The Celestial Temple According to the Aggada. In: *Tarbiz*, Vol II, no. 1 (1930), pp. 137–273 (Hebrew).

Perrone, Lorenzo. "The Mystery of Judaea" (Jerome Ep. 46). The Holy City of Jerusalem Between History and Symbol in Early Christian Thought. In: Levine, Lee I. (ed.). *Jerusalem: Its Sanctity and Centrality to Judaism, Christianity, and Islam.* New York, Continuum (1999), pp. 221–239.

Porat, Yehoshua. *The Emergence of the Arab Palestine National Movement.* London, Frank Cass (1974).

Porat, Yehoshua. *The Palestinian Arab National Movement, 1929–1939.* London, Frank Cass (1977).

Prawer, Joshua, Christianity Between Heavenly and Earthly Jerusalem. *Jerusalem Through the Ages: The Twenty-fifth Archaeological* Convention, *October 1967.* Jerusalem, Israel Exploration Society (1968), pp. 179–192 (Hebrew).

Prawer, Joshua. *The World of the Crusaders.* London, Weidenfeld & Nicolson (1972).

Prawer, Joshua. Jerusalem in Christian and Jewish Perspectives in the Early Middle Ages. In Ben-Arieh, Yehoshua (ed.), *Jerusalem from the Second Temple to the Modern Period.* Jerusalem, Yad Izhak Ben-Zvi (1981), pp. 96–128 (Hebrew).

Prawer, Joshua. Political History of Crusader and Ayyubid Jerusalem. In: Prawer, Joshua, and Ben-Shammai, Haggai (eds.), *The History of Jerusalem: Crusaders and Ayyubids (1099–1250).* Jerusalem, Yad Izhak Ben-Zvi Publications (1991), pp. 1–42 (Hebrew).

Ramon, Amnon. Beyond the Western Wall: The Attitude of the State of Israel and the Jewish Public Toward the Temple Mount. In: Reiter, Yitzhak (ed.), *Sovereignty of God and Man: Sanctity and Political Centrality on the Temple Mount.* Jerusalem, Jerusalem Institute for Israel Studies (2000), pp. 113–142 (Hebrew).

Reich, Roni. Suggestion for Identifying Two Ritual Baths on the Temple Mount. In: Schiller, Eli (ed.), *The Temple Mount and Its Sites.* Jerusalem, Ariel Publishing House (1989), pp. 182–183 (Hebrew).

Reiter, Yitzhak. *Har ha-bait/al-Haram al-Sharif.* Jerusalem, Jerusalem Institute for Israel Studies (1997).

Reiter, Yitzhak. The Status-Quo in the Temple Mount/Haram a-Sharif Under Israeli Rule (1967–2000). In: Reiter, Yitzhak (ed.), *Sovereignty of God and Man: Sanctity and Political Centrality on the Temple Mount.* Jerusalem, Jerusalem Institute for Israel Studies (2000), pp. 297–336 (Hebrew).

Reiter, Yitzhak. Third in Holiness, First in Politics: Al-Haram al-Sharif in the Eyes of the Muslims. In: Reiter, Yitzhak (ed.), *Sovereignty of God and Man: Sanctity and Political Centrality on the Temple Mount*. Jerusalem, Jerusalem Institute for Israel Studies (2000), pp. 155–179 (Hebrew).

Ritmayer, Leen. Locating the Original Temple Mount. *Biblical Archaeology Review,* Vol. XVIII, no. 2 (1992), pp. 24–45.

Ritmayer, Leen. The Ark of the Covenant: Where It Stood in Solomon's Temple. *Biblical Archaeology Review,* Vol. XXII, no. 1 (1996), pp. 46–55.

Rosen-Ayalon, Miriam. Art and Architecture in Jerusalem in the Early Islamic period. In: Prawer, Joshua, and Ben-Shammai, Haggai (eds.), *The History of Jerusalem: The Early Muslim Period (638–1009)*. Jerusalem, Yad Izhak Ben-Zvi Publications and New York, New York University Press (1996), pp. 386–412.

Rosen-Ayalon, Miriam. Three Perspectives on Jerusalem: Jewish, Christian and Muslim Pilgrims in the Twelfth Century. In: Levine, Lee I. (ed.), *Jerusalem: Its Sanctity and Centrality to Judaism, Christianity, and Islam*. New York, Continuum (1999), pp. 326–346.

Rubin, Rehav. Jerusalem and Its Environs: The Impact of Geographical and Physical Conditions on the Development of Jerusalem. In: Ahituv, Shmuel and Mazar, Amihai (eds.), *The History of Jerusalem: The Biblical Period*. Jerusalem, Yad Izhak Ben-Zvi (2000), pp. 1–12 (Hebrew).

Safrai, Shmuel. Pilgrimage to Jerusalem after the Destruction of the Second Temple. In: Oppenheimer, Aharon; Rappaport, Uriel; and Stern, Menahem (eds.), *Jerusalem in the Second Temple Period*. Jerusalem, Yad Itzhak ben Zvi (1980), pp. 376–393 (Hebrew).

Safrai, Shmuel. The Jews of Jerusalem During the Roman period. In: Tsafrir, Yoram and Safrai, Shmuel, *The History of Jerusalem: The Roman and Byzantine Periods (70–683 C.E.)*. Jerusalem, Yad Izhak Ben-Zvi (1999), pp. 15–34 (Hebrew).

Safrai, Shmuel, *Pilgrimage in the Second Temple period*. Tel Aviv, Am Hassefer Publishers (1965), (Hebrew).

Sagiv, Tuvia. *The Temples of Mount Moriah*. http://www.Templemount.org/mtmoriah.html' (2001).

Sanders, J.P. Jerusalem and Its Temple in Early Christian Thought and Practice. In: Levine, Lee I. (ed.). *Jerusalem: Its Sanctity and Centrality to Judaism, Christianity, and Islam*. New York, Continuum (1999), pp. 90–103.

Schein, Sylvia. Jerusalem in Christian Spirituality in the Crusader Period. In: Prawer, Joshua, and Ben-Shammai, Haggai (eds.), *The History of Jerusalem: Crusaders and Ayyubids (1099-1250)*. Jerusalem, Yad Izhak Ben-Zvi Publications (1991), pp. 213–263 (Hebrew).

Schiller, Eli (ed.). *The Temple Mount and Its Sites*. Jerusalem, Ariel Publishing House, (1989), (Hebrew).

Schure, Nathan. *The History of Jerusalem*. Tel Aviv, Dvir, 1987 (Hebrew).

Schwabe, Moshe. The Greek Inscriptions. In: Avi-Yonah Michael, *Sefer Yerushalayim*. Jerusalem, Bialik Institute and Dvir Publishing House (1955), pp. 358–368 (Hebrew).

Shragai, Nadav. *Mountain of Dispute: The Conflict over the Temple Mount*. Jerusalem, Keter (1995), (Hebrew).

Sivan, Emanuel. The Sanctity of Jerusalem in Islam during the Crusader Period. In: Prawer, Joshua and Ben-Shammai, Haggai (eds.), *The History of Jerusalem: Crusaders and Ayyubids (1099–1250)*. Jerusalem, Yad Izhak Ben-Zvi Publications (1991), pp. 287–303, (Hebrew).

Souchek, Priscilla. The Temple of Solomon in Islamic Legend and Art. In: Gutmann, Joseph (ed.), *The Temple of Solomon*. Missoula, Mont., Scholars Press (1976), pp. 73–123.

Steibel, Guy D. The Whereabouts of the Xth Legion and the Boundaries of Aelia Capitolina. In: In: Faust, Avraham, and Baruch, Eyal (eds.), *New Studies on Jerusalem*. Ramat Gan, Bar-Ilan University (1999), pp. 68–103 (Hebrew).

Stern, Menahem. "Jerusalem, the Most Famous of the Cities of the East" (Pliny, *Natural History* V, 70). In: Oppenheimer, Aharon; Rappaport, Uri; and Stern, Menahem (eds.), *Chapters in the History of Jerusalem in the Second Temple Period*. Jerusalem, Yad Izhak ben-Zvi (1980), pp. 257–270 (Hebrew).

Stroumsa, Guy G. Mystical Jerusalem. . In: Levine, Lee I. (ed.). *Jerusalem: Its Sanctity and Centrality to Judaism, Christianity and Islam*. New York, Continuum (1999), pp. 349–370.

Townsend, Richard F. Geography (Sacred). In: Eliade, Mircea (ed.), *The Encyclopedia of Religion*, Vol 5. New York, Macmillan Publishing Company (1987), pp. 508–512.

Tsafrir, Yoram. The Topography and Archaeology of Aelia Capitolina. Tsafrir, Yoram, and Safrai, Shmuel (eds.), *The History of Jerusalem: The Roman and Byzantine Periods (70–683 C.E.)*. Jerusalem, Yad Itzhak Ben-Zvi (1999):115–166 (Hebrew).

Turner Victor, and Turner, Edith. *Image and Pilgrimage in Christian Culture*. Oxford, Basil Blackwell (1978).

Uffenheimer, Benjamin. The Religious Significance of the Temple and Jerusalem. In: Ahituv, Shmuel and Mazar, Amihai (eds.), *The History of Jerusalem: The Biblical Period*. Jerusalem, Yad Izhak Ben-Zvi (2000), pp. 175–194 (Hebrew).

Ussishkin, David. King Solomon's Palaces. *Biblical Archaeology* 36 (1973), pp. 78–105.

Warren, Charles. *Underground Jerusalem*. London, Richard Bentley & Son (1876).

Wensink, Arent Jan. *Some Semitic Rites of Mourning and Religion,* Vol. XVII, no. 1. Chapter III: The Navel and the Universe. Amsterdam, Johannes Muller (1916).

Whalen, Robert K. Premillennialism. In: Landers, Richard (ed.) *Encyclopedia of Millennialism and Millennial Movements*. New York and London, Routledge (2000).

Wilson, R.E., and Warren, R.E. *The Recovery of Jerusalem*. London, Richard Bentley & Son (1871).

Yadin, Yigael, The First Temple. In: Avi-Yonah Michael (ed.), *Sefer Yerushalayim*. Bialik Institute and Dvir Publishing House (1955), pp. 176–190 (Hebrew).

Yadin, Yigael. *The Temple Scroll: The Hidden Law of the Dead Sea Sect*. New York, Random House (1985).

Zakovitch, Yair. The First Stages of Jerusalem's Sanctification Under David. In: Levine, Lee I. (ed.). Jerusalem: Its Sanctity and Centrality to Judaism, Christianity and Islam. New York, Continuum (1999), pp. 16–35.

Zeligman, I.A.. Jerusalem in Hellenistic Jewish Thought. In: Aviram Joseph (ed.), *Judah and Jerusalem*. Jerusalem, Israel Exploration Society (1969), pp. 156–171 (Hebrew).

Zilberman, Ifrah. The Conflict over a Mosque/Temple in Jerusalem and Ayodhya. In: Reiter, Yitzhak (ed.), *Sovereignty of God and Man: Sanctity and Political Centrality on the Temple Mount*. Jerusalem, Jerusalem Institute for Israel Studies (2000), pp. 241–268 (Hebrew).

Index

The index excluded the terms Temple Mount/Haram a-Sharif, Jerusalem, Arabs, Jews/Jewish, Christians, Muslims, as well as biblical books, prophets and apostles mentioned in quotations.